THE
MYSTERIOUS
SEA

Ferdinand C. Lane

Essay Index Reprint Series

BOOKS FOR LIBRARIES PRESS
FREEPORT, NEW YORK

INTERNATIONAL STANDARD BOOK NUMBER:
0-8369-1971-8

LIBRARY OF CONGRESS CATALOG CARD NUMBER:
73-128268

PRINTED IN THE UNITED STATES OF AMERICA

Foreword

The sea! the sea! the open sea!
The blue, the fresh, the ever free!

BRYAN W. PROCTER

The sea holds a perennial lure. Its immensity, its capricious moods, and its ungovernable power are a challenge to the spirit of adventure in each of us.

Somewhere in its far offings have lurked the Ultima Thules; somewhere beyond undiscovered shore lines have peered the "Mountains of the Moon" or gleamed the Eldorados or the Fountains of Perpetual Youth. The Fortunate Isles have always been hidden in sea mist.

The artist sees in the "countless dimpling smile of sea waves" that Aeschylus noted a canvas of ever changing color. The poet strives, as Shakespeare did, to catch the melody of "the murmuring surge, That on the unnumber'd idle pebbles chafes."

Even the prosy scientist beholds in the oceans one of Nature's grandest phenomena. He knows they are the original home of life, the present source of life-sustaining moisture, the controlling influence upon our global climate.

Peering into their deeps, he must continually adapt his lists to new species of life, strange, nightmarish, or of uncanny beauty. He also sees there a vast crucible in which the elements of erosion mingle to form the uplands of the fu-

v

ture. And he observes the shadow of some remote and overwhelming disaster. He knows that the great strait jacket of the tides will ultimately slow the spinning earth until the moon swings back to a perilous proximity. Or he forecasts a coming glacial age when the continents will groan anew beneath oceans of invading ice that disrupt sea levels and climatic averages the world over.

The man who gets his living from the sea is attracted by its boundless riches. To him it is a global larder or storage bin of food, or perhaps the last source of mineral wealth beyond the output of all the gold veins and copper lodes and mountains of iron ore. The merchant views it as the one broad highway of international commerce; the statesman as access to distant markets and supplies, or perhaps a widening sphere of influence in world affairs.

The sailor with all his superstitious dread of its krakens and specter barks, has been bewitched by its mermaids and sirens. Like Homer, he looks upon that "great gulf of the sea—so dread, so difficult," to realize, as did Horace, that "the greedy sea is death to sailors." True, such classical gold he coins in the sulphurous phrase, "that old Devil, the sea." Yet how many sailormen are contented unless they can listen to its surge?

The sea has developed a vocabulary of its own. Its slurring r's in "no'th by east" and "fo'c'sle"; its figureheads and capstans and binnacles; its spars and marlinspikes and belaying pins, all conjure up sagas of adventure. Its hoarse chanteys fairly echo the thrumming of the wind among the shrouds.

A vast battleground of elemental strife, the sea has brought out in sharp relief the utmost in human courage and exertion and self-sacrifice. Even its villains seem invested with glamor, like the ferocious pirate, Edward Teach, or Blackbeard, who arranged his long whiskers in three braids, carried three brace of pistols and two stilettos under his purple cloak, and, according to a contemporary, "was kind to his fourteen wives, as long as he was sober, and never murdered above three of them." No wonder salty tales of sea adventure fill a widening niche in our literature.

Meanwhile, the war has made millions of landsmen sea-minded. The farmer lad from Nebraska has caught a glimpse of far horizons on his voyage to Okinawa, while even his people at home have breathed an invigorating whiff of spray. Millions more, holiday strollers on the beaches, have been impressed by the sea's vastness, its unpredictability, and, above all, its mystery.

For the great waters of the globe, in spite of chemical analysis, the seinings and the dredgings, the probing of fathometers and the measurements of charts, remain the still mysterious sea.

Sir Isaac Newton realized this when, complimented upon his great achievements, he remarked, "I have only strolled a little while by the sea and picked up a few shells and pebbles," so vast, he knew, was the gulf that yawns between the known and the unknown.

Mystery is the sea's most enduring charm. But it has so many that doubtless every individual of the growing multitudes who have felt even a little of its spell may endorse the lines of William Wordsworth:

> Two voices are there: one is of the sea,
> One of the mountains,—each a mighty voice.

or share in spirit Byron's sonorous lines:

> There is a rapture on the lonely shore;
> There is society, where none intrudes,
> By the deep sea, and music in its roar:
> I love not Man the less, but Nature more.

Contents

The Mysterious Sea

CHAPTER I

How the Sea Began

This world was once a fluid maze of light
Till toward the center, set the starry tides.
                    TENNYSON
The rising world of waters dark and deep.
                    MILTON
Hail to thee, O Sea, ageless and eternal!
                    HEINRICH HEINE
If thou wouldst know the age of the earth look upon the sea in
a storm. The greyness of the whole immense surface, the wind-
furrows upon the faces of the waves, the great masses of foam,
tossed about and waving like matted white locks, give the sea
in a gale an appearance of hoary age, lustreless, dull, without
gleams, as though it had been created before light itself.
                    JOSEPH CONRAD

The origin of the oceans is obscure. According to primitive peoples everywhere—Chinese, Chaldeans, Hebrews—
they emerged from chaos at the command of Deity. Such a
momentous announcement occurs in the first chapter of
Genesis: "God said, Let the Waters under the heaven be
gathered together unto one place, and let the dry land appear"—an event once supposed to have taken place six
thousand years ago.

Science has thrust back the dawn of creation into a past
immeasurably more remote, but there fragmentary data and
incomplete knowledge of astronomy and physics leave us
to grope in a fog of speculation. The very axioms of mathe-

matics seem to break down, as Einstein shows, when applied to inconceivable speeds or distances. And so, upon the far horizon of geologic time, all explanations must remain conjectural. No wonder, when experts disagree over current events, the history of our planet two billion years ago becomes confused!

It was then, so astronomers believe, that the globe, torn from the parent sun by some cosmic cataclysm, went spinning off upon its own. Congealing slowly from incandescent gas to boiling mush, a crust coated its surface like that upon a vat of liquid steel.

Where were the oceans then? Not in their present positions, we may be sure, for the crust was far too hot. They must have floated with other substances in the denser air or remained undifferentiated in the molten earth.

That is where the two theories diverge. One school of thought pictures a primeval atmosphere, mainly oxygen, a thousand miles high, in which the oceans appeared as global clouds. These rained incessantly, ascending again in steam, for many millenniums. Meanwhile the deluge was intensified by the dizzy whirling of the earth, which rotated every four hours, generating furious hurricanes and no less appalling currents in the boiling seas. As cooling progressed the crust buckled to fit the shrunken interior; the folds became continents, the depressions the beds of seas. A world of waters had subdued a world of fire.

The known facts, however, are too complex for so simple an explanation. Other scientists contend that the primeval atmosphere contained little oxygen, while the oceans still mingled with global matter in one indistinguishable mass. Water, they remind us, breaks up into oxygen and hydrogen at a temperature of 1100 degrees. Hence the earth crust must have been mainly dry land. What little water then existed collected in abysmal pools, to be augmented through long aeons by moisture forming in the deeper rocks and oozing out in the steam of geysers and the vapors of volcanoes.

The first school would have us believe that the oceans are slowly diminishing. Water keeps penetrating lower strata to combine with minerals. When raindrops are shattered by lightning, some liberated hydrogen rising to the outer stratosphere may drift off into space. Other planets confirm the general theory. Venus, a younger world, is hidden by dense clouds suggesting seas still floating in the atmosphere. On more venerable Mars the dwindling waters collect as snow or ice about the poles to trickle in summer toward the equator. The grim conclusion is written on the moon, sterile and lifeless, whence all moisture has disappeared.

The second school, on the contrary, would have the oceans slowly increasing, a disquieting thought as one stands upon a low-lying beach to watch the tide come in. Must we eventually take to the hills or build arks like Noah? For water vapor does emerge through cracks in the earth's crust. The Valley of Ten Thousand Smokes in Alaska steams like a Titan's laundry, while on some of the islets of the Ryukyus natives distill much of their meager water supply from volcanic fumes. Such increments, though slight, would swell the seas over vast intervals of time, particularly since volcanoes and hot springs were once more numerous and active than at present.

Where experts differ, what may a layman believe? As often happens where opposing theories clash, both are doubtless partly true and neither completely so. For whether the volume of our oceans is in ebb or flood, no one knows.

As we turn for further light to the more comprehensive story of our globe, we find as sharp a cleavage among explanatory theories. Formerly the lava from volcanoes made a molten world beneath a thin veneer a reasonable supposition. Deep borings showed a rising temperature of one degree for every seventy feet of depth until in the lower shafts of Johannesburg workmen panted in a heat made endurable only by air conditioning. At earth's center a thermometer might well register twenty thousand degrees, were it not that both glass and metal would vaporize at such a temperature.

Here other physicists countered with the superior force of gravity. Sheer weight, they contended, in spite of increasing heat, must squeeze the interior into a solid. This assumption seemed established by Maskelyne in 1774 when he set out to weigh a mountain and weighed the earth instead. Six and two thirds sextillion tons was the impressive total, a figure that dwarfs even our national debt. Average density proved to be roughly five and one half times that of water, hence surface density of two and six tenths must increase correspondingly toward the center. Terrestrial magnetism indicated iron, while recent experiments have endowed the entire globe with an elasticity greater than that of solid steel.

And so our latest theories are compromises. A huge core, presumably iron, is overlaid with molten matter called magma. Floating upon this like the ice of Baffin Bay is a crust comprising two or more different strata. Some three quarters of this in turn is covered like a tattered quilt by the oceans, while over all is the more voluminous ocean of the air. Hence the globe is neither liquid nor solid but composed of layers like an onion.

To explain the continents Fairbairn, Green, and others have elaborated a tetrahedral theory not quite so forbidding as it sounds. When the molten globe cooled, land masses crystallized into great triangles, the broad base fronting north, the apex toward the south. The analogy is indeed striking in wedge-shaped Eurasia and South America. Such irregularities reveal the pattern of a globe that is not perfectly global; but they are slight while the tetrahedral form is not what the physicists consider "a figure of equilibrium for a rotating spheroid."

Suess studied the continents. These, he decided, must be very ancient because great layers of the oldest fossil-bearing rock remained undisturbed. The land masses, he thought, were composed of relatively lighter materials with a specific gravity of 2.6. This he named sial from the predominant constituents, silicon and aluminum. Between the sial and the semimolten magma lay a heavier stratum with a specific gravity of 2.9 which he named sima. This formed the ocean beds and sometimes intruded upon the surface in such excretions as the Giant's Causeway and the Palisades of the Hudson.

Wegener accepted this explanation but added a theory of his own, that of drifting continents. Composed of sial resting on a denser sima, they resemble ice fields that flowed slowly outward. They once formed, he thought, a single land mass, surrounded by a universal sea, that split asunder to go sidling off in various directions. The Pacific must therefore be gradually narrowing, while the Atlantic must be a widening crack of comparatively recent origin.

For evidence Wegener fitted the great bulge of South America into a corresponding depression in Africa. He also called attention to the fact that similar land plants and animals appeared in widely separated places. Fossil-bearing rocks in both continents are similar, while among living forms heather and land snails are common to both Scotland and northeastern North America, now separated by the Atlantic. Such similarities present a problem in biology, for which the theory of a continuous land mass offers a convenient explanation.

When the discovery of radium upset the very foundations of chemistry, Joly appropriated radioactivity as the basis of a new theory. According to him, heat thus generated, unable to escape through non-conducting rock, accumulates until it melts the undersurface of the sima. The molten matter supplies volcanic lava and explains those vast intrusions of igneous rock among sedimentary layers. The earth's crust first expands with heat, then, melting at the bottom, subsides again in gigantic pulsations over enormous intervals of time. Such pulsations, which have caused great areas to rise and fall, might even account for lost continents. Joly's theory is both interesting and plausible.

How thick is the earth's crust? Perhaps thirty miles, perhaps sixty, no one really knows. Daly thought that in the bowllike depression of interior Greenland he had detected a warping of this crust beneath the weight of ice a mile and a half thick. Timid persons wonder how Manhattan can support its ponderous skyscrapers, but the floor of the Pacific has not yielded to the far greater burden of Hawaii that culminates in the crest of Mauna Loa nearly thirty thousand feet above.

Earthquakes suggest continuous readjustments in sial and sima. Minor tremors are so frequent that Milne estimates there are thirty thousand annually or nearly two per minute. Those of historic prominence are of course much rarer. One of the best known destroyed Lisbon in 1755. Even more disastrous was the Japanese quake of 1923. Causing widespread conflagrations, it laid Tokyo in ruins with a quarter of a million casualties. The bottom of Sagami Bay was elevated in places nearly fifteen hundred feet and depressed in others twenty-five hundred, a total displacement of more than three quarters of a mile.

The focal point of an earthquake, as revealed by the seismograph, is of special interest. Numerous observations show that this lies from one to thirty-one miles beneath the surface. Violent convulsions, however, indicate much greater depths. The San Francisco quake of 1906 extended downward an estimated sixty-seven miles. Turner believes that major upheavals may start at depths ranging from a hundred and twenty-five to three hundred and seventy-five miles. The Assam quake of 1897, felt over an area of nearly two million square miles, has been ascribed to some vast readjustment perhaps eight hundred miles deep!

Those far mightier convulsions which gouged out the great African Rift, five thousand miles long, enclosing such bodies of water as Lake Tanganyika and the Red Sea, fortunately occurred when only dinosaurs or perhaps trilobites were alive to wonder what was going on. And those vaster alterations in the architecture of the globe, the rounding of the continents and the grooving of ocean beds, were mainly completed before the first flicker of life appeared in the primeval slime.

Pratt, in his theory of compensation, had foreshadowed more volatile continents upon a soggier floor. He maintained that equal surfaces cover roughly equal amounts of matter, the lighter fluffing up into mountains, the denser sagging like a fallen cake to accommodate the seas.

Experiments involving keen technical skill have seemed to verify this theory. A plumb line drawn straight downward by the earth's attraction is somewhat deflected by the sidewise pull of mountains or other land masses. This deflection is revealed by comparison with the true perpendicular found by sighting fixed stars overhead. Thus the boundary between the United States and Canada, when routed by ordinary surveying instruments through mountainous districts, shifts several miles north or south of its true parallel of latitude.

Investigators in Ecuador found that the Andean heights

overlay less matter than the coastal plain or even the bed of the Pacific. A study of the ocean floor presented special difficulties as wave motion disturbed the plumb line. To solve this problem a Dutch savant, Vening Meinesz, invented a double compensating pendulum mounted upon gimbals like a mariner's compass, which was carried down in a submarine for greater accuracy, though it worked well on the surface of the sea. The results, though fragmentary, indicate that the ocean floor is composed of heavier materials than the land rocks. The sial and sima hypothesis, if not definitely proven, is at least a plausible explanation of global phenomena.

And now to sum up the evidence. The continents and seas are not mere folds in the earth crust that conform to a shrinking globe. They are of different densities and seem to rest upon a layer of molten matter. Their undersurfaces are melted at long intervals by imprisoned heat partially produced by radioactivity, which causes continuous readjustments manifested by earthquakes and volcanic action. Into heavier depressions among lighter continents flowed the primordial seas. They condensed at first from global clouds but have been swollen through the aeons by water forming in the deeper rocks or the underlying magma and seeping upward through the crust.

To every square centimeter of earth's surface Goldschmidt assigned approximately 373 liters of water. A mere trace—three one-thousandths of a liter—floats in the air as water vapor. The contents of lakes and rivers comprises one tenth of a liter. Four and a half liters are locked in ice mainly in the glacial fields of Greenland and Antarctica. All the remainder, 268.45 liters, has accumulated in the oceans, the great reservoirs of life-sustaining moisture.

Shore lines between shallow seas and land masses of slight elevation are continually fluctuating. The British Isles were once a part of Europe, the East Indies part of Asia. On the other hand, great stretches of arctic tundra are so newly risen from the sea that they fairly drip with moisture, while the Mississippi River is but the skeleton of a vast oceanic gulf. But such changes, though impressive upon a map, register but slight modifications in global topography, for geologists now believe that both continents and ocean beds were pretty definitely fixed by the end of Archeozoic time and have changed but little during seven hundred million years!

CHAPTER II

Ocean Boundaries

Without a mark, without a bound,
It runneth the earth's wide regions round.
BARRY CORNWALL

The most ancient of ocean boundaries is the Isthmus of Suez. The builders of the Pyramids could not know that the Indian Ocean, which they understood so imperfectly, mingled with the Atlantic far away below the southernmost cliffs of Africa. The Isthmus of Panama seemed quite as definite a division between the Atlantic and the Pacific; at least Balboa thought so as he fought his way across those deadly jungles. Thus the three major oceans gained historic recognition.

From hardy whalers who followed the trail of the Vikings the world learned of the Arctic, while explorers battling storms around Cape Horn first ventured across the threshold of the Antarctic.

Romance is woven into the very names of these five oceans. The Greeks called the Mediterranean Thalassa, but beyond the Pillars of Hercules stretched the boisterous Atlantic, vague and terrible. This gained its name from Atlas, the Titan who bore the heavens upon his shoulders and had his station amid the snowy Atlas Mountains of Morocco. Schoolboys also became acquainted with him from their well-thumbed atlases.

The Indian Ocean was familiar to the Greeks as the Erythraean Sea; but it seems to have derived its present name from the Indus, and that in turn from the Sanskrit *sindhu*, or "river," which the Greeks corrupted into "India." This river valley marked the eastward boundary in the progress of Alexander the Great, that brash young man who set forth to conquer the world. Modern excavations have unearthed there evidences of a civilization perhaps as venerable as the more familiar cultures which flowered along the banks of the Euphrates and the Nile. The river gave its name to both country and people and, by a kind of poetic overflow, to the ocean also.

Balboa, "silent upon a peak in Darien," gazed due south into what he naturally termed the "Great South Sea"; but Magellan, battling storms through that evil strait which bears his name, found the waters beyond so relatively calm that he called them the "Mare Pacifico." This name may seem inappropriate to a region where typhoons rage among treacherous currents, but who had a better right to bestow it than the first navigator who ever crossed its interminable waters?

Arctic comes from *arktos*, the Greek "bear." This, of course, is not the captive of the zoo, ever homesick for his native bergs and blizzards, but the constellation Ursa Major which hovers above the polar regions. Part of this enormous figure, called the Great Dipper, is the most familiar star group in the sky. This Bear, prowling among the Northern Lights, was supposed to darken earth with his shadow and congeal its waters with his icy breath; hence the name still lingers in that sea which chills the coast of Greenland and the dreary shore line of Siberia.

The Antarctic is, of course, merely the Anti-bear, for no celestial animal brightens its skies and no living specimen from Baffin Land or the Barents Sea ever approaches within three thousand leagues of its still deadlier solitudes.

In deference to tradition we might list a few characteristics of these oceans. The Atlantic, best known to the ancient world, is still the most important because leading nations use its waters so freely in commerce. Its Gulf Stream is the mightiest of ocean currents, its Sargasso the most extensive of stagnant seas. Into its basin drain fully half the rivers of the globe, including the Amazon and the Congo, the Plata and the Mississippi. Though second in area, it is the longest ocean, twisting like a gigantic letter S to envelop one pole and reach almost to the other.

A certain glamor invests the Indian Ocean, famed for the voyages of Marco Polo, of Cheng Ho, the great Ming admiral, and of Vasco da Gama. Though scarcely half as long as the Atlantic, it is more than twice as broad, a vast bay between Africa and Australia, opening out like a funnel toward the South Pole. More than other oceans it is the sport of seasonal winds, for the monsoons not only torment its surface but actually reverse the flow of its shifting and mysterious currents. Nor have modern explorations wholly robbed it of the atmosphere of the Spice Islands and *The Arabian Nights*.

The Pacific is the true Father of Waters. Many geologists regard it as the oldest of oceans. Astronomers once toyed with the idea that it might be the global scar left when the moon tore loose from the earth, a theory no longer credited. It is so vast in area that it could cover all the continents and islands, so capacious that it could contain all other oceans and seas. Though studded with innumerable islands, it registers the profoundest depths. Widest of oceans, nearly ten thousand miles at its maximum, it narrows to thirty-six at Bering Strait. Because it has all the Orient on one shore and on the other endless leagues of undeveloped coast line along the Americas, it has been called the Ocean of the Future.

The Arctic conjures up visions of intrepid explorations, of gropings for the Northwest Passage, of savage hunts for whale and seal and walrus. Much of it is covered by never-melting ice. Birthplace of freezing winds and chill currents, its evil influence upon northern climates is just beginning to be understood.

The Antarctic is still more forbidding. Its polar continent, encased in ice, is washed by the loneliest seas on earth. Its floating ice islands dwarf the bergs of Greenland. Wandering albatross brave its fierce winds, penguins rear their colonies along its inlets, and its frosty air is startled by the spouting of the great blue whale; but essentially Antarctica is a dead continent, almost as lifeless as the moon.

This division into five oceans seems simple enough, but the drawing of boundaries has long baffled the experts. For one thing, an indeterminate territory has been set off into seas and bays and gulfs. This is well enough for landlocked waters like the Black Sea, but the Gulf of Senegal and the great Australian Bight are merely huge indentations in continental coast lines.

Some interocean boundaries are quite as ill defined. The Pacific, Atlantic, and Indian oceans, though outlined by continental land masses, are united below them. Their boundaries must be traced by arbitrary hand across wide-open spaces, and who shall trace them?

The International Hydrographic Bureau, with headquarters at Copenhagen, has tried to do so. But the reader who wades through the literature of that learned society will be bewildered by the conflict of opinion. A pamphlet issued in August 1928 set the boundaries of the Antarctic by drawing a line from Cape Horn to Cape Agulhas, the southern tip of Africa, thence along the shores of Australia, Tasmania, and New Zealand and back to the starting point. This was

definite enough, but it swelled enormously the area of the
Antarctic at the expense of the three major oceans.

In a later pamphlet His Highness the Prince of Monaco
attempted a compromise which led him into difficulties
quite as serious. A flair for science, financed by the roulette
wheels of Monte Carlo, had gained the prince recognition
as a leading geographer. While remaining close to land off
Cape Horn, he roamed far asea off Agulhas and Tasmania.
There he set arbitrary positions linked by a rhumb line
which went zigzagging around the globe at various latitudes.
With all due respect to the prince, no boundaries established by the late League of Nations were ever more high-
handed or less satisfactory.

More recently scientists have suggested bottom contours
as a guide. True, the oceans are traversed by shallows that
divide them into gigantic compartments. Whether these
shallows mark the graves of lost continents, however, or
earth wrinkles that failed to show through, they are too
hidden to provide even the most indefinite boundaries to
the seas.

Too much deference has been accorded to historic association. The Antarctic is not a separate ocean but a mere
name; hence modern oceanographers divide it like a hapless Poland among the major oceans of the world. Nor are
they less ruthless with the Arctic. True, this is remote from
the Indian Ocean and connects with the Pacific only by
the narrows of Bering Sea. But through the great gap between Greenland and Norway it mingles freely with the
Atlantic, so it is now considered only another subdivision
of that greater ocean, like the Caribbean or the North
Sea.

Even the simplified three oceans present some problems.
Visitors to the Cape of Good Hope are informed that off
its cliffs the waters of the Indian Ocean meet those of the

Atlantic. But the accepted boundary begins rather at Cape Agulhas, some distance to the eastward, thence down the 20th Meridian for twenty-four hundred miles to the shores of Antarctica. From South Cape in Tasmania a similar following of the 147th Meridian for sixteen hundred miles sets off the Indian Ocean from the Pacific, while the boundary between the latter and the Atlantic runs due south from Cape Horn six hundred miles to the icy ridges of Graham Land.

Some tables deduct fringing or landlocked seas from the grand totals, others include all adjacent waters. The latter seems the approved choice, for the Sea of Japan and the Persian Gulf are quite as "oceanic" as unlimited territories along the Equator. Recent measurements give the total area of the Indian Ocean as 74,917,000 square kilometers, the greater Atlantic as 106,463,000, and the Pacific as 179,679,-000. The ratio of 5:7:12 is easy to remember and accurate enough for practical purposes.

For these are only divisions of convenience in that universal sea which even Homer visualized dimly, long ago. Strabo called him "the father of geographical science" because he "stated that the earth is entirely encompassed by the ocean, which indeed it is."

This global ocean covers a little more than 71 per cent of earth's surface or roughly 140,000,000 square miles. The 57,000,000 square miles of continents and islands are most unevenly distributed. About 61 per cent of the Northern Hemisphere is water; 81 per cent of the Southern Hemisphere. An even more unequal division can be made. If we placed the pole of the land hemisphere near the mouth of the river Loire, water would still predominate in the ratio of 53:47, while the other hemisphere, with its pole southeast of New Zealand, would then be nearly 90 per cent water.

But it is in volume rather than area that the oceans reveal their commanding importance, for they comprise 324,-000,000 cubic miles or fourteen times as much as all the land above sea level!

CHAPTER III

Bottom Contours

> . . . the bottom of the deep,
> Where fathom-line could never touch the ground.
>
> SHAKESPEARE

If we could voyage to the moon and there survey our seas with X-ray sight that penetrated their profoundest depths, we would be impressed by three outstanding characteristics of the ocean floor. First, the great land masses would be enlarged to include those coastal waters that we call continental shelves; second, bottom irregularities, unlike mountain scenery, would appear generally smooth or gently undulating; and third, the oceans would be divided into compartments by enormous ridges or submerged plateaus.

The outer borders of the continental shelves mark the permanent outlines of the continents. The shelves themselves are the battleground of ceaseless warfare between sea and land. Such turmoil through the long ages of geological time has ground the mountains to sand and clay only to remodel them again; hence, while uprearing continents and subsiding ocean beds seem permanent features of the globe, the elemental strife persists along all the seacoasts of the world.

The continental shelves, scoured by wave action, tides, ocean currents, and the flux of rivers, are economically the most productive areas of the sea. There fish, shell fish, and crustaceans abound; there, too, flourishes all the rooted vegetation of the sea which dies out at greater depths.

The ebb tide reveals the threshold of this strange world which slopes outward at an' angle so nearly level that the eye could scarcely detect a change. Krümmel found that the continental shelves of the North Atlantic had an average declivity of but 1 foot in 124. But at depths which usually range around a hundred fathoms these curious sea prairies terminate and plunge far more abruptly to the ocean floor. The angle of this slope may be rather startling, as in the Bay of Biscay, where it exceeds 41 per cent, steeper than the sides of the Matterhorn.

Continental shelves may embrace whole seas like the Baltic and the Persian Gulf, or be entirely absent beyond such cliffs as rise along the eastern coasts of Formosa and Mindanao. As their average width is thirty miles, they embrace some 7.6 per cent of all oceans and seas. The division is unequal: 4 per cent for the Indian Ocean, 6 per cent for the Pacific, and 13 per cent for the Atlantic.

The flatness of the continental shelves is broken by extraordinary submerged canyons which present a problem to geologists. Some, like those off the Hudson, the Congo, and the Indus, are mere prolongations of river channels carved long ago when the coast-line levels were vastly different. During the ice age many rivers must have raced with flood-tide frenzy across plains now covered by the sea, but this is at best a partial explanation. Underwater seepage from the land aided such erosion, while raw surfaces were etched by waves and tides. Diastrophism may have played its part, such rending of earth's crust as gouged the titanic trough of the Dead Sea. One of the most precipitous of these canyons lies off Monterey in California, where, within a few miles, soundings dip from three hundred to eighty-four hundred feet. The Grand Canyon carved by the Colorado through painted rocks is neither so steep nor so abysmal as this appalling chasm under the sea. So as we sail along the coast we may be passing over scenes that excel in grandeur our wildest mountain gorges.

Beyond the continental shelves lies the Deep Sea. The Atlantic registers an average depth of 3332 meters, the Indian 3897, the Pacific 4028. As continental shelves are included, three quarters of the ocean area is at least two miles deep, half is three miles or better, while occasional abysses exceed six miles. The most arresting features are the vast submerged plateaus. One fairly bisects the Atlantic. From the Arctic beyond the southern latitude of Cape Horn it follows the twisting *S* formation of that ocean at an average depth somewhat under two miles, flanked by gulfs three miles deep or more. A similar plateau prongs northward from Antarctica to the coasts of Hindustan to divide the Indian Ocean, while another reaches upward from Antarctica across the southern Pacific to Central America.

Popular fancy has long pictured these immense areas as the graves of drowned continents. Thus the Azores have been called the mountain peaks of a lost Atlantis. The Indian Ocean, too, had its Lemuria, for how otherwise explain the presence of lemurs in Malaya and far-off Madagascar? In the Pacific the vanished world of Mu has intrigued even such hardheaded scientists as Darwin. Coral atolls may fringe subsiding mountain peaks, while the weird stone faces of Easter Island, called the strangest sky line in the world, hint at a larger population than could have been supported on isolated islets. Several books, more sensational than convincing, have been written on the subject of lost continents, but scientists now discredit such theories. More and more they are convinced that both continents and oceans were well established long before the development of mammalian life.

These great submerged plateaus are not the only impressive features of the ocean floor. Other considerable ridges create lesser but still gigantic compartments. They influence the flow of currents, temperature, and salinity even where the outlet or sill is relatively deep. The western Caribbean is roughly a mile deep where it merges with the Atlantic, but the partially enclosed basin reaches depths of nearly four miles and a half. Many such ridges fret the bottom of the sea.

More superficial irregularities are those either shallower or deeper than the average. Shallows of considerable extent, where passable by shipping, are called banks, like the Dogger Bank of the North Sea or the Grand Banks off Newfoundland; shallows more dangerous to navigation are shoals; those marked by the white froth of breakers, reefs.

Of special interest are volcanic peaks that do not quite show through. There is one off the California coast 7000 feet high with a crater 500 feet deep, yet no one has ever seen it, for its formidable crest lies more than half a mile below the waves.

Islands are welcome interruptions amid otherwise interminable waters. The South Pacific is a noticeably rich territory. Some of its islets have enormous bulk and altitude. The highest mountain in the world is really Mauna Kea in Hawaii, for, though partially submerged, it towers approximately 30,000 feet above the ocean floor.

Even more fascinating because more mysterious are those abysses which seem to have been gouged out by Titan fingers when the world was still plastic. Although they occupy scarcely 1 per cent of ocean's area, they are of peculiar significance. Many geologists view them as the roots of gigantic mountain ranges of the future, for deep inward folds in earth's crust seem prone to split and buckle into jagged peaks. These depressions are variously named basins,

troughs, trenches, and plain deeps. They are deep, too.
The lowest level in the Atlantic so far discovered is the Mil-
waukee Deep off Haiti, 30,246 feet. The Arctic, now generally incorporated with the Atlantic, attains its nadir at
18,456 feet, off the northeastern coast of Siberia. The Indian
Ocean, though generally deeper than the Atlantic, shows
no such aberrations, for its "low" is the Wharton Deep off
Java, 22,968 feet.

The Pacific is the grandest of oceans, largest and deepest,
with the profoundest abysses. One of these, off Guam, measured by piano wire, showed a depth of 31,614 feet. A more
cavernous gulf off Japan yawns 34,626 feet, but most impressive of all is the Mindanao Deep near the great southern
island of the Philippines. Here a fathometer on the German
cruiser *Emden* registered 35,400 feet, or more than six and
two thirds miles. Were Everest dumped into that enormous
sink, sounding devices would probe more than a mile of
water to touch its hitherto inaccessible crest.

Kossinna found the mean depth of oceans and seas to
be 3800 meters, or two and a third miles; the mean height
of land 800 meters, or slightly over half a mile. And so, if
all the continents were cast into the sea, they would form
only submerged plateaus like Atlantis and Lemuria and Mu,
for there is water enough to flood the globe to a depth of
more than a mile and a half.

CHAPTER IV

The Romance of Soundings

Deeper than e'er plummet sounded . . .

SHAKESPEARE

Ocean soundings are older than history. Herodotus mentions them, while there is a distinct nautical flavor in St. Paul's shipwreck as recounted in the Book of Acts. Deeming "that they drew near to some country," the shipmen "sounded, and found it twenty fathoms," sounded "again and found it fifteen." In alarm, "they cast four anchors out of the stern, and wished for the day."

Soundings, to the mariner, are the blind man's cane tapping along crowded streets. Thus Bering groped through the fogs of the Aleutians as did Captain Cook among the shoals of the Great Barrier Reef of Australia. Columbus, misled by the floating meadows of the Sargasso Sea, felt for a new world by letting down a cannon ball upon a rope for two hundred fathoms, but failed to find bottom. Magellan, doing the same in the Pacific, sagely concluded that "he must be over the deepest part of the ocean."

Once on a British trader, blundering at quarter speed into a nameless hamlet in the Philippines, I stood beside the captain as the midshipmen cast the lead. "Five fathoms —sir, four and a half, a half scant, four." Then we struck, fortunately on soft ooze whence the flood tide soon released us. Mark Twain, our greatest humorist, chose his pen name from the leadsman's cry in the mud-choked Mississippi.

Heaving the lead, "flying the blue pigeon"—what romance still lingers in those salty phrases. Not only depth of water but the nature of the bottom was investigated. Soft mud might mean a dragging anchor; rocks, a lost one. Hence fishermen, feeling their way through the fogs of the Grand Banks, still "grease" the lead. Whalers did the same, and legends have invested Nantucket skippers with almost occult powers in determining their whereabouts by "tasting" such samples. No wonder seamen, grown superstitious, believe in wonders.

In 1580 when Captain Arthur Pet sailed from London in the good "Barke George" of forty tons burden with a crew of nine men and a boy to explore the Northeast Passage, his instructions read: "At the end of every four glasses . . . sound with your dipsin lead and note diligently what depth you find and also the ground. But if it happens that you cannot get ground, yet note what depths you did prove and could find no ground."

Sounding lines are like enormously elongated fingers thrust into the depths by one who cannot see. Captain Cook, in his world wanderings, and Captain Ross, in the Antarctic, were perhaps the first to employ them systematically. Modern invention has improved greatly upon the lead or the cannon ball on a rope, but the problem remains unchanged: "How far is it to bottom?"

Tourists at Monte Carlo should inspect the museum, which is filled with elaborate sounding and dredging devices. It is more interesting and less expensive than a visit to the more famous casino, which, by the way, financed the investigations which employed this apparatus.

Soundings are the alphabet of the chart which navigators must learn to read. They spatter its surface like a spluttering pen, tracing the channel through a maze of rocks and shoals. More than 1,300,000 such soundings were required for a single contour map off the coast of California!

Few mechanisms show greater improvement than modern sounding devices. The lead—all the fisherman needs in five fathoms—is quite inadequate to plumb the five-mile abyss. The hempen cord, with all its virtues, is no longer standard. It was last used on an extensive scale on the famous *Challenger* voyage (1872–76), the greatest scientific expedition of all time. This stout ship of the British Admiralty, while sailing lonely seas around the globe, sometimes trailed more than eight miles of cord and rope!

Lord Kelvin, who pioneered in so many fields, introduced that piano wire which has been everywhere adopted. Less than one twentieth of an inch in diameter, it has enormous tensile strength, at least ten times that of hemp. For heavier operations a three-strand, seven-strand, or even stronger steel cord or rope is used. Machines have been invented which unreel six hundred feet of wire in a minute and rewind it nearly as rapidly. They usually operate from the bow of the ship, which is held at a fixed angle against wind and current, but in stormy weather the stern is more sheltered. A weight of thirty or forty pounds suffices for depths up to a mile, but in deeper waters a type of rod is preferred that was first employed nearly a hundred years ago. This is geared to still heavier weights, which are sometimes released and left upon the bottom. Ships engaged in cable surveys even cut the wire, less valuable than the time involved in its recovery.

The deepest sounding made by the *Challenger* on her leisurely voyage of three and a half years was 4475 fathoms, or something over five miles. To sound this depth required about two and a half hours. Such depths present special problems. Currents sway the enormously long line from the perpendicular, while contact with the bottom is not instantly recorded. The cable ship *Nero*, surveying a route across the Pacific, discovered near Guam that famous deep which bears her name. Here the wire ran out 5269 fathoms, or 31,614 feet. The whole operation required nearly six hours.

A useful device for revealing unknown shoals is the "sentry," consisting mainly of a spread-eagle affair called a "kite" which trails a moving ship at any required depth. Let the delicate trigger strike bottom and a gong rings on board, while the kite rises to the surface.

Still more ingenious are the echo machines or fathometers, which are carried by all big passenger liners and many other ships. These, though often complicated, involve the simple principle of the echo. The mechanism sends a sound downward and the interval before the echo returns measures the distance. The officer upon the bridge of the great liner, groping through the fog into Liverpool or New York, listens by earphones or scans on a revolving disk an almost continuous series of such reverberations. In great depths readings must be corrected for pressure and salinity in the water, as speed of transmission varies from about 1400 to 1620 meters per second. This marvelous listening robot can plumb depths of more than four miles in ten seconds, even in stormy weather, and while the ship is sailing at twenty knots. The war, with all its wreckage, has speeded invention so that sounding devices now disclose such lurking perils as submarines and icebergs.

Although echo machines may reveal to the trained ear the difference between a soft or a rocky bottom, their province is to register depth. Other apparatus is required to disclose the type of life below, as well as the nature of the water and underlying sediments. Hence a wealth of ever more complex equipment has been invented.

Silken tow nets sieve out the minute sea life at varying depths. The *Challenger* dragged oyster dredges along the bottom, and sometimes huge otter nets with a mouth spread of fifty feet. In the red clay abysses of the South Pacific a single operation required from twelve to fourteen hours. As the harvest was laboriously raised by winches still dripping with sediment so cold that the officers chilled their wine with it, even the humblest seaman wondered what strange creature might burst upon human sight for the first time.

Samples of water are brought up from varying depths in tubes which close automatically. They are tested for density and salinity. Thermometers record the temperature, usually at intervals of a hundred fathoms. In the early days delicate instruments were not only broken but the glass was ground literally to powder by the appalling pressure which, in the profoundest deeps, may exceed seven tons per square inch. Photometers record the penetration of light, which decreases rapidly and soon fades out altogether. Even those more subtle actinic rays, the ultraviolet, presently disappear. Below lie the regions of perpetual darkness and almost freezing cold.

The greased lead no longer suffices for bottom samples. Dredges scrape them off, while steel jaws bite out capacious mouthfuls. But the scientist seeking deeper borings now forces long tubes into the bottom. Professor Shepard, off the Pacific Coast, loaded such a tube with six hundred pounds of lead, equipped it with a penetrating nose, and sent it hurtling into the depths. Cores six feet deep or more were the usual result, while once the javelinlike rod, impelled by the giant hand of gravity, pierced twenty-four feet of sediment to bring up a compressed core seventeen feet long!

Dr. C. J. Piggott has even employed a curious cannon. Lowered far beneath the surface, it shoots such a rod into the bottom with high explosives. To go gunning for deep-sea sediments is, indeed, an innovation for the sportsman.

Improvements upon the customary type employ a square tube equipped with a removable side. This presents the oozy strata undisturbed.

Cores of material bored from the bottom of the sea may tell as much about former ages as rock ledges hundreds of feet in thickness. For the deposits of a muddy river in a single day may rival the sediment of a thousand years in the deeper abysses. Traps lowered to record the rate of sediment accumulation sometimes show not only the amount but even the direction from which it came. Well-nigh numberless are the devices for probing the secrets of the "hoary deep."

Current measurements, so vital about great harbors and in the leading commerce lanes across the seas, also reveal conditions in deeper waters. They present problems of their own, for the observer cannot sit beneath a tree to watch such currents glide by. On the contrary, he is sometimes a part of them. Nevertheless, much information has been gleaned about ocean's drifts and movements even to the very bottom.

Those Cretan or Phoenician mariners who began sounding long ago would marvel at the progress made since their day. Exploring the ocean is no longer left to hardy fishermen or sailors or even co-operative cable ships, but is directed by the leading governments of the world. Ships are specially designed and equipped for such research. They carry not only a bewildering assortment of winches, dredges, and other apparatus but complete laboratories where trained scientists record a multitude of findings, analyze specimens, and classify those grotesque forms of life which are continually emerging from the depths.

And yet, with all their probing into the world beneath the sea, there still remain large areas where not one sounding has ever been made!

CHAPTER V

Carpets on Ocean's Floor

> . . . doth suffer a sea change
> Into something rich and strange.
> SHAKESPEARE

The elements gnaw the land like famished wolves. As their assaults grow fiercer the higher we climb, what terrifying storms must rasp at Everest's icy peak! At lower levels the winds sweep away farms in clouds of dust, frost crumbles the rocks, while every raindrop filches substance from the soil. Fertility that might enrich whole counties swirls every year down the Ganges or the Mississippi to be swallowed up in the unresponsive sea.

This mineral content of the rivers amounts annually to some 3.7 cubic miles. At such a rate all the continents and islands, comprising twenty-three million cubic miles, would wear away in a little over six million years! Land, like water, seeks a common level—the dead flatness of a prairie.

This vast abrasion reveals to a geologist the life history of our uplands, but of what underlies the sea he knows pitifully little. It is a strange fact that we can observe the moon more clearly than our own earth. She turns toward us more than half her face veiled by no shred of vapor, while nearly three quarters of earth's surface lies hidden beneath waters which no human eye has ever penetrated.

The Paumotuan pearl diver thrusts down a rude contrivance by which to survey the gardens of his shallow seas, the branching corals, the sea fans, and the rainbow-tinted fish. But we can employ no such methods to examine those greater depths shrouded in perpetual darkness. Hence our meager information comes from specimens bored into or gouged out or scraped off for our inspection.

The continental shelves, as we have noted, are scoured continuously by waves and tides and currents. But in the depths beyond lies unbroken calm—the calm of death, we might infer, did we not know something of the fantastic life that gropes there in darkness and cold. No erosion deepens those abysses; on the contrary, they are slowly filling up. Steep cliffs and rugged valleys are few; ridges are smooth and gently sloping; enormous plains predominate.

What would ocean's floor look like if we could see it? No vegetation would enliven its monotony, for rooted plants disappear where the light fades out, but everywhere we would find a many-colored sediment, the dust of aeons settled undisturbed upon the bottom of the sea.

This sediment is of two kinds: terrigenous, or the wastage of the continents; and pelagic, the remains of numberless dead sea things. Terrigenous deposits drape the continental shelves and slopes and trail downward to the abysses. The millstones of earth and water grind the rocks to clay, which mingles with animal and vegetable detritus to settle as mud over all the coastal shallows of the globe. This mud is mainly of three types—blue, red, and green. Blue mud, far the most prevalent, is rather a slaty gray or sometimes a dull brown that may turn almost black. Red mud, ranging from yellow-brown to red-brown, though widely distributed, is most prevalent in the Yellow Sea and off the coasts of Brazil. Green mud occurs in scattered patches on the continental shelves, and is frequently encountered along the coasts of eastern North America, Australia, Japan, South Africa, and the Ceylon Sea. Its green tinge comes from glauconite, a product of dissolving minerals.

Less noteworthy is volcanic mud. Sometimes greenish, it is more often dark gray or brown. Many volcanoes never emerge above the surface but spill out their multitinted tiling upon the ocean floor. There is also coral mud, formed when coral rock or sand disintegrates, which ranges from light gray to almost pure white.

These various muds resemble stair carpeting upon the threshold of the great deep. The vaster areas beyond are covered by the oozes and the clays—the characteristic sediment. Though mingled with dust from the uplands, from volcanic outpourings and meteoric showers, they are mainly pelagic, the remains of that life which swarms above in inconceivable myriads.

The oozes fall into two great divisions, calcareous and silicious, determined by the shells of the creatures which produce them. Calcareous shells, like the valves of clams and oysters, have a limy base known to chemists as calcium carbonate (the few polar species which utilize strontium rather than calcium are relatively unimportant). Limy oozes are also augmented by the skeletons of fish and sea mammals, and certain minute seaweeds. The crustaceans have a protective armor from that complex substance chitin, familiar in the shells of crabs and lobsters. Other sea life, mainly microscopic, prefers the more rigid and durable silicon, manufacturing transparent cases of nearly pure glass.

The limy oozes, much the most prevalent, are divided into pteropod and globigerina oozes. Pteropoda, true mollusks like our muscles, dart about like butterflies. Dying, their fragile shells rain down upon the bottom to form a characteristic sediment which appears sparingly in all the oceans. A product of shallow waters from four hundred to fifteen hundred fathoms, it varies from white to light brown through medium shades of gray. In its purest form it is almost 100 per cent lime.

Much more abundant is globigerina ooze, composed of those minute Foraminifera which swim about in surface waters. Their fairylike shells flutter downward like showers of snowflakes. Of many shapes, one species looks for all the world like a microscopic golf ball covered with sharp spines. With them mingle curious little plants which form limy bodies called Coccoliths. In the depths all these disintegrate into a creamy paste overlying layers of firmer texture that tend to solidify, for globigerina ooze is only chalk in its initial stages that may form beds hundreds of feet in thickness, like the white cliffs of Dover.

This ooze is of many hues from almost pure white to deep brown. Samples dredged up dripping wet may be rose-tinted, pale yellow, gray, bluish, or even green. Though rarely found at depths of more than four miles, its natural range is from the edges of the continental shelves down to two and a half miles, where it tends to merge into even more curious sediments.

There is enough globigerina ooze to mantle all the continents and islands with millions of square miles to spare. It seems to cover roughly two thirds of the Atlantic bottom, one half the Indian, and a third of the vast Pacific. Combined with pteropod ooze, it carpets fully half the ocean floor.

Less common but even more interesting are the silicious oozes. Those minute floating plants called diatoms, each in its glassy case, create characteristic sediments. Since they prefer cold waters, vast beds of diatom ooze occur in the northern Pacific, while around Antarctica a broad band girdles the globe. In places this great belt spans twenty degrees of latitude to cover at least ten million square miles or more than three times the area of the United States. Usually white or straw-colored, the ooze may be dirty gray, though other tints are woven into the pattern. The city of Richmond is built upon a bed of such deposits many feet in thickness, while there are pockets in California more than two thousand feet deep.

More beautiful even than the diatoms are the Radiolaria, whose microscopic cases of spun glass far surpass the jeweler's craftsmanship. Many are studded with spines and spicules which withstand the pressure of the deeper sea. They form widely scattered patches which are most abundant in the Pacific. North of the Equator a broad band of radiolarian ooze bridges halfway across that vast ocean. Such ooze, solidified, is used in polishing gems under the trade name of Barbados earth.

Rarely found at levels which favor globigerina deposits, this more durable sediment is a product of the deeper seas. It has been dredged from depths of five miles or more, where iron oxide dyes it a reddish or red-brown tint.

Although the silicious oozes (diatom and radiolarian) cover some 14 per cent of the ocean floor, the only other sediment which rivals globigerina ooze in extent is the red clay of the profounder depths. Vast areas occur in the Atlantic and Indian Oceans, while it underlies perhaps three fifths of the Pacific. It is the characteristic flooring below the 2200-fathom mark. Since numberless globigerina swarm in the upper waters, their shells no doubt sift downward as in shallower seas. But only a few of the almost indestructible spicules mingle with the bottom sediment. To be sure, this may show a limy content of 10 per cent or more, but there are few traces of the shell formations so conspicuous in calcareous deposits. It is significant that globigerina ooze, when treated with a mild acid, dissolves save for a residue of from 1 to 2 per cent which closely resembles red clay. The latter is presumably just such a residue, for lime disintegrates in icy temperatures under appalling pressure. Red clay is composed of iron, aluminum, and other minerals common in the earth crust. Iron oxide imparts the reddish tint which varies from bright brick to chocolate brown, and may even be bluish near the continental shelves. There are also traces of meteoric iron, the star dust of outer space winnowed by the atmosphere and filtered by the seas, together with queer nodules of manganese peroxide. These encrust the ear bones of whales and the teeth of giant sharks which swam the seas millions of years ago. In short, red clay seems to be the irreducible minimum of all the rubbish accumulated through the ages on the very basement floor of creation.

From much shallower depths another strange substance called bathybius has been dredged. It forms a gelatinous mass which Huxley once thought was elemental life substance or unorganized protoplasm. Now scientists regard it as either a limy precipitate in the water or the partially decomposed remains of countless protozoa, lowliest of all animal life. Whatever its origin, it remains one of the unsolved mysteries of the sea.

And so we may picture ocean's floor as covered with a vast mosaic of colors ranging from nearly pure white to almost jet black through every shade of red, yellow, green, blue, gray, and brown. Largest and most wonderful of all carpets, its rich designs are lost upon the weird dwellers in those regions, for many of them are blind, while those with eyes grope through darkness broken only by luminescent flashes.

How rapidly these sediments accumulate no one knows. Rivers may build up several feet of terrigenous shoal in a single year. Submerged moorings indicate that Globigerina may deposit an inch of ooze in a decade, while a thousand years would probably not suffice for such a layer of red clay.

Nor can anyone tell how deep these deposits lie. Attempts to bore into them have yielded an average penetration of only a few feet. In some cases one sediment seems to overlie another like a rug spread out upon a larger carpet.

Beneath that carpet at some unknown level lies the ocean floor. The geologist cannot delve there with pick and hammer. It is thought that the hidden rock layers of earth's crust are denser and heavier than those on land, the sima of the geodesist, but this is still conjectural. For the startling fact remains that what lies hidden under those slowly deepening layers of ooze and clay has so far proved almost as inaccessible as though it were upon the planet Mars.

CHAPTER VI

How the Oceans Got Their Salt

The sea's a thief, whose liquid surge resolves
The moon into salt tears.
                              SHAKESPEARE
The unplumbed, salt, estranging sea.
          MATTHEW ARNOLD

Salt in windrows, in mountains, in continents! Salt enough to bury Mount Washington and the Great Smokies, to cover the whole United States beneath a layer of shining crystals a mile and a half deep; enough to form a continent as big as Africa! All this salt is dissolved in the sea. How did it get there, where did it come from? Surely not the least of ocean's mysteries is salt.

Curious stuff this, the only mineral required by man that he can appropriate directly. Others he gets from meat and vegetables, but Mr. Piltdown, long ago, licked his salt from the rocks at low tide.

The chemist calls it sodium chloride, a simple marriage between two elements, both poisonous. Sodium, a silvery metal, floats upon water; swallow a fragment and it would burn the throat like a red-hot iron. Chlorine, a heavy, greenish gas, would smother you. In nature's laboratory, however, they unite in table salt, the only type familiar to the layman. The chemist recognizes many more—salts of magnesium, potassium, calcium, and different metals besides sodium.

Not all the mineral content of the sea, however, is common salt. Nearly a quarter of that content is comprised of alien substances. Here are the proportions:

Sodium chloride (common salt) 77.7%
Magnesium chloride (source of much of the light metal
    used in airplane construction) 10.8
Magnesium sulphate (another source of this metal) 4.7
Calcium sulphate (calcium makes bones) 3.6
Potassium sulphate (enters into seaweeds) 2.7
Calcium carbonate (the lime in oyster shells) 3
Magnesium bromide (source of many bromides) 2

There are also traces of other things. More than fifty of the ninety-odd elements that make up all matter have been identified in sea water. Probably all are present in minute quantities. The above proportions for the saline content of the sea remain pretty constant all over the world, although the amount of this content fluctuates widely. The Atlantic is the "saltiest" of the major oceans, particularly just north and south of the Equator. Next come the Indian Ocean and the southern Pacific. Less salty are the northern Pacific, the Arctic, and the areas around Antarctica.

Thirty-five parts of mineral content dissolved in 1000 parts of water is the average for all the oceans and their fringing or landlocked seas. The Atlantic shows a ratio slightly above 36, reduced near shore by rivers. In the Gulf of Guinea, off Africa, it falls to about 32 because of the Niger and the still huger Congo. The seas show greater variations. Saltiest of all is the Red Sea. Hemmed in by burning deserts, under rapid evaporation, its saline content sometimes rises above 42. In the shallow Baltic, freshest of all seas, it may sink below 7.

Surface waters are diluted by torrential downpours. The Indian Ocean is thus "freshened" by the deluge of the monsoons, as are the polar seas by melting ice. And yet, contrary to what we might suppose, most seas are saltier near the surface than farther down. In fact the heavier mineral content may decrease slowly with the depth. This is particularly true in the Atlantic. To be sure, there is a vast churning upward complicated by great currents like the Gulf Stream. And yet not the least of the mysteries that concern the salt in the sea is its erratic distribution.

How did the oceans become salt? Here clashing theories on the formation of our globe offer quite different explanations. According to one school of thought, the oceans were originally fresh water, since they floated in global clouds above the earth. Another school as stoutly maintains that they were always salt, for water seeping upward through the earth's crust holds much mineral content in solution. There is evidence to support both theories and a strong presumption that both are partially correct. But whatever the primordial seas may have been, they are slowly getting saltier.

The rivers are largely responsible. Every year, so estimates assure us, they bear into the sea more than 2,700,000,000 tons of soluble mineral matter. However, only a small part of this huge total—slightly over 2 per cent—is salt. More than 50 per cent may comprise carbonates, which shrink to a mere fraction of 1 per cent in the mineral content of the sea. Moreover, rivers differ widely. The "contribution" of the Colorado, for example, is quite unlike that of the Columbia. The problem is not so simple as it seems.

Everything dissolves in water. The alchemists of the Middle Ages, who sought a universal solvent, might have found it in this commonest of liquids. Water of absolute purity does not exist in nature. Always it carries a trace of something else. Thus by erosion the solid rocks dissolve and are swept into the sea.

Silicon, the substance of window glass, aside from oxygen, is the commonest element in rock, more than five hundred times more abundant than chlorine. But in the sea chlorine is nearly five thousand times as abundant as silicon! This reversal is truly staggering. Where did all this chlorine come from, and what happened to the silicon? True, the latter element is not particularly soluble, but there is relatively far more of it in river water than in the sea.

Aluminum, the metal of pots and pans, is next in order among the elements. But the ratio between aluminum in the rocks and in the mineral content of the sea is over 100,000:1; in iron it is more than 1,000,000:1!

Among certain elements there exists a strange affinity; they seem to share family characteristics. One of these families is called the halogens, comprising chlorine, bromine, and iodine. But in the sea chlorine is nearly three hundred times as prevalent as bromine. It is more than a hundred and thirty thousand times as abundant as iodine.

A similar relationship exists between potassium and sodium. In some respects they are almost twins. They are nearly equal in igneous rocks. In river water, however, the ratio of sodium to potassium is about 3:1; in the sea it is 50:1.

Unlike silicon or aluminum, sulphur is more commonly found among ocean's minerals than in rock, while in chlorine the proportions become almost fantastic. In fact "salinity" is a poor name for ocean's mineral content. "Chlorinity" is a better one, for this muddy, noxious gas is the major partner not only in table salt but in magnesium chloride, the next most common mineral in brine. In short it is so abundant that it almost dominates the sea.

The oceans evidently do not passively accept what the

rivers give them. They stir that mineral matter with their tides and currents as in a gigantic crucible and make decided alterations. Three factors seem to determine their acceptance or rejection of any mineral: Does it readily dissolve? Is it subject to chemical reaction? Is it essential to living organisms in the sea?

Nitrogen, the predominant gas in air, serves merely to dilute the oxygen. Too much of the latter would make us drunk, more might prove fatal. Common salt is similarly an inert substance in the sea. Nothing extracts it, hence its slow accumulation. Marine life and ocean sediments want little of it. It stays put.

In contrast, potassium comprises some 10–14 per cent of dried kelp, those leathery cornstalks of our beaches. Silicon makes up nearly three quarters of dried diatoms, microscopic plants that swarm in countless trillions in all the oceans of the world. It also shapes the gemlike cases of the radiolarians that sprinkle the deepest gulfs. Aluminum compounds form much of the red clay of the Pacific, while iron and manganese impart the characteristic color. The carbonates so prominent in river waters form the shells of clams and the skeletons of whales. Sometimes they comprise nearly 100 per cent of that most prevalent of ocean carpetings, globigerina ooze.

All this reflects a vast program of creation and destruction as the oceans labor with the materials that the rivers thrust upon them. One portion is useful to the multitudinous life that swarms in their waters, another is sifted out for bottom sediments, while the perhaps unwelcome residue remains to accumulate as salt.

So much for the rivers and their varied gifts to the sea. Much of the sea's sulphur supply never drifted down the Amazon or the Nile. It was belched upward by volcanoes.

Both visible and submerged, they pour forth their acrid yellow powder from the earth's internal laboratory.

No such upheavals, however, or any mere melting of rock strata can account for all the chlorine in the ocean. We must go back to that remote geological time when boiling seas ascended in seething vapor to descend again in one continuous deluge. This frightful turmoil probably continued for millenniums until cooling brought peace to warring skies and seas. Earth's new-formed crust must have melted at a prodigious rate, so that, while the seas may have been fresh water in the beginning, they did not long remain so.

But even such rapid dissolution of mineral matter would not explain all the ocean's chlorine. We are led to suspect the atmosphere rather than the rocks as the source of some of the original supply. True, we cannot dogmatize about our planet two billion years ago. But we can well assume that chlorine was an important part of that tempestuous atmosphere. We can dimly see a sun glaring down through skies all green with chlorine gas at seas that boiled above rocks but recently red-hot. A vast absorption of such chlorine would have been inevitable. This, we may conjecture, marked the birth of ocean's salt, that original bank account which the contributions of the rivers and upward seepage from the hot interior have augmented ever since.

Evaporation promotes extreme saltiness in certain isolated waters. That weird lake, the Dead Sea, has become bitter not only through the inflow of the Jordan, but because it is the dried-up remnant of a larger lake. The same shrinkage has given Utah its Salt Lake. But such evaporation does not alter the salinity of the oceans, even though it lowers their surface some two and a half feet annually, enough to dry them up completely in a few thousand years; for all this moisture comes back again in rains and rivers to sustain the vast equilibrium of salt and sea.

Not everything that washes down from the uplands is mineral. Much is organic substance, the decay of plants or animals. This, too, is worked over to supply vital fertility to ocean life, as we shall observe later.

There are more volatile contributions also. Oxygen, the very breath of life, mingles at the surface and penetrates even to the abysses. Some gases are thus absorbed, others given forth. Carbon dioxide and nitrogen bubble upward to drift away with the winds. The oceans thus acquire or rid themselves of foreign substances simply by breathing.

Still more mysterious things are found in ocean depths. One of these is "heavy water," quite like the ordinary fluid in composition, but with some unknown adjustment of atoms or electrons which makes it "different." The hydrogen of this queer liquid is called deuterium. Yes, it is a far cry since Boyle, the brilliant amateur, or perhaps Lavoisier first made their crude analyses of sea water. Yet, with all the advances in our knowledge, neither chemistry nor her sister sciences have quite explained just how the ocean got its salt.

CHAPTER VII

Rivers in the Sea

Like to the Pontic sea,
Whose icy current and propulsive course
Ne'er feels retiring ebb, but keeps due on
To the Propontic and the Hellespont.
SHAKESPEARE

Earth's mightiest rivers are in the sea. Beside them the Amazon is but a meadow brook. They preserve the oceans from becoming vast, stagnant lakes and profoundly affect the continents. Because of them winter roses bloom in Oregon and daffodils in Cornwall; because of them drought parches the deserts of South Africa and the rainless coast of Peru.

Ponce de Leon, sailing south along the Florida coast to look for the Fountain of Youth, found instead, "a current such that, although they had a great wind, they could not proceed further." This was the white man's introduction to the Gulf Stream, the greatest of ocean currents. Off the coast of Yucatán it sometimes flows faster than five miles an hour. Past the Florida capes it carries nearly two billion tons of water a minute, a majestic torrent forty miles wide sweeping clear to the bottom—482 fathoms—at a speed of sixty to a hundred miles a day. At Hatteras, where it has cast up the dreaded Diamond Shoals, it has broadened to fifty miles, slackened to a speed of from fifty to seventy-three miles per day, and become three degrees colder, but it still hurries along more than ten cubic miles of water every hour. Off the Banks of Newfoundland it is sometimes swerved from its course by the downrush of icy waters from Baffin Bay. It has lost from twelve to nineteen degrees of temperature and slowed to little more than a mile an hour. Turning eastward, it sends off great branches. One which bathes the British Isles and the western coast of Europe has been traced as far north as Spitzbergen, within six hundred miles of the Pole. Part of this stream curves around North Cape to give Russia its ice-free Murmansk coast. Another great branch stems off by the Azores and Africa to redouble upon its course as the North Equatorial Current.

Vitus Bering, feeling his way along the Aleutian Islands, met but did not recognize the major stream of the Pacific, the Japanese Current. Perhaps he blamed instead the demons of fog and cold for his erratic longitude, for he had been carried more than eight degrees out of his reckoning. This vast ocean river, emerging from the warmer seas of Japan at a speed varying from forty-eight to seventy-two miles a day, swings on the path of a great circle down our own northwest coast, then back again in the North Pacific eddy.

The Mozambique Current, which sweeps down the east coast of Africa and around its southern tip, Agulhas, at an average speed of two miles an hour is perhaps the most dependable of the Indian Ocean variety. Marco Polo mentioned it when he wrote of Madagascar, "The currents in those parts are of exceeding force." Elsewhere in that ocean they follow the changing mood of the monsoons. These fierce winds may not only halt the currents but actually reverse their direction. One great stream flows past Ceylon at eighty miles a day, another along Arabia at a hundred miles. This latter current, near the Equator, sometimes speeds before the southwest monsoon at seven miles an hour, a veritable millrace. Some years ago when I was sailing through the Maldive Islands, the captain remained up all night for fear of such dangerous currents. For seafaring men long ago recognized their menace. Portuguese caravels, en route to the Spice Islands, were often baffled by them. Whalers' logbooks in the South Pacific bristle with complaints of "Strange motions of ye waters so that a shippe may split upon rocks even in the calmest wether." Because of such "motions" the coral atolls of the Tuamotus have been christened the "Dangerous Archipelago."

Currents can be helpful too. Cape Cod schooners beating northward in winter with loads of oysters from Virginia, when freezing seas sent them "down by the head," veered out into the Gulf Stream off Nantucket to melt the ice.

It was a Nantucket skipper in London who explained to Benjamin Franklin why certain ships made speedier passages from the New World to the Old. He even traced the Gulf Stream upon a chart which Franklin verified upon his return passage in 1775 by noting changes in the color of the water and taking temperatures.

Such tropic currents are not wholly warm. Ocean temperatures decline rapidly with depth. Even the Gulf Stream grows cool a hundred feet down. Its steamy surface is but a blanket upon a moving cradle of colder water. On the other hand, some currents are entirely cold. There is an eastward swirl about Antarctica driving endlessly around the globe before westerly gales. Cape Horn diverts some of this cold water northward in the leisurely Humboldt Current which flows little faster than half a mile an hour. Now and again it loses out in a wrestling match with El Niño, a warm current from the tropics, to upset the topsy-turvy climate of Peru. A similar stream, the Benguella Current, steals up along the southwest coast of Africa. That bold adventurer, Vasco da Gama, avoided it on his voyage to India by swinging far to the westward. Into steamship lanes cold drifts from both polar seas bear icebergs such as wrecked the *Titanic*. The Labrador Current helps to chill all northeastern America, including much of New England. Every few years a howling "nor'easter" drives a great field of floe ice miles long and many feet thick into Cape Cod Bay to blunder about until spring thaws.

These cold rivers of the sea are not so unpleasant in themselves as in their effects. Veered from the coast by offshore winds, they cause an upwelling of deeper water at the edges, like a board dragged across a mud puddle. This upwelling seldom comes from below six hundred feet, but it is cool enough to chill the fringing waters of Angola and California.

Unlike other rivers, ocean currents have neither source nor mouth. The Gulf Stream does not rise in the Gulf of Mexico: it merely hurries through on a continuing journey. Every drop of water that passes the Florida capes is replaced by a drop coming from south or east. Just as the blood does not flow merely from heart to finger tips, so ocean currents are but sections of the vast circulatory system of the sea.

Such surface meanderings produce great vortices or areas of relative "no motion." Most famous is the Sargasso Sea, onetime bourn of missing ships and theme of countless gruesome legends.

Mere surface patterns, however, give but a superficial idea of ocean currents. If we could see to the bottom, we would often find deep currents moving in quite different directions, while intervening layers drifted away at varying angles. This is noticeable in the outlets of landlocked areas, such as the Black Sea, which hastens out through the Bosporus while an unseen bottom current flows inward—two blue rivers in the same bed bound in opposite directions.

The Mediterranean is another example. Excessive evaporation lowers its level, causing an influx of the Atlantic past Gibraltar of from two to four miles per hour. Meanwhile a deeper current flows as steadily outward.

Broadly speaking, the surface waters of the three great oceans have a northerly drift while bottom currents creep southward. With many interruptions and reversals, such is the global trend. Intervening layers obey more complex impulses, for technically one drop of water cannot be displaced without affecting all the other drops; there is, moreover, a perceptible up-and-down motion, a sinking of waters in certain areas and an upsurging in others. Visible currents merely reveal a little of the vast turmoil and commotion of the sea.

Great cosmic forces are the motive power. First among these is gravity. Nearly two thousand years ago Strabo, noting that the earth was a sphere, observed that "things trend inward." Hence water seeks its level—seeks but never finds it, for something is always unsettling that level. The waters of the Gulf of Mexico are actually about eight inches higher than those of the outer Atlantic. One reason why the Gulf Stream is in such a hurry is because it is running downhill. Wherever such inequalities occur, ocean currents set forth to correct them in an endless quest for equilibrium.

Other cosmic forces interfere with gravity. One of these is temperature. Warm water expands and rises, cold water contracts and sinks. Salinity has somewhat the same effect. The oceans on either side of America have no common level. Measurements indicate that the Pacific is higher by more than a foot and a half, presumably because the Atlantic, the saltiest of oceans, is a trifle heavier. Yet salinity does not steadily increase with depth as we would suppose; on the contrary, the Atlantic is saltiest within a hundred yards of the surface. Below the hundred-fathom mark, however, salinity in all the oceans varies little more than one part in a thousand, from 34.5 to 35.5.

Temperature not only changes the weight of water but removes some of it by evaporation. Negligible at the polar regions, this is important at the Equator, but is most marked in certain confined areas like the Red Sea. That is one reason why surface waters flow into that sea from November to March and flow outward from June to September.

Atmospheric pressure is another disturber of the status quo. A barometric change of one inch means a corresponding change of more than a foot in water levels since the weight of the atmosphere presses down unevenly upon the sea.

The attraction of great land masses pulls neighboring waters out of plumb. The upper Bay of Bengal, for example, is thought to be many feet higher than normal because of the Himalaya Mountains.

The rotation of the earth is a major factor. This prevents all the oceans from piling up at the poles, for the globe, like an elderly gentleman, bulges at the waistline. The equatorial spin of more than a thousand miles an hour diminishes to zero at the poles. That is why surface waters in northern latitudes move clockwise, those in southern latitudes anti-clockwise. This global whirl makes the Mississippi River actually run uphill and helps to send the Gulf Stream and the Japanese Current sprawling generally eastward.

Then there are the waves and the tides, both so important that we must reserve them for other chapters.

Currents, on the surface, are governed most of all by the winds. The picture is clearer if we recall that the oceans are not one but two, a sea of air resting upon a sea of water.

The volatile air responds more readily to the great cosmic forces we have briefly considered. Warm air, expanding, piles up great masses of barometric high pressure which gravity pulls down to flatten out; these masses flow into depressions hundreds of miles distant, which become the whirling vortices of storm. Meanwhile the solid globe spins on beneath these moiling gases which struggle to catch up in trade winds and prevailing westerlies.

The currents of the atmospheric ocean are the winds which drag after them corresponding currents in the less responsive sea. As we observed, they sometimes not only arrest such currents but start them going in the opposite direction. They also pile up the waters in the Caribbean, which gives the Gulf Stream its original impetus.

Land masses interrupt the orderly working out of this vast program. The Gulf Stream is turned backward by Africa, the Japanese Current by America. Cape Horn, like a gigantic hook, plucks the Humboldt Current from the circumpolar whirl, while there are countless other obstacles to the free circulation of the waters. Most dominant of land masses is Antarctica. Around its desolate shores the major oceans mingle in one uninterrupted sweep. The spreading icecap, which there overlaps the sea in cliffs hundreds of feet high, breaks off in chunks many miles long to tumble fresh waters into that global caldron.

Submerged ridges, such as the fabled lost Atlantis, also play their part. They divert and partially confine bottom currents, which, vaulting over hidden obstructions, intrude upon the surface.

Still more important is temperature. The surface waters, which surround Antarctica sink slowly to spread along the bottom, reaching into the Atlantic, the Indian, and the Pacific oceans in great tongues. These meet the southward drift of bottom waters and, being less saline, slowly rise.

Around the North Pole, although there is no continent and no untrammeled whirl of the seas, low temperatures and melting ice cause similar drifts. Hence it has been estimated that the nearly enclosed Arctic changes its entire watery content in something over a hundred and fifty years. O. Pettersson believes that melting ice is the main cause of vertical circulation. He wrote, "There exists in every ice-filled region of the ocean an indraft of warmer and saltier water as an undercurrent from lower latitudes."

This vast flux of waters brings life to the abysmal sea. Oxygen is the essential element. Surface waters absorb it in that mutual mingling when liquids and gases come together, so that a liter of sea water on the average contains 18.7 cubic centimeters of gas; 34 per cent of this is oxygen, showing a more rapid absorption of that element by water than by air, of which it constitutes only about 21 per cent. Some oxygen in the deep seas drifts downward from the surface, but the great source is the bottom currents from the polar regions. This circulation is nowhere in sharper contrast than in the North Sea and the Black Sea. The former, scoured by ocean streams, swarms with life; the latter, isolated save for the feeble trickle of the Bosporus, is, in its deeper portions, a stagnant pond. Its depths disclose no oxygen and no life, only smelly hydrogen sulphide, the gaseous herald of decay. The Black Sea is like a human limb slowly gangrening from restricted circulation.

Ocean currents are charted in various ways. Vivid color contrasts may reveal them. When sailing from the Philippines out into the China Sea, I noted so sharp a division between a deep blue and an almost olive green that I could trace its outline along the ship's side.

Wave action also differs. On my first return voyage from England to America, I was seated at dinner when, almost as abruptly as though we had struck a rock, we entered the

Gulf Stream. Instantly the prolonged heave of the Atlantic was replaced by a crisscross shudder that sent more than one pale-faced passenger to the deck.

Temperatures are quite as decisive. A classic example is that of the Coast Guard cutter *Tampa*, which in 1922 paused long enough on the edge of the Gulf Stream to record a bow temperature of 34 degrees, a stern of 56.

Moving objects are silent witnesses of ocean drifts. Arthur Jenkinson, ambassador to Russia in the reign of Queen Elizabeth, while promoting a northeast passage to China, wrote, "There comes a continual stream or current through the Mare Glaciale [Frozen Sea] of such swiftness that if you cast anything upon it, it would presently be carried out of sight toward the west." This current was confirmed when ice cakes bearing equipment from the ill-fated *Jeannette* expedition to northern Siberia appeared three years later off southwestern Greenland.

The Japanese Current strews the floats of native fishermen along the California shores. In 1815 the whaling ship *Forrestal* picked up off Cape Conception a Japanese junk that had drifted disabled for seventeen months. Only three of the crew survived. Their experiences would have furnished material for a dozen ghastly sea tales.

Governments send out numberless bottles to trace currents. The United States Coast and Geodetic Survey provides ship captains with standard messages for such bottles in eight languages, including Esperanto. The date and position of launching are compared with those of the finders. One such bottle drifted more than fifteen thousand miles in six years.

Most accurate of all measurements are those taken from a fixed position. Lightships, ideal for the purpose, are not always or often in the desired position, but the survey ship *Meteor* once anchored for two days in three miles of water, sending down measuring apparatus to record current velocities at varying levels.

The first systematic investigation of the Gulf Stream was inaugurated by the United States Coast and Geodetic Survey in 1845. Through the intervening century much water has flowed by the Florida capes and from it no little information has been "seined and netted." But a deal of mystery, deep as Bering's fogs, still veils these vast, tireless rivers of the sea.

CHAPTER VIII

The Tides

> . . . like a mighty sea
> Forced by the tide to combat with the wind;
> Now sways it that way, like the selfsame sea
> Forc'd to retire by fury of the wind;
> Sometime the flood prevails, and then the wind.
>
> SHAKESPEARE

Julius Caesar, facing the Atlantic upon the northern coast of France, was amazed at "that vast and open sea with its strong tides." From the nearly tideless Mediterranean to St. Malo's maximum range of thirty-nine feet was indeed a startling change. Elsewhere he complained because the "tides had rushed in from the main ocean which always happens twice in twelve hours," a careless error on the part of the great conqueror. Herodotus, in his wanderings, was impressed by an arm of the Red Sea, where "every day the tide ebbs and flows." Numerous other allusions to the subject have survived from antiquity.

The Chinese, the Arabs, and the Norsemen knew something of the tides, but little of what caused them. They even thought them the "breathing of the earth monster," a not unnatural supposition. Caesar came near the truth when he wrote of Britain, "It happened that night to be full moon, which usually occasions very high tides in those oceans." Whether he considered our satellite as more than a spirit influence is doubtful, however, for farmers still plant turnips in the "dark of the moon." Pliny stated the case more correctly by giving credit to both sun and moon, but it remained for Sir Isaac Newton to solve the riddle in his law of gravitation: "Every particle of matter attracts every other particle directly with its mass and inversely with the square of the distance."

Although in mass the sun is 27,000,000 times greater than the moon, its distance is nearly 390 times greater, and 390 squared is a formidable figure. Proximity proving more potent than mass, the moon's influence is more than twice that of the sun's, or in the ratio 2.17:1.

The tides are exceedingly complex, involving many mathematical formulas, yet they manifest simply the pull of the moon and sun upon our planet. While the crust yields but slightly, the more volatile waters hump up toward the moon, flatten out on the sides, and hump up again on the opposite sector of the globe. These world-wide oscillations maintain a steadfast rhythm so that, should gravity suddenly cease, they would continue with diminishing magnitude for many days. As the moon's period of revolution is nearly twenty-eight days, while there are but twenty-four hours in the day, the times of high and low water shift progressively at any given locality. Nor, strictly speaking, are there two tides daily, but rather two in twenty-four hours, fifty minutes, thirty-eight seconds, so we need not be too critical of Julius Caesar.

The moon and sun are not always in harmony. Now they pull together; now at cross-purposes. At full moon, when they are on opposite sides of the globe, occur those "high course" tides which astronomers call "spring tides." Two weeks later, when both are on the same side, we have a similar situation, although their combined pull is not then so pronounced. In between are periods when they are dragging at right angles to cause what fishermen call "low course" and scientists "neap" tides.

If the globe were one vast sea, two orderly waves would girdle it in a little over twenty-four hours. How high those waves would be is conjectural, for there is no accurate method of measuring tidal altitudes in mid-ocean. Yet isolated islands furnish a clue. In Tahiti the rise is only a foot, in Hawaii about two. In the Azores and St. Helena it varies from one and a half to three feet.

This mighty rhythm, however, is disrupted by the intrusion of land masses. In mid-ocean tidal waters merely bob up and down or indulge in a vast merry-go-round; near shore disturbed levels set up powerful currents. Hence variations in both time and altitude may be considerable. In Chesapeake Bay the time of high water varies nearly twelve hours from one locality to another, or nearly as much as should occur from voyaging halfway around the globe. Tidal currents tear up and down the coast doing the weirdest things. High tide arrives at Nantucket Shoals Lightship nearly four hours earlier than at Boston, when we would expect a difference of but a few minutes. The currents seem to rotate endlessly. Two coming together at Edgartown on Martha's Vineyard so nearly balance that the rise and fall is only about ten inches. There actually are some twenty-five coastal localities in the world which have no tide at all.

Tides are also influenced by the moon's position relative to the earth's Equator. When she is directly overhead, morning and evening tides are roughly the same, but let the moon swing north or south of the Equator and the balance is upset. Then either the morning or evening tide is noticeably higher.

In Seattle, while two successive high waters may be nearly equal, the corresponding low-water marks may differ by as much as eight feet. In other localities low-water marks may be equal and high-water marks affected. Such aberrations are called "diurnal inequalities."

In certain places the flood tide is interrupted by a temporary ebb only to be resumed for a new maximum. But still queerer things occur. At Manila there is but one tide a day instead of the customary two. A similar situation prevails in certain localities along the China Sea, on the Alaskan coast, the Gulf of Mexico, and a few other places. There are localities where a single tide daily is the usual though not invariable program. Early voyagers noted such a situation in the Gulf of Carpentaria in northern Australia, while Russian scientists report a similar tide in Penzinsk Gulf which has reached the startling height of thirty-seven feet.

Sometimes, because of her eccentric orbit, the moon increases her tidal pull by approaching several thousand miles nearer the earth. This factor becomes noticeable along the eastern coast of Canada.

The Panama Canal well illustrates how land masses create tidal inequalities. The Atlantic side generally has but one tide daily, with a usual range of less than a foot, a maximum height under three feet. The Pacific end of the canal has the customary two tides with an average rise of over twelve feet, an extreme altitude of more than twenty.

There is an amazing thrust of the tides in narrowing straits or bays. Magellan was dismayed by a forty-foot tide at the mouth of the strait that he discovered; Captain Cook by a thirty-foot rise in Cook Inlet, Alaska. Some great seaports are subject to abnormal fluctuations. I once observed the *Baltic*, then the largest liner afloat, steam proudly up the Mersey River to Liverpool only to stick fast in the mud when the tide ebbed nearly thirty feet. The wash and scour of the seven-mile current which results there are major erosion factors.

There are enormous as well as freakish tides in the
Okhotsk Sea, but the highest known are in the Bay of Fundy.
There the flood comes in like a millrace, as Kipling noted
when he wrote, "the hogs from ebb tide mark run scamper-
ing back to shore." At Noel Bay, according to H. A. Mar-
mer, official measurements record a maximum of 50.5 feet,
although Moncton citizens, claiming to have the highest
tides on earth, assured me these had risen in their river inlet
72 feet. On Fundy shores one may observe a three-masted
schooner, stranded on a steep shingle beach, float away on
the next high water.

Although the moon is the major cause of tides, this is
not invariably so. At Tahiti the solar influence predomi-
nates, as it does along the southern coast of Australia. Nor
are tides exclusively marine. Lake Superior experiences a
surface variation of several inches. Even some wells have
tides, a phenomenon noted by the elder Pliny at Gades and
other regions. The artesian well at Longport, New Jersey,
which is 805 feet deep with a 6-inch bore, shows a daily tidal
range of over two feet. Moreover, those mysterious aberrations called seiches introduce further complications. These
were first observed in Alpine lakes in 1730. In October 1841
the waters on one shore of Lake Geneva actually rose over
six feet. There a longitudinal seiche seems to follow a schedule of seventy-two minutes, while a transverse seiche appears at briefer intervals.

Seiches are not confined to lakes, for they also occur in
semienclosed arms of the sea. They appear to be gigantic
tremors occurring at regular intervals. In Long Island Sound
the seiche interval between Hell Gate and Montauk Point
is roughly eleven and a half hours, or nearly that of the tides.
Where these intervals correspond, tidal action is increased.

The so-called "crazy tides" of Palawan are really seiches
in the Sulu Sea. They seem to follow a definite schedule

and are particularly marked along the lengthy shore line of Palawan Island. There they appear about every ninety minutes, though with a variable range of from a few inches to nearly four feet.

Seiches were first attributed to changes in barometric pressure, which is certainly a contributory cause. But the layman may understand them better if he recalls how difficult it is to carry a large panful of water without spilling. Similar oscillations swing back and forth across many bays and inlets.

Other spectacular phenomena may occur. At St. John's, New Brunswick, the river, rushing through a narrow gorge in a series of rapids, is reversed by the influx of a twenty-foot tide. I found it thrilling, after some hours' wait, to see a boatman careering up the river, merely steering his craft on the crest of the inrushing sea.

Some rivers have a tidal bore, a wave that speeds up the channel when the current has at last succumbed to the mightier sea. There is such a bore in the Petitcodiac River in New Brunswick, in the Severn in England, and in various other places. A formidable wall of water speeds up the Amazon when the tides have conquered that tremendous stream, while in the Tsientang River in China this foaming breaker is sometimes more than ten feet high.

The tides may rise higher on one side of an estuary than the other. At the mouth of the Hudson the tidal elevation on the New York shore is more than an inch above that on the Jersey coast. This variation is caused by the rotation of the earth, which swings the waters eastward.

Sea level, the basis of all altitude measurements, is really quite unstable. Mean low water is the standard, for incoming ships must know the minimum channel depths. But mean low-water marks shift over long periods, in some localities as much as 9 inches in twelve months. Such variations follow a curve that may exceed 1.1 feet over a period of years. The vast pattern of the tides is bewilderingly complex. O. Pettersson has elaborated a theory that, due to the relative positions of sun and moon, this pattern embraces cycles of nine, ninety, and eighteen hundred years!

The power of the tides has intrigued physicists for centuries. Attempts have been made to harness it in tide mills, which have proved rather cumbrous and inefficient. In its lush spending days the federal government squandered millions of dollars in trying to utilize the tides in Passamaquoddy Bay, an economic fiasco.

The measurement of coastal tides is relatively simple. To eliminate wave action, the water is introduced into a neighboring tube or reservoir. Not only the extreme of altitude is recorded, but the rate of movement is transcribed upon a revolving cylinder.

Sir Isaac Newton first investigated the tides in a scientific manner. To explain them he evolved his "equilibrium theory," while Laplace followed with his study of "waters in motion." Since that day prodigious masses of statistics have been accumulated, all throwing some light on what still remains an obscure and difficult subject.

Cotidal maps seem to have been introduced by Sir John Lubbock in 1839. He coined the name which he defined as the "series of points at which it is high water at the same instant." Nothing should more impress the layman than a glance at a modern cotidal map, with its confused and confusing jumble of curving lines. Among other perplexing details he would note that the course of the tides is not invariably westward.

Lord Kelvin invented the first tide-predicting machine based upon principles still recognized as standard. At Washington the intricate mechanism maintained by the Coast and Geodetic Survey can forecast tides anywhere on earth a year in advance, an operation which requires about seven hours.

The theory involved is simple. The lunar pull is first examined as though it were the only one. The crest of this tidal wave usually follows some distance behind the passage of the moon across the meridian, a "time lag" which may amount to several hours. In some localities, however, the tidal crest seems to precede rather than follow the moon. This time variation, whatever it may be, is known for every required locality. The pull of the sun is then plotted and the two combined in a chart which records all the aberrations which occur when our celestial neighbors are working together or at cross-purposes. Allowance is also made for local eccentricities and the whole elaborate computation appears in nautical almanacs and the daily press.

Atmospheric disturbances, however, work havoc with such predictions. Barometric pressure may alter the tidal level a foot or more by changing the weight of the superimposed air; hence in low-pressure storms tides are correspondingly high. Winds are even more potent and indeterminate. An offshore wind can hold back the tide; a seaward gale sends it roaring shoreward. The hurricane of September 1938 raised water levels in Narragansett Bay more than ten feet to flood the downtown section of the city of Providence.

Most interesting of tidal phenomena from a long-range viewpoint is their retarding influence upon the earth's rotation. They act as a gigantic brake. True, global mass and momentum are so prodigious that tidal inertia seems like an attempt to arrest a moving auto wheel by brushing it with a feather, but over endless time such a cumulative force will at last prevail.

When the moon had newly separated from earth, the tides in the infant oceans must have been terrific. Our day, so astronomers believe, was then but four hours long. During the intervening aeons, that day has increased to twenty-four hours, and the moon retreated to the safe distance of approximately 238,000 miles. But the program will continue, so many astronomers predict, until the day equals our present lunar month and the moon itself is drawn back to a dangerous proximity. All this would introduce alarming and doubtless deadly climatic changes, even if both worlds escaped destruction by ultimate collision.

Slowly but inexorably the great clock of diurnal time is running down. Instruments which are the last word in mechanical accuracy indicate that our day is lengthening by one thousandth of a second in a century. Such atoms of time might appear negligible until we reflect that they are continuous and cumulative. And so the oceans which were once the source of life and now make life possible by their sustaining moisture may, through tidal action, destroy all life at last.

CHAPTER IX

The Waves

The sea heaves up, hangs loaded o'er the land,
Breaks there and buries its tumultuous strength.
ROBERT BROWNING
And the waves bound beneath me as a steed
That knows his rider.

BYRON

To watch huge combers spout among the rocks or fling white surf across the sands is to witness one of nature's grandest spectacles. Then we can almost glimpse Poseidon rearing his foam-flecked whiskers above the surge to shake his dripping trident at us.

But here prosaic science reminds us that we are merely viewing one of those cosmic tremors that seem woven into the very fabric of the universe. In radio broadcasts such pulsations pierce the walls of our homes; in light they flame into color; in sound they burst into strains of music; in the ocean they become visible as waves.

Waves are a surface phenomenon. Tides dredge the deepest abysses, currents sweep the ocean floor, but the most furious storm creates only minor commotion a hundred yards below. Timid sea things need dive little lower to find regions of perpetual calm.

Currents move, waves stand still; at least their forward thrust is slight until they encounter the land, where disturbed gravity makes them perform many weird antics.

A mirror pool is ruffled instantly by the passing breeze; a calm sea is soon whipped into angry foam by a squall; yet the supposition that waves are caused merely by friction of the air is too casual. Physics discovers more obscure explanations. As Helmholz reminds us, "The boundary between two fluids of different density cannot remain in equilibrium when they travel with different velocities." Waves reveal such an upset equilibrium between air and water.

Discovering that wave action is essentially stationary is a common phenomenon at the seashore. Children waiting for a bit of wreckage to wash in see it perversely dancing up and down. Only in the forefront of the breakers is there a perceptible forward thrust. The flotsam follows the path of the typical drop of water. Forward, on top of the wave, it goes, then downward, back in the wash and up again in the glistening wall to repeat the journey endlessly. The circuit is roughly a circle whose diameter equals the wave height.

A wave has three important characteristics: height, interval or length, and velocity. Height is easy to see but difficult to measure accurately; length is the distance to the next wave; while velocity is the rate of wave motion through the water, not to be confused with the speed of the surf as it comes seething up the beach.

Many formulas have been worked out to express the relationships among these three characteristics. One simple enough to remember tells us that the height of the wave in feet equals, roughly, one half the wind velocity in miles per hour. A fifty-mile storm should produce twenty-five-foot waves, a statement that needs some elaboration.

The interval between waves increases far more rapidly than their height. In mid-ocean this interval may be very great. Another formula informs us that if the velocity of a wave is doubled the height doubles also, but the interval

increases fourfold; in other words, velocity and height increase directly, but the interval is squared. Cornish observed shore breakers with an interval of twenty-two and a
half seconds, from which he deduced a mid-ocean velocity
of seventy-eight and a half miles per hour. He sought in
vain for evidences of a hundred-mile velocity, yet this may
occur in typhoon-tormented seas.

Another simple formula might amuse jaded voyagers at
sea. Let them observe the rise and fall of a patch of distant
foam. The interval in seconds multiplied by three and a half
roughly expresses the wind velocity. But enough of techni-
calities.

The wind cuts like a two-edged sword. It not only stirs
the waves but levels them as well. A fierce squall slices off
the crests of breakers to shower them in spray. Even typhoons maintain a steadying influence. It is not when the
wind is strongest but rather in the calm vortices of those
terrifying storms that the billows seem to go mad. Sailors
who have survived that peril say that when the wind ceases
chaos breaks loose, for the waves, released from all restraint,
then rear in such wild frenzy that only the stoutest ship
can live.

Shore manifestations even in storm are but a faint indication of what is happening in the open sea. There foaming
breakers become vast moving ridges, for waves require both
time and space to attain maturity. A squall may kick up a
nasty sea in a few minutes, but only a two days' blow and a
thousand miles of elbow room can build up those rugged
hillocks of mid-ocean. Stevenson has worked out a table
which records with fair accuracy how waves increase in
height as we recede from land. A five-foot wave, ten miles
from shore, should be a seven-foot wave at twenty miles;
at fifty miles it should be eleven feet high; at a hundred
miles, fifteen; at a thousand miles, forty-seven.

How large can waves become? Few topics are a richer theme of nautical discussion. As a small boy I listened spellbound as old salts spun tales of the formidable "graybeards" off Cape Horn. These mountainous seas two hundred feet high roared on endlessly at intervals of a mile or more. An English captain told me that, as a young sailor, he left the wheel in panic when, glancing over his shoulder, he saw a vast cliff of water higher than the topmasts foaming down upon him. Older hands seized the wheel to prevent the ship from "broaching to," or turning broadside to the waves, which would instantly have engulfed her, for many ships have vanished because the helmsman fled from just such an appalling apparition. The logbook of the explorer Davis describes those "graybeards" as "seas such and so lofty and with continual breach that many times we were doubtful whether our ship did sink or swim"; and again: "We spooned before the wind, three men not being able to guide the helm." Another "ancient mariner," a lifelong friend, told me that in a North Atlantic storm he feared that his small schooner would "pitch pole"—that is, turn end over end—in plunging down one of these watery chasms.

Scientists, critical of untrained observers, discount such tales, since gravity, they remind us, works steadily to prevent waves from vaulting above a certain height. What that height may be, however, is still debatable.

Forty-five-foot waves seem fairly common in the Antarctic. The staff captain of the steamship *Majestic* assured me that he had observed waves at least that high off the Cape of Good Hope. Incidentally, it was the *Majestic* that yielded some reliable data on the subject. In December 1922, while "hove to" in a North Atlantic hurricane, officers upon her bridge measured neighboring waves with a height of at least thirty meters, or roughly a hundred feet.

Huge waves are usually difficult to estimate, for the horizon is blotted out in thick weather. The observer sees only three or four great ridges foaming at him, while on the downward slope from such distorted angles the oncoming waters loom all the more impressively. The "two-hundred-foot" graybeards of Cape Horn and their mile-long intervals might well be reduced one half without too much criticism of unskilled seamen who fought with them at peril of their lives.

But what about our formula that wave height equals one half the wind velocity in miles per hour? The officers on the *Majestic* bridge encountered no two-hundred-mile hurricane. On the contrary, their best measurements showed a seventy-five-mile wind that rose in gusts to perhaps a hundred. It is the gusts that may yield the hidden motive power. Hurricanes often do exceed a hundred and twenty miles. Sir Douglas Mawson, wintering in the Antarctic, measured wind velocities of a hundred and eighty miles and suspected that gusts surpassed the two-hundred mark. I recall the story of an old whaling captain who, encountering a West India hurricane on his very first voyage, remarked, "Anyway, the wind can't blow any harder"; to which the harassed captain replied, "The wind can blow just as hard as it wants to blow." This the young seaman learned on a later voyage when he drifted for three days lashed to the deckhouse, which had been shorn away as by giant shears.

Where two seas come together unusual altitudes are possible. The captain of a trading ship in which I once crossed the Indian Ocean pointed to the bridge, which had undergone extensive repairs. On the previous voyage a "mushrooming" sea had vaulted up higher than the masthead to tear away half this superstructure.

Even shore breakers may temporarily defy gravity. The keeper of Hatteras Light informed me that when the Gulf Stream meets a fierce "nor'easter" in winter the clash of waters beggars description. During such a storm he had observed, for ten miles out to sea, a wavering row of breakers like waterspouts rear a hundred feet high in a veritable dance of death along Diamond Shoals.

Whatever their maximum height, waves have incredible climbing power. Amateur photographers delight in snapping a wave breaking over the top of Minots Light, south of Boston, which rises eighty-nine feet above its rocky base. The foghorn on Bishops Rock, in the Scilly Isles, has been torn away though well over a hundred feet above sea level, while waves vaulting the steep sides of the Eddystone have plucked off doors by creating a vacuum and bursting them outward by air pressure from within. Fair-sized stones have also been hurled through the lantern of Tillamook Light, a hundred and thirty-five feet high, and even more amazing things are recorded on exposed seacoasts.

In the Faeroe Islands, which receive the full fury of North Atlantic gales, huge cliffs of hard basalt melt away like sugar. Hansen found there a boulder, which he estimated weighed forty tons, boosted by such wave action to a ledge a hundred and sixty feet above sea level. Mathematical formulas, after all, are fragile controls upon the ungovernable fury of the sea.

Waves rise higher above mean level than their troughs sink beneath. The latter remain relatively stable, but the crests are the sport of capricious gusts.

Experienced swimmers find waves rough but jovial playmates. There is no more thrilling sport than surfboard riding on the breakers off Waikiki Beach. Even small waves can show unexpected violence. While swimming off Peru, I discounted waves scarcely three feet in height until they knocked me down. With the full force of the Pacific behind them, they drove up the shelving beach like battering rams. Driven by a furious wind, waves become veritable engines of destruction. Stevenson estimated that a twelve-foot wave with an interval of two hundred feet struck with a pile-driver force of 113 tons for every foot of width. He mentions the breakwater at Wick, its outer end protected by a block of cement and rubble 45 feet long, 26 feet wide, and 11 feet thick, weighing 800 tons. Clamped to blocks of stone with iron rods 3½ inches in diameter, the whole mass weighed 1300 tons. Yet the waves wrenched it loose to deposit it inside the pier. Another block twice as heavy, weighing 2600 tons, clamped even more securely, was constructed in its place only to be torn away by a storm in 1877.

Lighthouse builders encounter such wave action in the course of their dangerous calling. On Dubh Artach Rock, which rises over thirty-seven feet above the wild Scottish sea, a foundation was constructed of 14 toggled stones each weighing 2 tons or more and clamped together by iron rods, yet vaulting waves swept them all away. Neither man-made structures nor cliffs of solid rock can withstand such battering. Crumbling pinnacles thus sculptured by the sea are monuments to wave erosion on many a lonely shore.

As waves approach the land, they feel the force of diminishing space, and the intervals between them narrow abruptly. Those in the front rank rear higher, find less water to build up their sides, and presently sprawl forward in a shower of foam. This breaking point usually occurs when the water depth equals the wave height, but waves may break even in mid-ocean.

Swells are a strange phenomenon of wave action. The smoothest sea is invariably marked by undulations, the tremors of some remote commotion, just as ripples in a pond widen from the splashing of a stone. Swells are particularly prevalent along the Moroccan coast. When visiting Casablanca some years ago, I was compelled to wait over an hour on the deck of a tender until I could negotiate the flying leap to the gangway of the waiting steamer. In January 1913 a prolonged series of such swells paralyzed commerce for months by disabling not only tenders but larger craft. For hours on a stretch they would come dashing in, fifteen feet or more high. They were traced to some disturbance between Ireland and Iceland, sixteen hundred miles away. The French Government established a meteorological station at Rabat, ancient capital of Morocco, to forecast the arrival of such unwelcome visitants. These curious weather predictions of purely marine phenomena have proved fairly reliable. Such swells may even announce a coming storm, for they travel faster than the storm center.

The most appalling of all waves, however, have their origin in earthquakes or volcanic eruption. When Krakatoa exploded in the Sunda Strait in 1883, it hurled several cubic miles of earth twenty thousand feet into the air. Dissolving into dust, this cloud trailed three times around the globe. Finer particles remained suspended for months in the upper atmosphere to produce a series of gorgeous sunsets. Sound waves were quite as impressive. At Manila, two thousand miles distant, residents thought a vessel in distress was signaling from sea, and proposed to send out a relief ship. The sound was heard distinctly three thousand miles away, as though people in New York paused a moment to listen to something happening in Los Angeles.

The ocean of water, less responsive than that of air, was, nonetheless, violently agitated. Enormous waves a hundred feet in height swept tens of thousands of natives to their death, along the neighboring Javanese coast; they bore a Dutch gunboat two miles inland, to leave it stranded thirty-five feet above high-water mark; they traveled across the Pacific with an initial speed estimated at seven hundred miles per hour to break in seven-inch wavelets on the beaches of San Francisco Bay.

Such demoniac outbursts are rare, for Old Ocean is usually in milder mood. But summer vacationists who hear in the wash of the surf only a melodious lullaby might spare a thought for sailors on stormy waters. No big-game hunter faces greater perils, for the roar of a lion would be lost in the roar of breakers and the charge of a rogue elephant would seem unimpressive, indeed, compared with that of a foaming "graybeard" off Cape Horn.

CHAPTER X

Where Life Began

Dark heaving;—boundless, endless, and sublime
The image of eternity, the throne
Of the Invisible; even from out thy slime
The monsters of the deep are made; each zone
Obeys thee; thou goest forth dread, fathomless, alone.
LORD BYRON

Life began in the sea. Just when Nature's alchemy combined the essential elements in the exact proportions to kindle the spark of life, no one can say. Perhaps our giant new electron microscopes have discovered in the viruses those weird molecules, neither inert nor normally alive, life's first awakening from elemental matter.

The basic substance of life is protoplasm. Its principal ingredients are carbon combined with the invisible gases, oxygen, nitrogen, and hydrogen. A specialized form called chlorophyl, characteristic of plants, adds another gas, chlorine, to impart the familiar green to grass and trees. Chlorophyl also occurs in some primitive organisms where the bacteria, lowliest of the plants, separate from the protozoa, humblest of animal forms, in that twilight zone whence both emerge as though uncertain which path to choose. Life's earliest types were just such organisms of a single cell as still swim in the seas in astronomical numbers that defy all computation.

The earliest fossils in the Cambrian rocks were exclusively marine. That was nearly half a billion years ago, and life even then had doubtless been climbing for many ages up the great ladder of evolution. One of the numerous trilobites, a three-lobed creature called *Paradoxides harlani*, was the largest and most advanced of animal types. Yet he measured scarcely eighteen inches and weighed at most ten pounds. The only living relics of the more than two thousand species of fossil trilobites are the horsefoot or king crabs, found along the eastern coast of North America from Maine to Yucatán and in the Malayan Indies, that have died out everywhere else. These have few enemies except the larger sharks and rays and man, the ruthless destroyer who slaughters the harmless creatures by the thousands for chicken feed and fertilizer.

No doubt the mountain peaks had been visible a long time before life, invading the brackish waters and becoming acclimated to streams and ponds, crawled sluggishly from the primeval slime to begin the vast drama of upland diversification.

A recent biological classification divides all animal life into seventeen grand divisions or phyla. These differ enormously in importance. One phylum, the Phoronidea, those wormlike sea creatures that inhabit leathery tubes, has only a dozen or fifteen species; another, the Chaetognatha, or arrowworms, has but thirty. In vivid contrast the phylum Chordata, or vertebrates, which includes man, numbers sixty thousand species; the Mollusca, the clams, oysters, and snails, are even more numerous, with seventy thousand or better, while the phylum Arthropoda, which embraces the insects, is overwhelmingly the most diversified with over six hundred and forty thousand species!

All seventeen phyla are still represented in their ancestral home, the sea. Of the forty-five classes into which they have been subdivided, twenty-one, nearly half, remain exclusively

marine. Only three of the forty-five have no ocean representative. Of these the most important are the amphibians: the
toads, frogs, and salamanders. Fishes are mainly marine,
while birds, reptiles, and above all mammals are predomi-
nantly land types.

As we ascend the tree of animal life through its many
subdivisions, however, we seem to glimpse another picture.
Pratt, who listed 822,000 species, found that nearly four
fifths were land dwellers. This was due, however, to a single
order, the insects, so amazingly diversified that they number nearly half a million species, more than all the others
combined. These crawling, flying, boring creatures, Nature's favorite experiment, dispute the mastery of the planet
with man himself. However, with all their fertility of design, insects show no such contrasts in size or shape as
the marine phylum Coelenterata with its few thousand
corals, anemones, and jellyfishes.

Life seems to invade all possible environments and there
conform to unavoidable restrictions, hence a comparison of
land and sea habitats is illuminating.

First of all, there is far more room in the sea. Life upon
land is confined within a shallow envelope scarcely a hundred feet in depth. Most forms live upon the surface. A
motley population infests the trees: insects, bats, birds,
sloths, and monkeys. True, some of these make excursions
into the upper air but they do not long remain there. A few
species delve a little way underground: the earthworms,
moles, and woodchucks. On the other hand, the seas, which
cover nearly three quarters of the globe, support living forms
even to their profoundest depths. Hence the space they
offer for the development of life is roughly three hundred
times that upon the land.

Structural problems are simpler in the sea. The elephant
suffers some impairment of efficiency through sheer bulk.

Beyond a certain size, gravity imposes a breaking strain upon bone and sinew. The hugest of the extinct dinosaurs were apparently semiaquatic. The sea curbs gravity with buoyancy. Sharks, with only rubbery skeletons, may exceed fifty feet in length; the great blue whale sometimes grows beyond a hundred and weighs three hundred thousand pounds. Though several times larger than the largest dinosaur which ever existed, he roams easily for thousands of miles. The sea also develops tenuous forms that could not exist apart from its buoyancy and moisture. Norris, in the sea jelly aequorea, found less than 1 per cent of organic substance—the rest was water; Beebe, immersed in his bathysphere, observed jellied networks drifting past that seemed like elemental threads of living matter.

Oxygen is the very breath of animal life. Here the land would seem to offer a more favorable environment, for the 207 cubic centimeters of oxygen in a liter of air at sea level dwindles to a beggarly 7 centimeters below the surface. Yet the sea has enough. Dr. Günther estimated that a tench one foot long absorbed only one fifty-thousandth of the oxygen required by a man; furthermore, as this minimum decreased with the temperature, there is sufficient even upon the ocean floor for such life as exists there.

Land types must hustle for their food. Only a few are like the spider, which spins its web, or the ant lion, which digs its gruesome pit to await developments. But in the sea, where friendly currents are food distributors, the barnacle and the coral polyp have innumerable imitators.

Drought is the specter of arid regions, where wild things starve from shrinking food supplies or perish from thirst. Conversely, excess of water creates disastrous floods. Both perils are unknown in the sea.

Fierce winds that culminate in hurricanes and tornadoes afflict the land; sea creatures find a refuge but a few hundred feet down. Climatic changes have far greater influence upon land life. The temperature range from wintry Siberia to the Libyan Desert is 230 degrees. Such extremes may prove formidable barriers to life. Intense heat, coupled with drought, makes dreary wastes of much of the Sahara and interior Australia; intense cold locks Greenland and Antarctica in icy tombs. Hence land areas, already limited, are still further curtailed by climate. There are few such deserts in the sea.

Climatic extremes are not only harmful to life but play havoc with food supplies. Bears and ground hogs hibernate in winter not only to keep warm but because there is little for them to eat. Daily fluctuations may also be disturbing. In desert regions the mercury that soared above a hundred at noon may skirt the freezing mark at night.

In contrast with such extremes, the highest temperature ever recorded for sea water is 96 in the Persian Gulf; the lowest about 27 or somewhat below 28.6 degrees, the normal freezing point of salt water. Hence, the range from the Poles to the Equator, from the surface to the Mindanao Deep, is scarcely 70 degrees, or less than the Sahara may register during twenty-four hours.

G. Schott records the widest fluctuations in any one spot on the open sea northeast of Japan, where temperatures varied according to depth from 83 to 27 degrees. He also found the widest fluctuations in surface temperatures about North Latitude 40, where they varied a little over 18 degrees in twelve months. South of the Equator the maximum range, little more than 9 degrees, occurred around Latitude 30. Hence, he concluded that nowhere on earth does the surface temperature of the open ocean change as much as a single degree during twenty-four hours.

Siberian lakes and streams in winter may congeal to the very bottom, but the sea does not. Even through the long arctic night sea ice forms to a depth of little more than two or three meters. A poor conductor, this surface layer protects lower levels. The profoundest abysses register a cold slightly above the freezing point, but they do not freeze. The oceans seem to absorb and hold heat like gigantic sponges. Currents circulate the cold waters of the polar regions amid the warmer waters of the tropics in an endless mingling which maintains a livable temperature and supplies necessary food and oxygen.

Nordenskjöld, Stefansson, and others have found that cold sea water is rich in marine life. This is particularly true of such pelagic forms as the minuter algae and crustaceans. That is why the great blue whale goes to the Antarctic to wax fat upon the inexhaustible larder of the brit.

The bulk of the seas has a temperature range from 35 to 60, or only 25 degrees. Four fifths of all the water in the oceans never rises above 40 degrees. This might seem uninviting to land forms other than polar bears or reindeer, but marine life is cold-blooded. Still, the ocean has well-marked climatic zones. Most organisms cannot survive a temperature change beyond a few degrees, while, oddly enough, a rising temperature is more deadly than a falling one. Even where species survive in unfavorable environments, spawning may be restricted or prevented; thus oysters do not flourish in northern waters or soft-shelled clams in the tropics. That is why the Pacific salmon, introduced into Chilean waters, never crosses the Equator to revisit his native Alaska.

The depth of water forms well-marked zones. That coastal ribbon of alternate sea and land called the Kingdom of the Tides swarms with a life all its own, as do the continental shelves, which are usually limited to a hundred fathoms or less. More curious is the pelagic life which floats in a watery world without a bottom and seldom ventures far beneath the surface. Such an environment has no counterpart on land, nor have the more spacious abysses, where forms of uncanny beauty or ferocity have evolved in darkness and cold.

Another zonal division peculiarly marine is determined by salinity. Many species would perish in brackish water and vice versa. Certain sea urchins along the Patagonian coasts never venture north of the river Plata. The fresh water of that great stream is an impassable boundary. For the same reason marine types seem to be dying out in the semifresh Baltic.

Just as mountain ranges are natural barriers, so are the ridges of the ocean floor. One of these connects the Shetland Islands with the Orkneys. Though it is submerged to a depth of fifteen hundred feet, the Gulf Stream, flowing over its unseen escarpment, divides the slopes into quite different spheres. Of the hundreds of species dredged up from this area, only eleven are common to both.

The sea, like the land, has its localized life and its vast migrations. The flight of the wild geese is matched by the far roving of the salmon. Some of these living tides seek fresher pastures, others more favorable breeding grounds.

Just as winds scatter birds and insects far from their native haunts, so do the currents of the sea. The Gulf Stream bears Far North tropical species that could not long survive in colder waters. A tiny sea snail, Littorina, which congregates on tidal flats, seems to have found its way from native European waters across the Arctic and down our northeastern coast line.

Though the law of the jungle to "eat or be eaten" governs the sea, there are also strange affinities between species quite unlike. Pelagic fish find shelter beneath the deadly nettles of the Portuguese man-of-war, and scale worms seek snug berths in limpet shells. Such curious partnerships, which benefit one without injury to the other, are called commensalism.

Other associations beneficial to both are called symbiosis. Such is the strange partnership between the shark and the little striped pilot fish. When fishing for sharks in Delaware Bay, and again in the Mozambique Channel, I repeatedly observed their frantic efforts to push the shark's nose away from the pork-baited hook. Nor did they nibble at this bait themselves, though they commonly share the fragments of a larger feast. Another example of this cooperative spirit is furnished by the minute zooxanthellae which infest the mantle of the ponderous Tridacna, the largest of shelled mollusks, to their mutual advantage.

A third and less attractive association finds one form preying upon another. Our familiar parasites, the fleas and flies and lice, have numerous prototypes in the sea. Life finds there its farthest range and widest diversification from the microscopic bacterium to the great blue whale. There are sea snakes more venomous than cobras; killers more terrible than tigers. Earth's fireflies are but a faint reflection of the boundless phosphorescence of the sea. Few floral displays rival the coral reef, few upland creatures are half as terrible as the nightmare shapes that haunt the abysses; while over all is a veil of mystery. For a hundred facts are known about bees and birds and land animals for every one so far revealed about that life which swarms in such infinite profusion in the sea.

CHAPTER XI

Seaweeds

> When descends on the Atlantic
>   The gigantic
> Storm-wind of the equinox,
> Landward in his wrath he scourges
>   The toiling surges,
> Laden with sea-weed from the rocks.
> LONGFELLOW

The sea, as we have observed, is the great mother of life. To animal forms she offers commodious quarters far more spacious than the land affords, but to the plants she has been an indifferent stepmother. Their development was soon arrested, nor have they ever advanced beyond the stage of such primitive algae as skim our ponds with unwholesome browns and greens. Even their common name connotes indifference or contempt: "Seaweeds"!

The land is the favored habitat of the plant world. Only the higher mountain peaks and the frozen polar wastes are destitute of verdure, while even rocks have their lichens and deserts their fantastic cacti. Elsewhere innumerable species burst into bloom. Some are minute and quickly fading; others, like the giant sequoia, tower hundreds of feet and measure their sluggish growth not by years or even centuries, but by millenniums.

Sunlight is the explanation. Radiant energy transforms inert elements into chlorophyl, the basic plant substance.

Almost everywhere the land is flooded with sunlight. So is the sea, but beneath the surface life-giving rays soon become feeble and diffuse. Hence rooted sea plants are confined to the zone of shallow waters. Beyond a depth of three hundred feet they fade from the picture, while even the limited areas where they might flourish have waters less translucent than the open sea. Waves and currents roil the mud and silt to restrict fertile territory, and so scarcely 2 per cent of the ocean floor can support fixed vegetation.

Unlike most land plants, seaweeds have neither blossoms nor roots. Clinging to the bottom merely for anchorage, they derive nourishment from the waters in which they are immersed. Hence they avoid the soft mud or silt which land plants might prefer and grow best on rocky bottom where stones afford dependable moorings.

And yet such vegetation, though primitive and restricted, is of much greater importance than is commonly supposed. Botanists recognize several thousand species which fall naturally into color divisions.

Most primitive are the blue-green algae which may also be purple or red. They encrust rocks and wharf piling and give the mud its varicolored coating. All are too minute to distinguish without a magnifying glass.

Next in order are the grass-green algae. Most beach rovers are familiar with one of these, the common Ulva, or sea lettuce, which so resembles green cellophane.

Higher in the scale are the olive-green or brown seaweeds. Some species resemble upland plants with their rootlike "holdfasts," long stems, and branching appendages. Such are the Fucus and Aschophyllum, equipped with air bladders to impart buoyancy, which drape half-submerged rocks like yellow-brown wigs. Such, also, are the kelps, those rubbery stalks, terminating in a single leaflike process, known familiarly as "devil's aprons," and those other slender stems, like leather shoe laces, called "dead man's hair"!

Most highly developed of all, from the viewpoint of re-production, are the red algae, which number hundreds of species. Seldom more than a few inches in length, they often have a delicate fuzzy or threadlike structure. A product of offshore waters, they are found in the Mediterranean to a depth of 450 feet. At least two varieties are eaten by fastidious Americans. One is the *Chondrus crispus*, or Irish moss, from which puddings are made. This beautiful plant grows in clusters on tidal rocks in varied colors from cream-white to nearly black through shades of red, yellow, green, brown, and purple. Another species, the dulse of commerce, is reddish purple. Dried specimens are chewed raw, though Scotchmen relish them in broths or stews.

Most rooted varieties either ripen or are wrenched from their moorings to be strewn in windrows along the beach. Red algae, washed ashore and drying upon the sand, resemble etchings of the most delicate tracery. Nantucket lobstermen call this the "harvest of the sea": gales are the reapers and waves their sickles.

More impressive are the giant kelps of remoter seas. More than two thousand years ago Scylax of Caryandra mentioned regions where "the seaweed is the width of a palm and is sheer toward the points so as to prick." John Neun, shipwrecked on desolate Kerguelen Island, in the early 1800s, observed kelp in "seven fathoms of water in the most exposed places," while Pigafetta, Magellan's chronicler, wrote of the East Indies, "We found the sea to be full of grass although the depth was very great." Around Tristan da Cunha, the loneliest inhabited island on earth, great beds of kelp break the fury of the seas and even impede the navigation of small boats.

Looking southward from the extreme tip of the Cape of Good Hope, I was impressed by undulating fields of Ecklonia, or sea bamboo, with stalks rather larger than my leg. Cape Horn also has its kelp jungles which seem to thrive in what are perhaps the stormiest of all seas. One species called Lessonia resembles full-grown palm trees. Sir Joseph Hooker found windrows of this singular plant many feet high and miles in length along Falkland Island beaches.

Even more impressive is the giant kelp (Macrocystis). This serves as a natural breakwater along Chilean shores to a depth of at least two hundred and forty feet. Great beds are also scattered from California to Alaska. Rocky bottom is required to provide firm anchorage. Scientists frown upon reported lengths of twelve hundred feet, but they are a skeptical breed, seldom present when record specimens appear. This great alga certainly develops a stalk some hundreds of feet in length, terminating in leaflike fifty-foot fronds. Hence, we may perhaps assume that it is the longest of all plants on land or sea.

Another genus, Nereocystis, is found off the Aleutian Islands. A huge central bladder, which may be seven feet in diameter, surrounded by fifty or more fronds thirty feet in length, floats upon the surface like an enormous blossom. A slender, rubbery stem, which may be two hundred feet long, is anchored to the bottom; a stem so tough and tensile that natives once used it for fishline! This marine giant was called sea-otter's-cabbage, for that rarest of fur-bearing animals found it a natural cradle. Snug among the branching laminae, it loved to doze on the pulsing swells of the North Pacific.

How large marine algae may grow no one knows. While they never rival California redwoods, colossal specimens are occasionally encountered. In December 1848, Captain Smith of the good ship *Peking*, while cruising off the South African coast, sighted what he mistook for some unknown sea monster. Of an inquiring mind, he launched a boat to investigate and discovered instead an enormous stalk of floating seaweed which proved to be over a hundred feet long and quite four feet in diameter. It was, he added, "covered with every conceivable kind of marine growth."

Kelp beds harbor much animal life. Mollusks burrow into their "holdfasts"; sea worms construct limy dwellings on stem and fronds, where Bryozoa also build miniature cities. Crabs and fishes of many kinds seek shelter. Darwin wrote, "I can only compare these great aquatic forests of the southern hemisphere with the terrestrial ones in the inter tropical regions. Yet if in any country a forest were destroyed I do not believe nearly so many species of animals would perish as would here from the destruction of the kelp."

A once abundant sea growth is eelgrass (*Zostera marina*). Its narrow green ribbons of verdure have real roots and tiny blossoms, for long ages ago this was a marsh plant. Preferring the sea, it waded out into the shallows, sometimes to depths of forty feet, where it spread along the coasts of Europe, eastern Asia, and North America. Great windrows washed ashore, to be piled about the foundations of fishermen's houses as insulation against winter cold. Innumerable sea things lurked in its dense thickets. Then, some years ago, it was all but annihilated by a mysterious malady. Black ducks that browsed upon its fertile meadows perished by the thousands. Years of fruitless investigation by the federal government left only one more unsolved mystery of the sea. Recently the causative organism of this disease has been tentatively identified and it is hoped that eelgrass will stage a slow but persistent comeback.

Far more important than fixed varieties both in bulk and number is floating or pelagic vegetation. In contrast with a meager 2 per cent of available bottom, the entire surface of the sea, except where covered by floating ice, is adapted to plant growth, often to a depth of a hundred fathoms. In this vast surface layer swarm those microscopic plants, the diatoms, so numberless that they tinge arctic seas a definite green. Another pelagic form, the red alga Trichodesmium, in suspension like brick dust, gives the Red Sea its name.

More interesting still are larger forms, once rooted, that have drifted away to propagate in areas of almost continental size. Voyagers to the West Indies often encounter floating patches of brown Gulfweed, or sargassum. Although there are said to be a hundred and fifty species, only two comprise the bulk of the visible vegetation in the Sargasso, weirdest of all seas. A. E. Parr, recently returned from an exploring cruise in the *Atlantis*, found that *Sargassum natans* and *S. fluitans* accounted for nearly all this migratory weed. Highly developed brown algae, their air bladders furnish buoyancy. Over an ill-defined area of two million square miles which stretches from north of the West Indies toward the Azores, great floating islands collect, hundreds of feet long and sometimes a foot or more in thickness, the flotsam of the tropics. Morbid imagination has invested the region with tales of rotting Spanish galleons and sailors driven mad in the uncanny solitude. Certain areas have also been pictured as nearly impassable to navigation. To relegate such picturesque sea lore to the realm of the kraken and the mermaiden, however, is by no means to divest the Sargasso of all glamor, for it remains a region of enduring strangeness and mystery.

Columbus, who sailed through it without difficulty, was presumably "the first who ever burst Into that silent sea," although Aristotle may have caught a faint glimpse of it through the fog of sailors' fancies when he wrote, more than two thousand years ago, "It is said that the Phoenicians of Gades sailing with an east wind five days from the Pillars of Hercules, come to a lonely region full of tangle and seaweed."

Columbus's sailors were terrified by these forlorn meadows, but the admiral, much encouraged, decided, erroneously, that land could not be far away. He observed a queer crustacean, still called in his honor Columbus crab, and may also have noted the grotesque insects that stride about and the chameleonlike fish, pterophryne, with prehensile fins like fingers, that lurks in watery glades.

It has been estimated that from five to twenty million tons of sargassum is collected here, renewing its rubbery fronds, then dying, sinking down to feed the weird dwellers in the abyss.

Incidentally, this sea, though by far the largest and best known, is not the only weed-strewn area. There is a somewhat similar region in the Gulf of Mexico that, Parr estimated, covers two hundred thousand square miles, another south of Australia, and still others elsewhere in the almost boundless wastes of Old Ocean.

And now let us try to correct a misstatement of long standing. Webster defines a weed as "an unsightly, useless or injurious plant." Seaweeds, miscalled, far from being unsightly, are quite as interesting as oaks or orchids. They are certainly not injurious, however bathers may be annoyed at beaches cluttered by August gales; and, far from being useless, they furnish food and shelter to countless sea creatures. In short, drab and unimpressive as they are, they play an important role in Nature's vast economy.

CHAPTER XII

With Silken Seine

In water, in the earth, in air,
In wet, dry, warm, cold, everywhere
Germs without number are unfurled.
                    GOETHE
So close behind some promontory lie
    The huge Leviathans to attend their prey
And give no chance, but swallow in the fry
    Which through their gaping jaws, mistake the way.
                    JOHN DRYDEN

A conical net of finely woven silk, when dragged through sea water, collects a residue upon the inner surface. This residue, composed of minute organisms, is called plankton, from the Greek word "wandering"; there are two classifications—phytoplankton, or plants, and zooplankton, or animals.

Tiniest of all are the bacteria. Some of these vegetable mites hover upon the border of visibility even in a compound microscope, for they may be scarcely one fifty-thousandth of an inch in diameter! Smallest of living things except the viruses, if those uncanny life particles are indeed alive, they are found almost everywhere in the sea. Near the surface they seem most numerous at depths of sixty feet, diminishing in the middle depths until, toward the bottom, they reappear in such myriads that four hundred and twenty million find living room in a single gram of mud. They break down tissue cells and absorb inert elements like nitrogen; many are luminous. They have been likened to the numberless grains of sand in the foundations of the living world.

Larger, though mostly microscopic, are the diatoms, atomies which resemble cut-glass containers rather than plants. Clots of chlorophyl, gray, green, or brownish, interspersed with oily globules are enclosed in cases of nearly pure glass, one cover fitting snugly over the other and both elaborately etched and ridged and embossed. They are of many shapes: circles, triangles, parallelograms, boats and sticks and spindles. Some are almost as minute as the larger bacteria, a few are visible as specks to the unaided eye. One genus, Pleurosigma, which resembles an airplane propeller, may be nearly a millimeter long.

Diatoms usually reproduce by division, occasionally by spore formation. A single individual in one month may multiply into a billion! A liter of water from the Kiel Canal has yielded 6,336,000 specimens. One species, Cocconeis, forms extensive gardens that appear as yellow splotches upon the belly of the great blue whale; hence the latter's common name—sulphur-bottom. Like bacteria, diatoms are prolific in bottom ooze. I have examined samples of chocolate-colored mud that were veritable diatom gardens, for a cubic centimeter contained well over twenty-five million!

Diatoms, though global in distribution, prefer a cold habitat. In polar seas they reproduce in such numbers that they impart a green tint and a "smooth" feel to the water.

They are the basic food supply of many animal forms, particularly those tiny crustaceans called copepods. One of these, C. *Eurytemora*, according to Harvey, consumes one hundred and twenty thousand diatoms daily. But there are other minute algae in phytoplankton. Such are the halimeda that absorb lime rather than glass and contribute not a little to the development of oceanic oozes and coral reefs. Sir Douglas Mawson found incredible numbers of fossil forms in limestone formations in the South Seas, where great tufted masses of living specimens flourished to a depth of two hundred feet.

Quite as fascinating are the zooplankton. The radiolarians, which number forty-four hundred species, are the most beautiful, for like the diatoms they live in glass houses even more varied and richly chased. Sometimes, for further protection, these cases are lined with chitin, the lobster's coat of mail. There are apertures through which protrude footlike processes called pseudopodia. Many are covered with spines which survive in the radiolarian ooze of the abysmal sea.

Another extensive class prefers lime to silicon. Though less gemlike than the radiolarians, they too show a multiplicity of ornament, and their remains comprise much of the globigerina ooze. Some are visible to the eye like grains of quartz, while one variety, the nummulites, may be quite an inch in diameter.

Most prominent, however, are the copepods. Though far less numerous, their greater bulk makes up some 70 per cent of all plankton. Tiny shrimplike creatures, cousins to the crayfish, they form a branch of that most prolific of phyla, the Arthropoda, which includes the insects. They are the food of many surface-feeding fishes. The stomach of a single herring has yielded sixty thousand. As "brit" they strew the polar seas with reddish areas as though to verify Shakespeare's imagery and "the multitudinous seas incarnadine." Baleen whales skim the surface waters with open mouths, straining the copepods through their fringing whiskers to gulp them down by the barrel. More than three hundred gallons of this nourishing soup has been recovered from the stomach of a giant sulphur-bottom. Here are the grazing grounds of the sea, and the creatures that feed there, be they herring or whales, are as truly browsers as cows in a clover patch. But there are fundamental differences between upland and marine meadows; ocean verdure, being unattached, drifts at the sport of winds and currents; besides, it is rather more animal than vegetable. But its importance was emphasized by the Swedish Hydrographic Commission in the statement: "All fishing in the North Atlantic depends upon the great currents in the upper layers of the sea—and the presence in those layers of the food required by the fishes, viz.—Plankton."

Plankton nets sieve out many other organisms. There are fish eggs and the embryos of mollusks and larger crustaceans which usually have a floating stage before settling down; there are Hydrozoa, fragile flowerlike creatures, and Bryozoa, that so much resemble mosses frozen into lime, and, particularly in tropic seas, coral polyps. Few of man's works would be visible from the moon to the unaided eye, but the corals have built not only innumerable islands but the Great Barrier Reef of Australia, twelve hundred miles long and in places sixty miles wide!

Coral polyps are of many colors: black, red, orange, green, lavender, and white. Secreting lime from the water and toiling through countless generations, they construct their own world of fantastically carved stone.

Pictures sometimes show a greatly magnified drop of water teeming with bizarre life. This might give a fair impression of water from a stagnant pool, but in examining hundreds of samples of sea water I have often been impressed by its seeming sterility. To be sure, a plankton net skims something tangible from a considerable volume. But a quart of surface water may prove nearly lifeless, particularly on a hot, sunny day. This is partially due to the roving habits of the plankton. In the full glare, they seek the cooler gloom a hundred fathoms down, just as cows love the shade of the pasture oak.

Perhaps the first scientist to study plankton intensively was Müller in 1846. Since his day the silken sieve has proved a favorite with marine biologists. Some have even sampled plankton soup, which, though relished by herring and whales, proved too gritty for human consumption.

Sea pastures, like upland meadows, have their seasons, determined by sunlight, however, rather than by temperature. In February a plankton net dragged through the waters of the North Sea yielded four hundred specimens of a certain copepod, Calanus. Two months later a similar drag netted four million. That harvest had increased ten thousandfold!

Falling temperatures which change rich uplands into frozen wastes, cast no such blight upon the sea. On the contrary, Lohman found that the seven hundred specimens in a liter of warm sea water increased to twenty-five hundred in colder waters.

Also unlike the uplands, marine pastures are not exclusively upon the surface. The bottoms of coastal shallows may be even more prolific. There oysters prefer a diatom diet, though other species are not so particular. These feed also upon detritus, the sweepings of the ocean floor, including much cellular tissue from larger organisms, which they share with ground-feeding fishes. Marine worms are less discriminating. Many swallow the mud whole, leaving digestive processes to sort out the available nutriment.

Plankton are ephemeral creatures with a brief span of life. Dying, they rain slowly down to the bottom, in their leisurely transit helping to nourish other dwellers in the dark, while the residue adds continuously to bottom sediments. Hence plankton are the living carpets of the sea, or the carpets are dead plankton, whichever seems the more appropriate way of expressing Nature's handiwork.

"Through the slow lapse of ages" these minute organisms build up the limestones and the finer marbles of our quarries. The hills of Palestine, with all their associations, once slowly accumulated beneath the shallows; the highest pinnacle of Mount Everest is thought to be capped with limestone! The city of Paris is largely constructed from such materials. A single ounce may contain the remains of four million protozoa; thus plankton, quite as truly as Phidias, created the statues which once adorned the Parthenon. And those ponderous Egyptian structures for which some proud Pharaoh assumed credit were equally the work of myriads of tiny creatures that lived and died long ago in the sea.

CHAPTER XIII

Sponges, Jellies, and Worms

When leagued about the 'wildered boat
The rainbow Jellies fill and float.
                                        KIPLING

A long step above the globigerina and radiolarians of our plankton net are the sponges, the first animal type to develop from the single cell to a multicellular complexity. Aristotle was courageous enough to assert that they were not marine plants but animals, an opinion that won for him only the derision of his contemporaries.

Sponges comprise the phylum of the Porifera. According to Harvey they number over three thousand species. Though subtropical by preference, they are found in temperate waters as red or yellow incrustations or branches, suggesting their common name, "dead man's fingers." Elsewhere they are of many shapes and sizes. Some clothe submerged surfaces like fungus growths, others resemble puffballs, still others branching shrubbery. The huge cup sponges may be five feet in diameter and nearly six feet high.

The familiar skeletons of our bathtubs are of chitin, although certain species incorporate lime in their bodies, others silicon. The latter are hard as flint and their spicules sprinkle huge areas of sea bottom. Glassmakers long before the Egyptians mastered that art, they spin lustrous threads of exquisite beauty.

Though usually harmless, there are destructive species. A particularly bad actor is the boring sponge (Cliona) which flourishes from Cape Cod to the Carolinas. Its lemon-yellow masses not only suffocate oysters but bore into their shells for the limy content. The oyster labors to reinforce the inner surfaces but frequently succumbs. One often finds oyster shells pitted like smallpox and so brittle that they crumble in the fingers. Boring sponges also probe into rock or cement, causing damage to breakwaters. In contrast, many sponges give shelter to small crabs and fishes.

Another step upward brings us to the phylum Coelenterata, a long name for jellyfishes and their kindred. There are more than ten thousand species, ranging from almost microscopic forms to giants that trail their filaments a hundred feet or more.

Visitors to the beaches often observe translucent disks a few inches in diameter shrivel to mere crusts upon the sand. In autumn they may even find much larger masses, like coagulated blood, awash in the surf. These are among the commoner jellyfishes.

More spectacular are the Portuguese men-of-war that flit across tropic seas. A frail pear-shaped bladder, inflated at will, trails from the larger end a tangle of tentacles that may stretch fifty feet. The bladder, iridescent as a soap bubble, catches every breeze, and like a clipper ship can make headway into the wind. To see a flotilla of these singular craft tacking across an opal sea is to catch a glimpse of fairyland. Far more truly than the Chambered Nautilus of Oliver Wendell Holmes, this is "the venturous bark that flings On the sweet summer wind its purpled wings," only the wings are a delicate pastel shade of pink or blue.

These fascinating apparitions are formed not of individuals but of colonies, each member with separate functions, as though nature had assembled the necessary parts without fusing them into a living unit. Some tentacles absorb food, others are purely reproductive, still others defensive. The stinging nettles not only paralyze small fishes and crustaceans but are painful to human beings. The Sherlock Holmes tale of a formidable sea jelly called the Lion's Mane has a foundation in fact.

Such creatures would seem to offer perilous sanctuary to others, yet an Australian fish, the nomeus, seeks such protection, as do our common whiting and the young of the huge tuna fish.

Many jellies which cannot spread their sails swim with gentle undulations of the body fringes like the opening and shutting of a Chinese parasol. Once in Delagoa Bay and again in the chill Humboldt Current off Peru, I sailed for miles over seas that were a veritable mosaic of such creatures with delicate hues of red, blue, green, and yellow.

Little is known of the life history of most sea jellies. They appear in myriads from nowhere in particular to disappear as suddenly. The larger species devour small crustaceans and fish, a savagery that seems ill placed in animals that are little better than diffuse protoplasm and water.

Enemies are few. The spiral-shelled Janthina, constructing a raft of gelatinous bubbles, puts out from shore to attack the jellies with astonishing ferocity. As human food they would seem to offer the minimum in nutriment, yet the Japanese salt and dry some species for future consumption.

The largest specimens prefer colder waters. Agassiz observed one off Boston Harbor, with a bell-shaped body, seven and a half feet in diameter, with filaments one hundred and twenty feet long!

Ephemeral as they seem, some Coelenterata build enduring monuments. Such are the coral polyps, whose branching
treelike formations are found in the Temperate Zone,
though they are far more prolific in the tropics, where the
lime in sea water is more readily precipitated. Each polyp
adds its skeleton to the communal structure. These, ground
by the waves and strewn by the winds, fuse into rock called
aeolian limestone, the foundation of Bermuda, the Bahamas, and countless islets in the South Pacific. At Funafuti
in the Ellice group one boring penetrated 1114 feet without finding other rock formation.

Under favorable environments coral growth is rapid. In
the Persian Gulf Darwin found that a wreck, submerged for
twenty months, was encrusted with coral to a depth of two
feet.

Quite as beautiful and more delicate are the sea anemones, the true blossoms of the sea. Some resemble garden
pinks, others dahlias, while less colorful species adorn many
a tidal pool in temperate waters, where observing their
activities well repays an idle hour. Their tentacles sometimes
sting as fishermen learn to their sorrow when their hooks
become fouled with them. Kent's anemone, native to Australia, measures eighteen inches across the expanded disk.
No wonder small fishes find its open mouth a snug haven.

Allied species are so curious in structure that they have
been incorporated into a phylum all their own—the Cte-
nophora, or comb jellies. Compared with their diaphanous
transparency, other species seem substantial, for they fairly
wreathe and undulate through warm seas like wisps of
smoke. Best known of the hundred or more species is the
Cestus or girdle of Venus, abundant in the Mediterranean.
Perhaps five feet in length and several inches broad, it is
alive for all its filmy nothingness, and worthy of adorning

the goddess who, according to legend, rose from the foam of that very sea. Strangely enough, some of these sentient gossamers use their filaments to lasso their prey!

Worms are the pariahs of the animal kingdom. To most of us they seem unattractive if not positively repulsive. But what a prominent role they play in the grand panorama of life! For they comprise no fewer than six of the seventeen phyla, those rungs in the ladder up which mammals have climbed from the humblest one-celled organism. Evidently Nature does not share our repugnance for these crawling creatures, nor would we if we but knew them better. For all are interesting and some as beautiful as anemones or corals.

Most primitive is the phylum Platyhelminthes, from the Greek words *helmins*, worms, and *platy*, broad or flat. Some are excessively elongated. A nemertean species reaches a reported length of ninety feet. The body is a living fishline with which it plays small fishes as skillfully as any human angler. Though slender and of little bulk, it exceeds in length all other animal forms except the great blue whale.

Such passing notice seems quite inadequate for a phylum in which Harvey places over three thousand species, but only rigid condensation can prevent this chapter from lengthening into a volume, if not an entire library.

The Nemathelminthes, or roundworms, have a phylum to themselves, as have the Trochelminthes, or Rotifera, those tiny whirligigs, common in stagnant pools, which seem to be the very whirling dervishes of the animal kingdom.

The deeper seas reveal strange forms of life which do not fit into the general pattern, hence two new phyla have been set apart, like concentration camps, for their accommodation. One of these phyla, the Phoronidea, is so far limited to fifteen species of wormlike creatures inhabiting leathery tubes; another phylum, the Chaetognatha, of thirty species, comprises the so-called arrowworms that dart about like animated torches in the subsurface gloom.

After thus striding with seven-league boots through five entire phyla, we come to the Annelida, or true worms, which number some sixty-five hundred species. These have developed the more elaborate nerve and sense organs which foreshadow superior types of life. Body segments contain complete and separate sets of organs. Where one breaks off another develops; in fact certain species discard segments at will. What a boon it would be thus easily to slough off corns and infected teeth!

One of the most interesting of the Annelida is the sea mouse. Six inches long and three broad, the flattened body is covered with cilia which resemble fur. These are so iridescent that the creature has been named Aphrodite for the goddess of beauty!

More familiar is the nereis, or clam worm, quite as popular for fish bait as his distant cousin in our gardens. Growing to a length of eighteen inches with a beak like a beetle, he is really a most voracious creature.

Some annelids are anything but wormlike, for their threadlike cilia, vivid red or orange, resemble a tangled maze of embroidery silk. These cilia are both gills and rudimentary eyes, as they react instantly to sunlight. Others with wormlike bodies terminate in similar frills which suggest blossoms in the mud.

Many worms construct permanent dwellings. The crudest are mere tunnels which certain species line with bits of shell or seaweed until they protrude an inch or more above the surface. Still others cement grains of sand in hollow cones that suggest wigwams and offer better protection than the rude windbreaks that Patagonian natives erect against the storms of that bleak region. The Serpula trace their sinuous homes of porcelain, like strange ocean script, upon shells and bits of wood. A tiny cousin, the Spirorbis, attaches his snaillike coil less than two millimeters in diameter to stalks or fronds of brown algae. A magnifying glass reveals the occupant seeking food with his fringing tentacles.

Some worms are carnivorous and in their restricted world as fierce as tigers; some browse upon marine vegetation as placidly as sheep. Still others of less discriminating taste swallow mouthfuls of soft mud, allowing the alimentary canal to pick and choose.

Many sea worms swim about at night, when they fall prey to surface-feeding fishes, but the more timid who stay at home fare little better. Sturgeon, cod, and halibut plow them out to devour them greedily. Sea birds are just as appreciative, particularly herons with their rapier beaks. We would scarcely expect humans at such a banqueting board, but some worms are considered delicacies in various parts of the world. Strangest of these is the palolo of the South Pacific. Frequenting certain islands, these worms are endowed with a phenomenal gift of time, as they appear in October and November and then only when the moon is in its final quarter. Emerging from their unknown habitats, the egg-bearing segments of the body break away to cover the sea for miles with a shimmering glow of yellow, green, blue, and purple. Natives, familiar with this phenomenon, fill their canoes with the tasty tidbits, which they devour raw or cooked with equal zest, while white travelers, overcoming a foolish prejudice, have found the palolo appetizing. Doubtless there are innumerable other delicacies still unrecognized in ocean's inexhaustible larder.

We must pass hurriedly over another phylum, the Bryozoa, for our observations are quite as fragmentary as those of the brown gull which wings his way slowly over tidal flats with an appraising glance at the life that swarms below.

The Bryozoa, which number three thousand species, are the sea mosses, which neither fade nor wither, as they are enclosed in limy, segmented cases. More delicate than most land plants, a brief hour among them with a magnifying glass would usher the explorer into a new and different world. Inoffensive, with few enemies, these creatures lead a cloistered life, creating beauty in the sea.

Another phylum, the Brachiopoda, suggest mollusks with their two shells fitted together, but structurally are aeons apart. Resembling the olive-oil lamps of ancient Rome, they are commonly called lamp shells. They live mostly on sea bottom at considerable depths, where the thirty-five hundred species in fossil-bearing rock have dwindled to one hundred and twenty. A dying race, they still cling to a precarious existence in dim regions of the sea, pushed into the background by more efficient and vigorous types.

With this brief survey we come to a new phylum better fitted to survive, the spiny creatures, the starfish and their kindred. But they deserve a chapter of their own.

CHAPTER XIV

The Spiny Skins

. . . the heavens
Thronged with constellations and the seas
Strewn with their images.
MONTGOMERY

Few phyla are more interesting than the Echinodermata. This formidable name, combined from Greek words meaning "hedgehog skin," becomes clear when we examine one of these curious creatures called sea urchins or sea eggs, for they live in strong boxes bristling with bayonets.

Together with the sand dabs, sea biscuits, and other spiny relatives, they number over six hundred species. Some are small, others many inches in diameter. They resemble a flattened hemisphere composed of nearly six hundred plates loosely fitted together like the pieces of a jigsaw puzzle. These plates, scarcely a millimeter thick, are covered with spines that may number nearly four thousand. In some species these spines are longer than the body diameter, sharp as needles, and may be poisonous to the touch; in others they are as bulky as slate pencils and even used as such. All are attached to the shell by ball-and-socket joints, are movable, and provide a cumbrous method of locomotion. The circular opening beneath is filled with bony mouth parts called Aristotle's lantern, terminating in five small teeth that meet at a point.

Though sometimes scavengers, sea urchins prefer a diet of seaweeds and small worms. In some mysterious manner they enlarge rock crevices even in granite for snug shelters from the pounding waves. Their eggs, which may number twenty million, are relished as "sea fruit" by Mediterranean peoples.

A grass-green species common to New England has been burdened with one of the longest names in the biological dictionary—*Strongylocentrotus drobachiensis*—more appropriate to a dinosaur than a tiny marine hedgehog!

Few enemies care to penetrate the sea urchin's protective armor. One of these is the sea otter, which lies on its back, tosses urchins from paw to paw like a juggler, than crushes two shells together to nibble the contents.

The sand dab or sand dollar resembles a small urchin that has been stepped upon. The chocolate-colored spines, like coarse plush, enable the disk-shaped body to burrow into the bottom. Tropic varieties have apertures in the shell-like keyholes, while an African species is notched on one rim like a cog wheel. They sometimes cover ocean shallows with a queer mosaic.

Sea hearts or biscuits, stripped of their spines, resemble balls of dough. The five-pointed figure etched upon the shell, however, reveals kinship with the starfish. Though more fragile than eggshells, I have seen Philippine beaches strewn with their empty cases.

Even more abundant are the sea stars. Their eleven hundred species range from tiny starlets to Pacific giants thirty inches in diameter. Some are fragile, others thick and fleshy, while in color they vary like the true stars of the sky.

The commoner varieties, constructed upon the ground plan of the Pentagon Building, are often called "five-fingers," but many species are more liberally endowed, while the notched outline of the "sun star" suggests a circular saw.

The undersurface of each grooved arm is filled with tiny tubes ending in sucker disks. With these the creature gropes about, though rarely progressing thirty feet in an hour. Starfish are the bane of the oyster grower. Gripping an oyster like bodiless hands, they exert a steady, persistent pull. The result is a triumph of patience over power. The oyster's adductor muscle, with a resistance of many pounds, gradually wearies. A half hour passes, the valves open slightly —fatal error! The camel has his nose in the tent, or rather, the stomach of the starfish, which he turns inside out like the finger of a glove, thrusts within the opening and consumes the soft flesh at leisure. Since a good-sized specimen may devour several oysters daily, his depredations are ruinous. In Essex Harbor I once saw a moving column of starfish piled one on top of the other, five feet wide and three fifths of a mile in length, sweeping in from the sea along the margin of a great bed of edible mussels. Unfortunately these pests have few enemies and are tenacious of life. An injured arm is speedily replaced; more curious still, cut a five-finger in equal fifths and a new animal will develop from each severed member.

Less familiar are the brittle stars and the basket stars, which number hundreds of species. The brittle stars are equipped with tenuous arms that writhe like those of an octopus, or may resemble plumed and tufted worms. The extremities of the basket stars are connected by an open meshwork like heavy embroidery which converts them into living fish traps. Shallow waters in which they congregate are called "spider beds" by disgusted fishermen.

Among the oldest known fossils are the crinoids, or sea lilies. Once regarded as a type of marine vegetation, their kinship with the sand dab and the starfish has long been established. Ancient species, resembling palm trees, grew to a height of twenty feet or more. All were supposed to be extinct until a living specimen was dredged up in 1864, followed by several others. These discoveries roused so much interest in England that the famous *Challenger* expedition was fitted out to study the oceans and their life.

Crinoids are now recognized as world-wide in distribution. Though once far more numerous and prolific, they still grace many an underseas garden with their fragile stems and drooping fronds. Although most species are firmly rooted or cemented to rock or coral, some drift about like wraiths of a remote antiquity.

Perhaps the strangest of spiny creatures, however, are the holothurians, which have no spines at all! Better known as sea cucumbers, some resemble that vegetable in both shape and color, others are more like the sea jellies, while still others are quite snakelike in action and appearance. Their proper place among the Echinodermata, however, is revealed both by internal anatomy and by the singular limy plates embedded in their skins. These often resemble minute gratings or fishhooks or even perfect little anchors!

Equipped with tube feet and sucker tentacles about the mouth, sea cucumbers may eject internal organs at will, to grow a new set. They turn themselves almost inside out as though with a violent spasm of seasickness. What an effective method of treating a diseased liver or pancreas!

In some parts of the world sea cucumbers are a popular article of food. In the East Indies one may frequently observe specimens in native fish stalls, writhing about like animated sausages, while old women split them open for dinner as they would herring. A particularly large species which grows to a length of two feet or more is dried, cured, and shipped to China under the trade name of trepang or bêche-de-mer. Doubtless sea cucumbers are as tasty and far more nutritious than the more familiar product of our pickle canneries.

CHAPTER XV

The Crusty Creatures

But what an endless work have I in hand
To count the sea's abundant progeny
Whose fruitful seeds farre passeth those on land.
EDMUND SPENSER

The crustaceans, known chiefly through their edible
varieties—the shrimp, prawns, crabs, crayfish, and lobsters—
form a prominent class of the great phylum of the Arthropoda which includes the insects.

As the name suggests, they are "crusted" with a protective
substance called chitin. This is carbon combined with the
three gases—hydrogen, oxygen, and nitrogen—in the complex chemical formula $C_{15}H_{26}N_2O_{10}$. In its pure form
chitin is whitish, impervious to water, resistant to alkalis
and some acids, hard, durable, much lighter than limy
cases and more flexible than glass ones. These virtues,
however, are partially offset by its unyielding rigidity. In
order to grow, the crustacean must shed its shell at intervals.
The soft body, freed from its strait jacket, thereupon swells
up an additional 15 per cent and proceeds to form a new
shell. Meanwhile the defenseless creature mopes under a
rock, a prey to voracious fishes which share with man a fondness for soft-shelled crabs. At length, fully armed, he sallies
forth, like a knight of Arthur's court, with segmented legs
and jointed body, equipped to repel the "vile blows and
buffets of the world."

As we have already noted, minute crustaceans make up 70 per cent of plankton. The annual progeny of a single individual, could all survive, would exceed four billion! The magnifying glass reveals numerous specimens in any bit of tidal mud. Their province seems to be to cleanse the seas as scavengers and to furnish an inexhaustible food supply for higher forms from herring to whales. In retaliation certain types infest the bodies of their hunters either in harmless symbiosis or as true parasites. The haddock, for example, is said to harbor no fewer than a dozen species. Such crustaceans are usually degenerate forms. One of the most curious is the "pea" crab that affects a strange partnership with various shellfish. The female, in an early swimming stage, may enter the valves of an oyster, where she spends the remainder of her life. She does the mollusk no injury but, in return for keeping his dwelling tidy, shares his food. Thus protected, she develops no shell, as does the smaller male, which swims about from one mollusk to another, seeking feminine companionship.

Edible shrimps and their larger relatives the prawns are too well known for comment. But there are less familiar varieties. One of these, the mantis shrimp, like its savage prototype of the insect world, has a pair of bent appendages armed with spines to grasp his prey, while even more bizarre forms inhabit deeper waters.

The crabs are much maligned. True, they seem churlish to bathers whose bare toes are nipped, but what gentleman of spirit would not resent being stepped upon? Active, courageous, often comic, with their upturned claws, their stalked and twitching eyes, crabs register alarm or anger quite as unmistakably as the human visage. One species that hugs itself like a box turtle is called the shamefaced crab; a Japanese species whose back resembles a sorcerer's mask is known as the goblin. The ancients regarded this crustacean with favor, for one of the twelve constellations of the zodiac is Cancer, the crab.

The typical crab is rounded, flattened, with ten jointed appendages. The upper and larger are claws for fighting or grasping prey; another pair may terminate in paddles, for some species are expert swimmers, others crawlers, burrowers, and climbers. Some have cylindrical bodies like the shrimps; others are square or heart-shaped, but bodily contours are enormously varied.

Most crabs are slow-moving, though capable of quick sidewise darts, but some are definite racers. While exploring a tidal flat in South Africa, I encountered a Nile-green specimen scarcely three inches in length that eluded my utmost efforts at capture by lightning sprints and dodges that would have done credit to a sandpiper.

Crabs are pretty nearly omnivorous. Some lie buried in the sand awaiting passing prey; others stalk it like leopards. The Indian species, Melia, goes a-hunting with a sea anemone on each claw, appropriating a share of what the latter's stinging tentacles collect. Mankind's employment of falcons, hunting dogs, and other dumb assistants seems reflected in this enlistment of a lower by a higher form of life.

A popular tidbit at shore dinners is the blue crab of the Chesapeake, caught literally by the millions. A larger species, Cancer magister, of the Pacific, may be nearly a foot across, as are several varieties common to western Europe.

A small crab (Uca) of the Temperate Zone is called the fiddler from the large claw it extends as menace or protection. Scarce two inches in length, it digs elaborate burrows, piling the sand and mud outside in neat pellets, and carrying down bits of seaweed. It is nearly as efficient as the earthworm in working over tidal soil. A Far Eastern species is a true empire builder, for it extends the shore line of many a tropic isle. Forbes counted no fewer than a hundred and twenty burrows in two square feet of exposed flat. It is known locally as the beckoning crab, from its fancied gestures to the oncoming tide.

Drollest of all the crab family are the hermits, which are really social creatures. They are the clowns of the tide flats and their antics are as diverting as puppies. Shrimplike in form, the abdomen has lost its chitin, so the hermit must seek other protection. His choice is usually an empty snail shell, though he will also appropriate the bottom of a broken bottle, the bowl of a clay pipe, or even living shelters such as a sponge or a mat of sea anemones. Anderson's hermit, which lives in the Indian Ocean at hundred-fathom depths, adopts the latter covering, pulling the tentacles about him like the tatters of an old quilt. As some of these anemones are luminescent, they light him about as he gropes through the dim world in which he lives.

Most hermits are confirmed house hunters. They squabble like humans over a desirable dwelling, but they never carry too big a house or one plastered with mortgages!

The largest of the hermits has climbed out upon the land, developing a tough skin where natural armor failed him. He is the famous robber crab, and his depredations are legendary. A foot and a half long and weighing perhaps eight pounds, he climbs palm trees, shreds the tough coconut husk, and breaks in the shell around the familiar eyes to get at the meat. His claws, though smaller than those of a lobster, are incredibly powerful. Darwin relates that a specimen "confined in a strong tin box, the lid being secured with wire,—actually punched many small holes right through the tin" and, bending down one edge, made his escape. Well named the robber, this crab steals useless articles with all the indiscriminate kleptomania of the crow.

Other crabs of the more familiar flattened type are also capable climbers. The Grapsus scales nearly vertical cliffs to rob birds' nests of their eggs and even young.

Crabs sometimes overrun the low atolls of the Pacific, piling themselves in heaps several feet high. The sound of their claws rasping on the coral is most irritating; still more so are their efforts to share the bunks of disgusted sleepers.

Most dignified of the family are the spider crabs. The heart-shaped body, studded with knobs and spicules, is ill balanced on absurdly elongated legs. One species, common in New England waters, has a leg spread of well over a foot. To observe one wading ashore, pausing to scratch his chin with an upper claw, is to encounter a veritable old man of the sea. Some specimens plant bits of sponge, hydroids, or seaweeds upon their backs for camouflage against appraising gulls. Hence they were perhaps the first of all the gardeners. A different species, the gnome crab of the Mediterranean, has two claws so modified that he can hold sponges behind his body, which resembles a ball covered with velvet.

The largest of the crabs is a member of the spider clan, the Kämpferi, from deep waters off Japan. Museum specimens show a claw spread of eleven feet, while an extreme of eighteen feet has been reported. In oriental markets a single joint from a leg is often sold as a portion. Since the heart-shaped body is comparatively small, however, it is doubtful whether one of these unwieldy monstrosities ever weighs as much as our largest lobsters.

The latter are certainly the most prized of crustaceans. Of the several species, the American (*Homarus americanus*) is the largest. A big female may glue seventy-five thousand eggs to the undersurface of her body, to carry them about for ten months. Resembling bird shot in size, these are dark green, becoming brick-red as hatching time approaches. The tiny lobster, called a zoea, bears upon his back a spine much larger in proportion than a rhinoceros horn. From this weird shape he emerges as a megalops with two lustrous eyes, a flattened body like a crab, and a bushy tail. Casting off this disguise, he assumes at length a lobster form, shedding repeatedly. Upon attaining fair proportions, shedding becomes an annual unpleasantness that more venerable individuals may postpone for several seasons.

The typical color, dark green (sometimes mottled or even blue), changes to red on boiling. The lobster swims backward with spasmodic hooking of his tail. Of his two large claws, the "cutter" is sharp, the "crusher" blunt. They serve him as knife, fork, and false teeth!

Like other crustaceans, lobsters replace missing parts, a wise provision since they are notoriously quarrelsome. A lobster fresh from the water is far more active than the moribund creatures on ice. While studying them on Nantucket Shoals, I once saw an individual bite off his own thumb in futile rage. Another had his body half torn away, perhaps by shark bite; but the injured thorax was rounding into form while four tiny legs and a new claw were developing to be renewed at the next "molt." Crabs shed by a zipper opening around the edge through which they elbow their way out into wider horizons. The lobster's shell "unbuttons" down the back, but how he ever drags his heavy claws through the narrow wrist openings is a mystery.

Preferring moderately cold water, lobsters are numerous along the Maine and Nova Scotia coasts. They seem to keep on growing indefinitely. Two specimens, Mike and Ike, caught off the Virginia Capes and exhibited for a long time in the Boston Museum of Natural History, weighed respectively over thirty-eight and forty-two pounds. New England newspapers recently reported one caught off Chatham on Cape Cod that weighed forty-eight. The age of such patriarchs is pure conjecture—fifty years? A hundred? Who knows?

Other types are the spiny lobsters of tropic seas which lack the big claws, and the crayfish that have become acclimated to fresh water.

Monarch of all crustaceans, as his name implies, is the king crab, the familiar horsefoot of our Eastern seaboard and the Malayan region, which may attain a length of eighteen inches. Hardly a crab at all, he more closely resembles the scorpions. His daggerlike tail, once used as arrowheads by the Indians, helps him to right himself, like a turtle, when overturned. His food, mainly marine worms, is chewed between his knees or elbows, he breathes through bookplates tucked under his body, surveys creation through two compound and two simple eyes; in short, is a most unusual creature. Visiting shallow water in early summer to breed, he shuffles off into a safer five or six fathoms. His age is uncertain, but I once found a battered veteran with a three-year-old oyster growing on his back. His most recent shedding was at least that far behind him. Another specimen carried over a hundred Crepidula, or "half decks," attached to his body together with numerous mussels and barnacles. Few sea creatures are so interesting as the lumbering old Limulus, so like an armored truck, wrapped in a dignity all his own. And why not? His muddy trail meanders back toward the Trilobites of Cambrian times, perhaps half a billion years ago!

Other grotesque forms are the pycnogonoids, or sea spiders. Their bodies are so attenuated that the stomach extends into the elongated legs, while the males bear an extra pair as receptacles for the eggs of the female. There are more than a hundred and fifty species which clamber over tidal vegetation like daddy longlegs, or blunder down to the abysmal sea three miles below the surface!

Few laymen would class barnacles with crabs, yet they are true crustaceans which, in their free-swimming stage, resemble shrimps. Their eyes are discarded as useless impediments when they construct their limestone houses. These have no windows, but through the collapsible roof the inmate thrusts out a tuft of chocolate-brown appendages not unlike ostrich plumes. This led Huxley to remark that "the barnacle stands on his head and kicks food into his mouth with his feet."

Barnacles are of two kinds. The Lepas, or gooseneck, variety grows on slender stalks that may be six inches long to form great masses on submerged buoys. The more familiar "acorns," which encrust tidal rock to the detriment of bare feet, have kept more than one shipwrecked sailor from starving. A huge species, the parrot barnacle of Australia, may be three inches high and five or more in circumference. A common article of diet, it resembles shrimp in taste.

Although barnacles are among the most sedentary of animals, one species fairly rivals the wanderings of Marco Polo. This is the *Coronula diadema*, or "little crown," more commonly called the whale barnacle. Though not a true parasite, his presence is irritating to the huge mammal, which vainly strives to free himself by dragging his ponderous bulk over submerged rocks. While collecting in South Africa, I was obliged, in detaching them, to tear the dead whale's skin to shreds. There are few queerer associations than this colossal steed and his diminutive but most unwelcome rider.

CHAPTER XVI

Shellfish

Green grocers rise at dawn of day
August the fifth, come haste away
To Billingsgate the thousands run
'Tis oyster day! 'tis oyster day!
HONE

Shellfish, to most of us, are clams, oysters, and scallops. Quite as appetizing are razor clams (Ensis) and the larger sea clam (Spisula). In California abalones are popular, and farther north the huge gweduc, that may weigh eighteen pounds and extend a leathery snout two feet or more. Gourmets would add mussels to the list, more popular in Europe, where snails, limpets, whelks, and less familiar species are common food items. Mediterranean peoples esteem both squid and octopus and make soup of snails and bivalves too tiny to be removed from the shell. The Indians smoked clams as a Chinaman does his ducks, spitting them on reeds for future reference. Interior tribes came from far distances, like the Pilgrim Fathers, to "suck the abundance of the seas," and left shell heaps as big as bungalows. The kitchen middens of Europe trace shore dinners back to the ice age, when, according to the poet's notion of primitive man, "He lived upon oysters and foes and dwelt in a cave by the seas." Let us hope he found oysters the more appetizing of the two.

Shellfish, of course, are not really fish, while many lack

shells. They belong to the mollusks, next to the Arthropoda the richest of all phyla in species. Even experts disagree on the exact number, but recent lists of over seventy thousand are being continually revised upward.

The mollusks originated long ago in the sea, where most of them remain. Some emigrated to fresh-water streams to supply us with the cheaper grade of pearl buttons, while others graduated to dry land to infest our gardens as snails and slugs. Soft-bodied, they developed shells partly as external skeletons like the insects, but more for protection. Two types proved efficient and have thrived enormously. The single-shelled creatures comprise most of the gastropods, with over fifty thousand species. The shell may be nearly flat or convex or spiral like the snail or an elongated spindle.

Less numerous are the bivalves with two shells hinged together. Sometimes these close tightly; sometimes they do not close at all. A few species, the chitons, experimented with eight plates down the back and resemble sow bugs or armadillos. Many others, the nudibranchiates, or sea slugs, carry the rudimentary shell concealed within the body, or have dispensed with it entirely. The squid have such internal plates, brittle, chalky, and much appreciated by canaries, which whet their beaks upon them.

Mollusks have an extensive range. Snails are found above the snow line in the Himalayas, and 16,000 feet under the sea. Squids probe even deeper, as one specimen has been dredged from an icy darkness of 17,694 feet. Tropical species are varied in form and color, cold-water species of drabber hue and more fragile. Some are pelagic, the pteropods, whose tenuous wings suggest butterflies as they dart about; others prefer the deep sea, while many inhabit the littoral zone. Tidewater forms in northern climates are often winter-killed. Blegvad found that a severe Danish winter which froze the sand killed all exposed mussels, four fifths of the clams, but only 30 per cent of a hardier mollusk, *Macoma Baltica*. The common clam (Mya) flourishes among Greenland rocks, where walruses dig them out with grunts of pleasure. These clams survive ice crystals frozen in their shells. The common oyster, however, objects to cold baths, while salinity limits his range. Hence, while he prefers brackish water, he would die out of the mouths of French rivers, unless replenished from outside sources. Other marine forms, once abundant in the ever freshening Baltic, have disappeared or become atrophied.

Mollusks are of an ancient lineage. Innumerable species have become extinct and are remembered only as fossils. One great bivalve of this type had shells six feet across and must have weighed hundreds of pounds.

Surviving species, however, are sufficiently abundant. An acre of clam flat may produce a thousand bushels of the toothsome "steamer"; an acre of quahogs, the adult little neck of the hotel bar, might yield fifteen hundred. A great bed of *Spisula truncata*, another variety of clam, covers seven hundred square miles on the Dogger Bank in the North Sea. Its population has been estimated at between four and five quadrillion! Who would care to count the oysters, which are of several hundred species? Of the familiar edible variety, the state of Maryland harvested in a single season over ten million bushels!

Many mollusks are thought to prefer diatoms, those glass-encased plants of our plankton nets, as food, but Scandinavian investigators have found a favorite food source in bottom detritus, which is comprised of many living organisms as well as disintegrating cellular matter. Some gastropods are vegetarians, consuming minute seaweeds; others are scavengers like marine vultures, still others are as predatory as wolves. Squid dart murderously into a school of mackerel, larger types are fond of crabs.

All marine mollusks pass through a free-swimming stage. As they develop a rudimentary shell most of them sink to the bottom. The oyster is a true clinging vine that, once attached to a rock or an old boot, never willingly moves again. The common clam digs a burrow in which he may possibly ascend or descend, but otherwise stays put. The bay scallop (Pecten), however, is a natural rover. Perhaps this is because he has eyes, a whole row of them, around the edges of his shells. By opening and closing his shells rapidly, he goes skittering over the surface. In marine experiments I have tagged specimens that traveled to points fourteen miles distant.

Nature has made some of the mollusks skilled artisans. The mussel (Mytilus) is a weaver which spins brown threads of attachment, so tough that in Italy they have been woven into gloves. The gastropod Purpura is an expert color mixer, yielding the rich dye that clothed the Roman emperors in royal purple. He is even mentioned in the Book of Acts. A squid (Sepia) was the first ink maker, and manufactures a superior product. Michelangelo outlined some of his masterpieces with the aid of this lowly mollusk. Some mollusks are carpenters; some stonemasons, for the piddock drills holes in the hardest granite. The Janthina, a fragile violet snail, which puts to sea on a raft of gelatinous bubbles, was doubtless the first Argonaut. The pearl oyster is a jeweler so efficient that his gems are the only ones which need no retouching. There are criminal mollusks which prey upon their fellows. With a tongue coated with chitin teeth like a rasp, they drill a countersunk hole through another's shell as accurately as any machinist. English scientists believe they secrete an acid to assist the operation, so perhaps they are also the first etchers. If one went exploring through the multitudinous phylum of the mollusks he would find many another trade represented among these humble toilers of the sea.

Mollusks have many enemies. In the free-swimming stage the mortality among them is prodigious, and the development of a shell offers no adequate protection. Gulls not only devour young clams like grains of corn, they prey upon adults, bearing them aloft to shatter them upon a convenient stone, just as the fabled eagle dropped a tortoise on the bald head of the poet Aeschylus. Glacial rocks on tidal flats are often fringed with broken shells. A neighbor of mine once watched a gull drop a large quahog thirteen times before the stony casing was broken. Ground-feeding fishes assist the shell collector, for the stomach of a large cod may contain many species from deeper waters swallowed whole and digested at leisure. Carnivorous mollusks prey upon others, while man is often the worst of despoilers, as many a depleted clam flat bears witness.

To offset such depredations, shellfish are extraordinarily prolific. I once dissected a large clam (Mya) that bore over nine million eggs. A recent reference in a scientific journal mentions an oyster with a hundred and twenty-five million! Certain European oysters have the bewildering faculty of changing from one sex to another and back again. Many mollusks develop both sexes in the same individual. Nature's expedients to preserve the germs of life are well-nigh numberless.

The egg, once fertilized, divides and subdivides with great rapidity. The living organism, launched upon the sea, drifts with winds and currents. The odds against survival are tremendous, but the favored few, borne by chance to some safe haven, take root, as it were, to begin the struggle for existence that never ends in the sea.

As the oyster is the most valuable among edible shellfish,

his habits have been more thoroughly investigated. Chill waters retard his growth, so that north of Cape Cod it requires four or five years for him to attain a stature for which a year and a half would suffice in Chesapeake Bay. In the Gulf of Mexico oysters spawn when but three or four months old; one year is the rule in Long Island Sound; northern specimens seldom spawn until the end of the second season, while farther north they do not spawn at all.

The life span of most shellfish is a matter of conjecture. Even large oysters conceal their age, like cautious spinsters. Shells a foot long have been dug up in the Charles River. Layer upon layer, they developed perhaps for decades. A quahog may show growth rings upon his shell, like those in a tree stump, to an age of eight or nine years. Then the edges turn inward, become blunted, and the inmate enters that autumn of his years which is reflected in the orange color of his flesh. In the Museum of Natural History at Boston is a huge quahog whose valves weigh over two pounds. The caption suggests an age of thirty-five years, which the curator confessed was a mere estimate. In a few species age limits have been worked out with fair accuracy. When bay scallops became depleted, shore towns passed drastic restrictions, until science found that these short-lived mollusks rarely survive eighteen months. From an economic standpoint it was better that they be eaten than suffered to perish from old age. A huge Tridacna shell that I brought back from Mindanao was branded as a hundred and fifty years old by the curator of a famous Eastern museum, and not over twenty-five by another equally eminent. Both gentlemen were guessing!

Shellfish are seldom considered dangerous to man unless cuts become infected or ptomaine poisoning follows the eating of tainted chowders. Yet these harmless creatures do sometimes retaliate for countless injuries suffered.

This may be indirect, as in the destruction wrought by the teredo, that wormlike creature whose tiny shells reveal his kinship with the mollusks. He drills neat tunnels in wood which he lines with the finest porcelain. Unlike the termite, another secretive borer, he is not a wood eater but a house builder. Sir Isambard Brunel, who constructed the first tunnel under the Thames, is said to have learned useful lessons from observing the teredo. These busy excavators so honeycomb the stoutest timber that it crumbles at the touch. Some specimens are nearly two feet long. Many an ancient galleon foundered at sea because her bottom fell to pieces. One of Magellan's ships was so damaged by teredos that it was abandoned in the Far East. Sir Hugh Willoughby, sailing for the Northeast Passage in 1553, sheathed his ship with lead plates; copper is now used for that purpose. For some reason teredos dislike teak as moths do cedar. One of the grim convict ships from the bad old days of penal servitude in Australia was constructed of this durable wood. When more than a century old she was quite as seaworthy as on the day she was launched.

Many shellfish, harmless themselves, harbor organisms dangerous to man. Oysters in sewage-polluted waters may carry typhoid germs; transplanted to cleansing seas, they become edible once more. Other mollusks like the horse mussel (Modiolus) are infested at certain seasons with minute organisms which are also dangerous. There are even specimens of the beautiful Cone genus that possess true fangs and poison glands. Bites from these fair but treacherous vipers of the sea have proved fatal.

The ponderous Tridacna has been called the "man eating clam." Though guiltless of that charge, he is a living bear trap as he rests among coral ridges with valves partly distended. Let the pearl diver, groping amid a tangle of brilliantly colored sea growth, thrust his hand between those valves and his only hope is a speedy and merciful drowning. How large Tridacnas grow no one can say. There is a specimen in the museum at New York whose shells weigh 576 pounds. Dr. Minor, the curator, thought that somewhere along the Great Barrier Reef of Australia individuals might occasionally tip the beam at half a ton.

This is large indeed, compared with the bulkiest of the single-shelled gastropods, the Fusus of the South Pacific, which may be two feet long and weigh twenty-five pounds, but even Tridacnas yield to the biggest of the cephalopods.

A few of these have shells. Most notable is the chambered nautilus, immortalized by Oliver Wendell Holmes. In the paper nautilus the fragile container is carried exclusively by the female as a receptacle for her eggs and young. It has been termed the "most beautiful cradle in the world."

The cephalopods fall into two great divisions. Typical are the octopus, like a bloated spider with eight tentacles; and the squid, an animated torpedo, with ten. Both carry ink sacs which are discharged as protective smoke screens.

The *Octopus punctatus* of the South Pacific has a known arm spread of twenty-eight feet. Boulenger even mentions a specimen from Australia reported to be forty feet across! Natives occasionally fall victim to these grisly horrors whose sucker-crusted arms are more formidable than a python's coils. But even the hugest of these are less ponderous than the giant squid (*Architeuthis princeps*). This weird monster lives far below the hundred-fathom mark. He never willingly visits the surface; dead specimens are speedily torn to pieces by hungry fishes. Yet a few have been observed and measured. In the Peabody Museum at Cambridge hangs a life-sized reproduction of an individual which weighed half a ton and measured fifty-four feet. How large they grow no one knows, but they have been a theme of direful speculation for two thousand years. Pliny mentions one whose body, "big as a cask," weighed seven hundred pounds, and was equipped with arms thirty feet long. The fabled kraken of the Dark Ages, which overturned ships by gripping their masts, was doubtless a mariner's exaggeration of a giant squid. The French steamship *Alecto* in December 1861 encountered a specimen evidently ill or dying. A rope was actually passed around the body, which was estimated to be twenty feet in circumference and weigh at least two tons, but the soft flesh cut like cheese. Sometimes these great cephalopods invade shallower fishing grounds. In October 1875 Gloucester fishermen on the Grand Banks captured at least twenty-five, which were used for bait! Captain J. W. Collins of the schooner *Howard* caught five, another schooner three in one afternoon. A specimen taken some years ago off Cape Cod by Azores Islanders had a body reported to be "as long as a dory."

The sperm whale dives to a great depth for this, his favorite food, as he requires a daily ration of at least a ton and a half. His body is always scarred by the suckers, fringed with claws like leopards, which arm the tentacles of the giant squid. The two longest of these, the "feelers," which may measure forty feet, shoot forward like the tongue of a chameleon with incredible swiftness. Rarely the whale drags his prey to the surface, for sailors have watched him churn the sea to foam while encircled in writhing tentacles. Death, to the formidable mollusk, was inevitable, for his soft body offered no protection against a toothed jaw powerful enough to bite a whaler's boat in two. Whales, when harpooned, often disgorge fragments of giant squid which whalemen assert are "bigger than oil casks."

In this huge creature, the most terrifying and perhaps the most mysterious of ocean life, the mollusks reached their peak. With a brain superior to that of any of the fishes and surpassed only by the higher mammals, he peers into his dimly lighted world through eyes that may be fifteen inches in diameter. Of his life history and habits we know next to nothing, but the vengeance he wreaks upon his hereditary foe is strange beyond belief. His parrotlike beak sometimes inflames the whale's intestines, which, it is thought, secrete as a waxy antidote the ambergris much valued by perfumers; and so one of these terrific battles in the abyss may survive in the lingering odor of violet or rose!

CHAPTER XVII

The Fishes

In the free element beneath the sea
Floundered and dived, in play, in chase, in battle
Fishes of every color, form and kind
Which language cannot paint.
MONTGOMERY

Far back in the dreary stretches of Paleozoic time Nature, groping for improvements upon the mechanism of life, evolved a streamlined creature with a backbone and lower jaw—the crude forefather of all the fishes. Fossils have been found by the Smithsonian Institution in sandstones nearly three hundred million years old. Superior types have since developed, but the fishes remain the most numerous of the vertebrates, for science recognizes more than twenty thousand species!

As life overflowed the oceans many fishes invaded rivers, streams, and lakes. A few still divide their time between fresh and salt water. Three fifths of all the species, however, and a far greater proportion of individuals remain in their ancestral home—the sea.

Yet there are sterile regions like Hudson Bay and much of mid-ocean where fish are scarce. Discounting wanderers like sharks and flying fish and ignoring for the moment the grotesque dwellers in the abysses, our familiar ocean fishes are mainly confined within a surface shell a hundred fathoms deep, while almost all are to be found within the two-hundred-fathom limit. Temperature restricts many within still narrower bounds. Though cold-blooded—except the tuna, whose bodily warmth exceeds that of the surrounding water—variations of but a few degrees compel most species to migrate or perish.

In 1879 a trawler seeking cod off Nantucket brought in five thousand pounds of an unknown species which became known as the tilefish. Of delicate flavor, it proved popular and increasing catches were reported. Then, three years later, a trawler sailed for a hundred and fifty miles through dead and floating tilefish. They were strewn over an area of several thousand square miles, and in places from Long Island to New England lay piled upon the bottom six to eight feet deep. For ten years they vanished, then, in 1892, a fisherman brought in eight specimens. Since that date the tilefish has been staging a slow, uncertain comeback. What had happened? A shifting of the Gulf Stream, unusual warmth followed by a sudden chill, and the tilefish appeared only to die by uncounted millions.

Next to temperature, food is the most prominent regional factor. Here ocean currents play a major role, accounting for the inexhaustible fishing grounds of the North Sea.

Salinity may also prove decisive, as when the herring forsook the steadily freshening waters of the Baltic.

Enemies, though restrictive, were governed by natural checks until man upset the balance. Where are the shad and salmon that once shoaled along the North Atlantic seaboard? Overfishing and contaminated streams are the answer.

Most favorable for species diversifications are the shallows surrounding tropic islands. No fewer than 780 species are known around Amboina in the East Indies, nearly as many as are found in all Europe. Fresh-water species show a similar trend, for the Ganges-Brahmaputra system has 170; the comparable Mackenzie River only 23. Of all ocean fishes the herring is most widely distributed, while tiny coral islands have specialized types known nowhere else. The oxygen supply, though limited, seems sufficient except in a few isolated regions like the depths of the Black Sea.

Food preferences divide the fishes into two great divisions: the surface feeders, which browse upon the infinite meadows of diatoms, copepods, and other minute organisms; and the bottom feeders, which grub for marine worms, mollusks, and crustaceans along shallow banks or littoral areas. Many species prey upon others, although none are quite so gruesome as the hagfishes, or slime eels, primitive or degenerate forms which fasten their hideous mouths to living fish, rasp holes in their flesh, and literally devour them alive. Beautiful, fascinating, but sometimes terrible is life in the sea.

Feeding habits determine both form and coloration in fishes. Surface feeders are swift-moving to capture prey or avoid enemies, while blue with a silvery sheen beneath is their characteristic color, like the mackerel or the herring. Bottom feeders, more sluggish, groping in dim light, blend with their surroundings, and are gray, brown, or mottled, like the cod, the haddock, and the halibut. The summer flounder even changes color, while some tropical varieties are veritable chameleons. Among coral reefs rainbow fish reproduce almost every tint of sea fan or anemone.

Many fishes have become highly specialized. The swordfish flails about among a school of mackerel like a living Excalibur. Truculent and fearless, he attacks whales or even vessels in sheer wantonness. The British Museum displays a sword of his piercing twenty-seven inches of solid timber. H.M.S. *Leopard*, repaired in 1795, disclosed another driven through metal sheathing, a three-inch plank, and a six-inch timber. Nine strokes of a twenty-five-pound sledge hammer barely equaled this one tremendous thrust. In tropic waters the larger sawfish mows down victims with his spiked and bony snout, while the huge manta stuns his with the hook-like projections above his eyes. The thresher shark lashes about with his lethal tail; the sting ray carries a barbed dagger in his tail made more dangerous by poison glands; while the torpedo and the electric eel paralyze their prey.

Certain fishes are toothless, others have bony plates, while the white shark displays rows of razor-edged triangles that could tear any living thing to shreds. Hence, while some fish cannot bite at all, others can clip steel wire. The filefish even crunches pieces of solid coral.

Body coverings are quite as varied. Scales, fitting one above another like the shingles on a roof, are characteristic, but the sturgeon is encased in bony plates that hark back to primeval forms, while the gar pike is almost as well armored as the crocodile. The shark family have tough, rasping hides, while many fishes have no protection other than a slippery slime.

Fins, variable in position and number, and the tail are means of locomotion. Fins are not always confined to paddling the water, however, for mud skippers and climbing perches use theirs to crawl up the roots of mangrove trees, the better to survey the world. Fins may even be protective and highly poisonous. Oddest of all, perhaps, are the flying fishes, whose pectoral fins, much enlarged, give them the appearance of animated hydroplanes. They may glide through the air for nearly a hundred yards, falling upon the decks of ships or even darting through open portholes to befuddle sleeping passengers.

Although most fishes swim in a horizontal position, sea horses and rainbow gar hold themselves stiffly erect like drum majors. The needlefish assumes the same position, but with his head down. Some catfishes swim upside down. The flat fishes, flounders, plaice, and halibut, lie upon one side, the buried eye migrating in infancy to the upper surface of the body.

While the tail of the thresher shark rather exceeds the bodily length, the ponderous sunfish, which may weigh two tons or more, has no tail at all. Seemingly all tail is the mysterious oarfish, which flashes through the water like a silvery ribbon, scarcely two inches in thickness for all its thirty feet of length. The fishermen call him the King of the Herring. In tracing fifty-six recorded specimens, Dr. Günther found this curious denizen of deep waters of world-wide distribution. With feeble jaws, or none at all, it contrasts vividly with the bulky angler, which is more than half facial orifice. Lying half concealed in muddy shallows, he is a living trap. A bony rod projecting from the head, with a bit of pendant skin dangling like bait, lures other fishes to their doom. From the stomach of a single five-foot angler seventy herring were taken, so recently swallowed as to be still salable. Sea gulls and even foxes are sometimes gripped by his formidable jaws.

Bizarre forms are not uncommon. The billfish is almost lancelike; the globefish "huffs and puffs" himself into a sphere studded with prickly spines. Some of the weird Chimaera genus of polar seas have a bony projection suggesting an elephant's trunk. The head of a hammerhead shark is crescent-shaped, with eyes at the extremities. Pigafetta observed a strange fish in the Far East with "two horns and a head like a horse," while marine freaks are often mentioned in the daily press. The sea has its angel fishes and its devil fishes.

Some fishes seem to hibernate. Nordenskjöld, marooned for a winter on Siberian shores, found that a shallow lake, frozen to the bottom, yielded excellent fish with summer thaws. Lungfishes, curled up in cavities of sun-baked mud, survive for months.

There are blind fishes and others gifted with keen vision. Only two types seem to look above the surface rather than below, the archerfish and the so-called four-eyed fish. The former squirts a stream of water at a fly with deadly marksmanship; the latter has but two eyes, but these are so divided that as he swims along he can survey the world both above and beneath the surface.

In size, fishes vary from a fraction of an inch to the whale shark, which is thought to reach a length of seventy feet and a weight of twenty tons! White sharks have been known to exceed forty feet in length. The manta, hugest of the skate family, may be over twenty feet across and weigh a ton and a half. Equally heavy is the great sturgeon of the Caspian, which sometimes attains a length of twenty feet. The clumsy jewfish may weigh six hundred pounds. Swordfish and sailfish may be larger, and tunas reach half a ton. Some years ago, off Boston Light, a halibut dragged a line fisherman overboard with a rush like a runaway horse. He tipped the scales at a good five hundred pounds. But halibut ten feet long and weighing over seven hundred have been caught. The largest cod on record measured over six feet and weighed two hundred and eleven pounds.

Age in fishes is largely indeterminate, yet some fishes bear a time index on each individual scale, which is ringed like the trunk of a tree. Flat fishes bear similar telltale markings on their ear bones. An Atlantic salmon eleven years old is a patriarch. The cod is not thought to survive beyond twenty. Haddock, herring, halibut, and sting rays are believed to range between fifteen and thirty, but evidence is fragmentary. According to Major Glower, an eel has been kept in a tank for forty-two years, a carp at least fifty, and a catfish sixty-one.

Fish are enormously prolific. A flounder may lay a million eggs, a halibut three and a half million, a cod nine million. A ling (Molva), twelve feet long, has been known to produce thirty million eggs; a sunfish over three hundred million! Fish eggs vary in size from almost microscopic smallness to rubbery cases six inches long with a well-defined "white" and "yolk" produced by certain sharks. A few species are viviparous. Sex unbalance is the rule. There are three female herring for every male, and no fewer than fourteen conger eels!

Fish eggs are of two types: floating, or pelagic; sinking, or dimersal. Those which sift to the bottom encounter perils enough, but those which float face even greater dangers from fishes, birds, and countless other forms of ever hungry life. Man shares with these his fondness for shad roe and caviar. But Nature, though prodigal, is also wise. Such fabulous destruction holds in check a too exuberant life. The progeny of a single cod, could all survive through several generations, would fill the oceans and drown the world.

Fish spawning is generally a haphazard affair. The germs of life are poured into the waters to mingle as they may. Yet there are notable exceptions. The eggs of the angler fish make a purple ribbon forty feet long. The stickleback constructs a rude nest of pebbles; some tropic species build rafts of bubbles; certain catfish carry their eggs in their mouths for safekeeping; while the male sea horse places the eggs of the female in a tiny pouch in his own body not unlike a kangaroo's.

Mysterious migrations are the most striking phenomena in the breeding habits of fish. Herring, shad, and salmon return, no one knows whence or how, to the ancestral stream to spawn. Salmon fight their way against the torrents of the Yukon for two thousand miles. Streams become living tides of fish. Birds of prey, otters, even the great brown bear, indulge in an indiscriminate slaughter in which man excels them all. The Indians still spear many thousands, but the white man's traps and nets take heavier toll. When and if the salmon's goal is won, and eggs are laid and fertilized, both male and female drift tail foremost down the current to die.

Still more remarkable are the spawning habits of the eel. No wonder Aristotle and Pliny thought they evolved from the mud, for their origin has been a mystery for two thousand years. And then a Danish expedition under Dr. Johannes Schmidt, after years of investigation, traced adult eels to their natural breeding grounds in the deep waters between the Bahamas and the Sargasso Sea. The eels in English ponds, when perhaps eight years old, grow strangely restless. Wriggling snakelike through the wet grass at night, they find some outlet to the sea, swim nearly across the Atlantic, dive into deep water, lay their eggs, and die. The newly hatched eels, tiny transparent ribbons with two dots for eyes, come to the surface and start back on the long, long trail. They have never traveled it before and the journey requires the better part of three years. But the survivors find their way, in some uncanny manner, back to native coves and streams and ponds to complete the life cycle. American eels use similar breeding grounds. In a shorter return journey, which they accomplish in about a year, their paths may cross those of their European cousins, but each seems to maintain its destined course. Few phenomena of nature are so incredible as the migrations of the eel.

Some species form strange partnerships. While fishing for sharks off Delaware Bay, I observed that pilot fish strove to push the shark's nose from a baited hook, but readily accepted smaller hooks themselves. Our Portuguese cook fried some which proved rather unappetizing. Another fish, the shark sucker (Naucrates) steals a ride by attaching the suckerlike disk on top of his head to the undersurface of the shark. Japanese fishermen employ these singular creatures to capture sea turtles.

Enemies of man are the fierce barracuda, whose pikelike body may be ten feet long, and certain poisonous species. But most feared and detested are the sharks. Pigafetta mentioned them as "fishes with teeth of a terrible kind that eat people." Most sharks are harmless, but there are a few man-killers; hence in South Africa, Australia, and elsewhere nets are stretched across shallow waters to protect bathers.

In contrast to these savage enemies of the sea, fish have been kept as pets for centuries. Familiar are the perches, which Chinese patience developed into the gold- and silver-fish of our aquaria, while more recently tiny tropical fish have proved popular. One species, long famous in Siam, are trained fighters and quite as pugnacious as gamecocks.

When Izaak Walton wrote his masterpiece for anglers, he had in mind fresh-water varieties. But trout and salmon offer no thrills like a battle with a big tuna or sailfish. To master such monsters with rod and reel taxes nerve and endurance to the utmost, and is akin to big-game hunting in Africa, where the bag may be a lion or rhino rather than a hare or partridge.

Volumes might be written on the romance of fish and fisheries. The famous Hanseatic League had its foundations in the herring fishery and declined when the herring disappeared from the Baltic. No wonder Lübeck, the capital, carried three herring upon its shield. The League currency, called easterling, still survives in the pound sterling of Great Britain.

When herring migrated again across the North Sea, Dutch fishing boats followed and came into collision with English boats. There arose a long struggle for maritime supremacy. For a time the Dutch Admiral Van Tromp carried a broom at his masthead to sweep the English from the Channel. Such efforts laid the foundation for that mastery of oriental waters which wrested the East Indies from Portugal and gave to Holland the second richest colonial empire in the world.

The search for fish led hardy Irish explorers to discover Iceland, nor should we forget that Newfoundland, the cornerstone of England's world empire, was only the fogbound hinterland beyond the rich fishing grounds of the Grand Banks. For more than a century after the voyages of the Cabots much of North America was valued only for its fish, and fishing was its only industry!

Two small islets off Newfoundland were withheld by France as outposts of transatlantic fishing, and remain the sole remnants of her once vast dominions in this part of the Western Hemisphere.

Incidentally, these fishing grounds have bred more than one international dispute that threatened war, while similar wranglings with Japan over salmon and halibut fisheries fanned that smoldering ill will which later flamed into open hostility.

The fish was one of the first insignia of the early Christian Church, while fisheries have prospered greatly because of religious fasts and holy days. It was gold that lured the Spanish conquistadors just as spices led Columbus and Da Gama and Magellan to embark on their momentous voyagings, but the lowly fish has done quite as much to set the boundaries of empires and remodel the map of the world.

CHAPTER XVIII

Regions of Darkness and Strange Light

The reign of Chaos and old Night.
                    MILTON
The water, like a witch's oils,
Burnt green, and blue, and white.
                    COLERIDGE

Ocean abysses were once believed to be as lifeless as outer space. Of course there could be neither food nor oxygen in such icy gloom. And yet deep-sea dredgings have given us glimpses into a world where life abounds, a different life than ours, to be sure, but life fantastic, frightful, and grotesque.

First of all, it is almost purely animal. Save for bacteria, no vegetation flourishes where the light fades out. Scientists, suspending a white disk over six feet in diameter, could see it at depths little greater than two hundred feet even in the transparent Sargasso Sea. Elsewhere visibility was more restricted. In tropic waters it rarely exceeded a hundred and fifty feet, while in polar seas, where plankton reduced the light rays more than a third, it sometimes fell below sixty.

Color variations are quite as striking. Red light fades first, then yellow, then green. Below depths of a hundred and fifty feet only blue rays illuminate a weird world at which the living organisms peer as through blue glasses. Dr. Beebe, in his historic descents in a bathysphere, was barely able to decipher the printed page at four hundred feet, while around nineteen hundred the last azure ray faded into inky blackness. True, Murray found that photographic plates immersed for two hours at fifteen hundred meters became darkly clouded; but this may well have been caused by that ghostly phosphorescence which is the only light that ever penetrates such depths.

As the light decreases, the cold becomes more intense. In the equatorial Pacific a surface temperature of 82 sinks to 52 a hundred fathoms down. Thereafter it usually declines gradually to the very bottom. But there are exceptions. In polar seas surface waters congeal, but deeper waters do not. There are also great ocean pockets partially confined within submerged ridges where the temperature remains fairly constant. The Bartlett Deep, for example, maintains a frigid equilibrium of 39.6 down to depths of nineteen thousand feet, where it would normally approach the freezing point.

Although some warmth it supplied by radioactive rocks upon the bottom, this can scarcely equal a half degree. The sun is the great source of that heat which is so uniformly distributed throughout the oceans by the complex system of circulatory currents. Surface temperatures which range from slightly under the freezing point, or 27 degrees, to 96 in the steaming Persian Gulf, are far more equable at lower levels. Three hundred fathoms down there is a variation of only 22 degrees, as we swing along the arc of a great circle from 60 degrees north of the Equator to 60 degrees south. At eight hundred fathoms that variation is 15 degrees; at fifteen hundred fathoms it is only 7. The mean average of all the seas from surface to bottom and from pole to pole has been estimated at 39.6 degrees. A deadly chill which approaches but never quite attains freezing is the unchanging climate of the depths.

The polar seas are the vast motor which aerates the abysses. At hundred-fathom depths they contain more oxygen than do tropic waters. Cold currents, sweeping downward as heated layers rise, creep along the ocean floor toward the Equator. The oxygen requirements of marine life, always meager, decrease with falling temperatures and growing pressures, so that enough remains to keep aglow that spark of life which animates even the profoundest abysses.

Poisonous carbon dioxide gas is seldom a hazard save in stagnant areas like the deeper portions of the Black Sea, which shows twelve times as much as similar levels elsewhere with a corresponding decrease of oxygen. Hence the deeper positions in this great natural bowl are almost as devoid of life as are the salt-impregnated waters of the Dead Sea.

Enormous pressures, once thought to be insuperable obstacles to life, present few difficulties. Imperceptible at the surface, pressure becomes fifteen pounds to the square inch at a depth of thirty-three feet. A thousand fathoms finds it increased to twenty-seven hundred, which nearly doubles with every additional mile. In the Mindanao Deep it becomes more than seven tons per square inch. A blue whale, could he dive that far, would be gripped as in a vise by a force of millions of tons!

So terrific is this pressure that water, though nearly incompressible, is squeezed into reduced volume. Were this not so, the surface of the ocean would rise nearly a hundred feet to inundate vast areas of upland. And yet life, even the most fragile and ephemeral, is readily adjusted to such pressure. To be sure, deep-sea fishes, venturing too near the surface, sometimes come within the deadly surge of buoyancy and fall upward, their swimming bladders forced through gaping mouths. But for the most part pressure seems to offer slight barriers even to migratory life. Not a few deep-water forms visit the surface at night, while surface forms make similar excursions downward. Dr. Beebe carried down for more than half a mile a Bermuda lobster confined outside the bathysphere, which showed no discomfort at sudden pressure changes. Old whalers assert that a sperm whale may sound a mile or more in the effort to shake off his tormentors. Though this is probably an exaggeration, the cable-repair ship *All America* in April 1932 found the body of a sperm whale entangled in the cable at a depth of 3240 feet. In fact temperature may prove a more important factor than pressure. A species of sea spider, or pycnogonoid, which frequents thirty-foot shallows around Spitsbergen, seeks similar temperature in the Norwegian Sea at depths of a mile or more.

The study of abysmal life presents special difficulties, for netted trophies may have been intercepted at median levels. Professional divers had long explored ocean shallows, but it was not until August 15, 1934, that Dr. Beebe and his assistant, in a specially constructed steel spheroid, descended to a depth of 3028 feet. This voyage was more adventurous than that of Columbus, for it led to a stranger world.

Jellyfishes seem to abound at all levels, some of gossamer texture. Squids are many and bizarre, many entangled in a maze of attenuated tentacles. Mollusks seem out of place, but pteropods, with winglike shells, dart about like dragonflies, while arrowworms of vivid scarlet sweep by in troops. All life here is carnivorous. "Eat or be eaten" is the one law of survival.

Most abundant are the crustaceans, which swarm like veritable insects of the sea. Many are minute and almost transparent. The shrimp family has numerous representatives. Some are highly colored, some have claws enormously elongated, and one curious specimen has eyes set upon stalks that are actually longer than the body. In descending through the beautiful blue world of sapphire light into regions of darkness, prevalent colorings are either a jet black or brilliant scarlet.

Life here follows divergent roads. One branch develops sensitive feelers like the blind man's cane; the other carries lanterns to light the gloom. Some species appropriate both aids to navigation. The deep-water fish lamprotoxu, though self-luminous, has attached to the underjaw a barbel several times as long as the body, which is thrust before it like an insect's antenna.

Minuter species feed upon the food which filters down from above to fall prey in turn to larger species. Life is always in suspension, for this queer world has neither roof nor floor. Here nature, adapting form to environment, has evolved nightmare shapes. Since food is an unending problem, and meals infrequent, a ferocity unmatched on land prevails. Some fishes are equipped with teeth so long and needlelike that they can never close their mouths. Most have distensible jaws like a python. One species (Chiasmodon) can swallow and coil in its distensible stomach, which resembles a grotesque bag, a fish three times its own length. The very names of such fishes are descriptive—the black gulper, the swallower, the sea viper, the dragonfish. Among the oddest are certain anglers dredged up from depths of nearly two miles. No wonder they are called anglers. From a cartilaginous rod above the head is suspended a fibrous line terminating in three barbed hooks!

Propagation is a problem in the darkness and cold. One monstrosity, a female fish several feet long, solves it by dragging about with her the diminutive male attached permanently to the undersurface of her body.

Down to a depth of 1200 feet marine life abounds. Specimens from greater depths are less numerous, for the difficulty of collecting becomes enormously enhanced. Some sea spiders (pycnogonoids) live three miles below the surface. Snaillike mollusks have been dredged from a depth of 16,000 feet, a squid (Chiroteuthis) from 17,694. In abysses over 18,000 feet down a fish with wraithlike eyes (Collettia) was snared and an annelid worm dragged from his burrow in the red clay. The deepest specimen so far recorded was a fish captured by an expedition under the Prince of Monaco from an appalling gulf of 19,806 feet!

Many deep-sea specimens are blind; others have huge eyes, out of all proportion. The mysterious light which the glowworm kindles on summer evenings is far more prevalent in the sea. So-called phosphorescence was doubtless observed long before the days of the Phoenicians. The name, from phosphor, the morning star, unfortunately suggests that quite different substance, phosphorus, which ignites our matches. A more accurate choice would be luminescence, or rather bioluminescence. The source is luciferin, which Webster defines as "a diffusible . . . compound . . . heatless light . . . undergoing oxidation, promoted by an enzyme, luciferase." Evidently the weird substance will not dispense its beams save in the presence of an equally weird associate.

Tropic waters sometimes fall from oar blades in flakes of light or reveal passing fish in trails of flame. The illumination may be so brilliant that the stars fade and the sky becomes a cavernous black. Nor are such manifestations confined to the tropics, nor even to the sea itself. Nordenskjöld wrote of an uncanny phenomenon of Siberian coasts: "If, during winter, one walks along the beach on the snow at ebb tide, there arises at every step an exceedingly intense, beautifully bluish white flash of light, so that he may fear that his shoes or clothing will take fire." This display is caused by a minute luminous crustacean which lives in snow sludge drenched with brine.

Of the seventeen grand phyla of animal life, eleven contain self-luminous species, while another is in doubt. This function, according to Professor Harvey, seems quite haphazard and not invariably useful. Many creatures not self-luminous carry lesser forms which are, either as parasites or incorporated into their very tissues. The glow becomes truly spectral when associated with death, as Aristotle observed that decaying fish were enveloped in a faintly luminous cloud, while Dickens mentions a similar ghostly emanation from a "bad lobster."

Such phenomena involve lesser living forms, either fungoid or bacterial. The latter are the tiniest lamps in creation, for only the combined light from thousands of individuals becomes faintly visible. Man's search for a "cold light" has been surpassed by these humblest of one-celled organisms.

Usually harmless, some luminous bacteria are heralds of decay. That tiny beach hopper, the sand flea, shines from a bacterial infection that invariably proves fatal.

Stranger still is the inclusion of great colonies of luminous bacteria in the organs of larger creatures. A peculiar fish (Photoblepheron) swims the Banda Sea and nowhere else. A section under each eye is filled with luminous bacteria which are operated as dark lanterns by a fold of tissue manipulated at will. Natives cut out these sections for bait, since they remain luminous for hours. A similar fish, also in the Banda Sea, is more widely distributed.

Surface conflagrations are often due to the presence of myriads of *Noctiluca miliaris*, a minute organism visible to the naked eye like suspended brick dust. It contributes to the characteristic color of the Red Sea by day and illuminates its waters by night.

Although such displays may seem quite as unproductive as the aurora borealis, bioluminescence supplies the sole lighting system of the deep sea. There its uses are manifold. A polynoid worm with a luminous tail sacrifices this member to a voracious crab while seeking a place of safety to grow a new one. The small squid, Heteroteuthis, which inhabits the Mediterranean Sea at depths of half a mile, where the characteristic inky cloud would be invisible in the darkness, discharges instead a luminous fog which temporarily blinds his assailant. Certain deep-sea shrimp have the same amazing gift.

For it is in regions of perpetual darkness that we find the most extraordinary manifestations. Many deep-sea fishes show parallel rows of lights along the body like the blazing portholes of some great liner. Others suspend tiny bulbs on long streamers. These may vary in color, for bioluminescence, though usually a ghostly white, may range through red, yellow, green, blue, purple, even to violet. One curious fish carries red light bulbs suspended from the head and blue ones, like taillights, trailing behind. A deep-sea squid (Lycoteuthis) brightens the gloom at nearly two miles depth by flashing from various areas of the body, blue, white, and ruby-red lights, the colors of the American Flag! Some fishes have illuminated teeth and must present a terrifying appearance to prospective victims. But, indeed, both lighting arrangements and color effects almost surpass the bounds of belief. Bioluminescence may be a steady glow or explosive like sparks from a battery, and is frequently switched on or off at will.

Impressive, indeed, is the panorama of marine fireflies comprising so many species of bacteria, radiolarians, bryozoans, hydroids, jellies, worms, brittle stars, mollusks, crustaceans, and fishes. The phylum of the Coelenterata, the sea jellies and their kindred, have more light-giving species than any other; the mollusks have but few, mainly nudibranchs, or shell-less forms. Even the highest phylum, the Chordata, which includes the mammals, has at least one representative, the Balanoglossus, which exudes a luminous slime.

Nature's wayward prodigality has endowed some species with this strange power for no obvious reason. Alcock found an electric ray, dredged from half-mile depths in the Pacific, which lacked functional eyes, although the body was studded with luminous spots. Other species have been catalogued with the same contradictory equipment. Even one bivalve, the rock-boring Pholas, is luminescent, for what purpose seems problematical.

The amount of light generated by bioluminescence is sometimes amazing. Linnaeus observed submerged sea pens that lighted up fishes swimming about them. Harvey, experimenting with a deep-sea crustacean (Cypridium) found that a minute portion of the dried body would raise four hundred million volumes of sea water to the range of visibility. In favorable cases a ratio of one part to forty billion proved sufficient!

Doubtless many unknown species still lurk in the abyss. Recorded specimens have been small and feeble, but huge hulks of flesh, twenty feet long and forty feet in circumference, weighing many tons, tough, fibrous, unlike any known creature, have washed ashore. New species have compelled a general revision of orders and even phyla, for they defied all other classification.

Thus the biology of the deep sea remains in a fluid state of readjustment, for there the great stream of life with which we are familiar flows through channels far deeper and more obscure.

CHAPTER XIX

Border Dwellers

> . . . the seal
> And bended dolphins play; part, huge of bulk,
> Wallowing unwieldily, enormous in their gait,
> Tempest the ocean.
>
> MILTON

The tides of life which long ago welled up from the sea to overflow the land have ebbed many times. Some plants still linger on the shifting border where beach grass holds the unruly dunes in check, coconut palms drink in tonic from the salt air, and mangroves dip their roots in the brine. According to oriental folklore, the clove tree "is never happy unless it can hear the wash of the surf," while at least one plant, the eelgrass, has actually "gone to sea."

More significant is the interchange of animal life. The Melampus of tidal areas, like some other mollusks, seems slowly evolving into a land type. Dozens of marine crabs have forsaken the sea, returning only to spawn, where their paths cross those of the sea turtles as they wade ashore to lay their eggs.

Most impressive of the land animals which have returned to their original habitat are the Cetacea—the porpoises, the dolphins, and the whales. These, so science tells us, were once land types. Many, losing their teeth, have developed fringes of ribbonlike "whalebone" suspended from the upper jaw, through which they strain the minute organisms which form their food. Of such is the blue whale, or sulphur-bottom, the true Leviathan of the great deep. Whalers speak of specimens 120 feet long, but truth needs no embellishment. One individual captured off desolate South Georgia Island measured 107 feet and weighed an estimated 125 tons.

Other bearded, or "baleen," whales are the finback, the humpback, the bowhead, the right whale, mercilessly hunted for a thousand years, the gray whale, the sei whale, and less familiar species. The bowhead and right whale, with enormous heads and ribbons of baleen that may be twelve feet long, are slow, ponderous, and bulky. The finback, on the contrary, is streamlined and so speedy that Nantucket whalers learned to leave him severely alone. A large whale swimming at a ten-knot speed has been estimated to generate nearly fifty horsepower.

All these species have relatively small throats and subsist largely upon brit, or tiny crustaceans. Over a ton of these sea atomies have been taken from the stomach of a sulphurbottom. The humpback, however, will plow through a school of herring, gulping them down by the barrel.

Most other cetaceans are equipped with teeth, though True's beaked whale has only two left. Smaller editions of the family are the pygmy right whale, the pygmy sperm whale, the white whale, the bottlenose, and others. Lord of the clan and undisputed monarch of the seas is the sperm whale. Though seldom exceeding sixty-five feet in length, his sovereignty rests in his massive head, tough as a tanker's bow, in the crushing power of his tail, and in his lower jaw, armed with massive teeth. The giant squid of the deep seas in his favorite food, though a twelve-foot shark was removed from one stomach.

Another toothed whale, smaller but more ferocious, is the dreaded killer (*Grampus orca*). Sometimes thirty feet long, stocky and powerful, both jaws are studded with murderous teeth. He swallows seals whole, while polar bears flee from his very shadow. In packs like wolves he assaults the great baleen whales, ripping off their fleshy lower lips to get at their tongues. Only the sperm whale seems immune, though an old sea captain once told me of a thrilling battle he witnessed when three killers, probably reckless from hunger, attacked an unsuspecting bull. The outraged giant promptly bit one in two, flattened another with a single sweep of his tail, and when last seen was leaping half out of water in his frantic efforts to overtake the third. Herman Melville made a huge sperm whale the hero, or rather villain, of his well-known romance, *Moby Dick*.

The "blackfish" (*Globicephela ventricosa*), slenderer than the killer, though sometimes twenty-eight feet long, travels in schools following a leader. One such school, which numbered over eighteen hundred individuals, was stranded, years ago, on Cape Cod beaches. Huge, harmless creatures, I have heard them crying in the night like babies from pain and fear.

Friendly spirits of the foam are the dolphins and their smaller cousins, the porpoises. Since the days of the Phoenicians their antics about a moving ship have been harbingers of good fortune. Of world-wide fame was Pelorus Jack, a Risso's dolphin, some thirteen feet long, which once piloted incoming ships into French Pass, New Zealand. The legislature granted him government protection. Dolphins roam all the seas, although some species favor restricted areas. Commerson's dolphin, for example, prefers the icy waters about Cape Horn. In addition to the common dolphin of world distribution, there are bottle-nosed dolphins, white-beaked dolphins, long-snouted dolphins, and various others. Oddest of all is the narwhal, which has no baleen, or functional teeth, yet readily captures salmon and halibut. The male has a single (rarely two) spiral tusk projecting from the upper jaw to an extreme length of nine feet. Quite useless to the animal, these tusks are prized by remoter tribes of Eskimos; as Kipling reminds us: "Their spears are made of Narwhal horn and they are the last of the men."

Tiniest of the Cetaceae are the porpoises, which may be only five feet long. There are several species: the harbor porpoise, Dall's porpoise, the black finless, and others. Sailors, calling them "sea pigs," once harpooned them for fresh meat. Most unusual are the porpoises and dolphins which have turned their backs on the sea to invade rivers and even lakes. There they have become so specialized as to develop new species. Such is the Guiana River dolphin of the Caribbean coast and rivers, and the La Plata dolphin. The Irrawaddy porpoise breasts that swirling current for nine hundred miles, while the Ganges dolphin has been made almost sightless by the mud of the Sacred River. The white dolphin, related to the bouto of the Amazon and its tributaries, is found in China's Tungting Lake and nowhere else! Marooned in this body of fresh water, it is viewed with special veneration by the Chinese.

Modern science has dispelled some of the mystery which long surrounded these interesting mammals. Whales, once thought to survive for centuries, have had their span of life perhaps too greatly reduced by reasoning from insufficient data. A baby blue whale may measure twenty-five feet at birth and is nursed by the mother until more than fifty feet long. Its life span is supposed to be twenty years; that of the sperm whale much less, but no one really knows. Pelorus Jack, a mere dolphin, was an active pilot for thirty-two years!

A true border dweller is the walrus, that grotesque monstrosity with exaggerated canines. Nordenskjöld found in Siberia a pair more than thirty-two inches long that weighed nearly fifteen pounds! The Norseman Octhere, of King

Alfred's reign, first mentioned them when, in recounting his famous voyage around North Cape, he spoke of "Horse Whales which have in their teeth bones of great price and excellence—their skins are also very good to make cables for ships." Sir Hugh Willoughby in 1553 saw in the Arctic "divers strange beasts—to us unknown and also wonderful." That these included walruses is confirmed by a fellow voyager, Sir Richard Chancellor, who wrote, "There are also a fishes teeth which fish is called the Morse." Barents, exploring the frigid sea which bears his name, observed several hundred of these uncouth creatures upon an ice floe. When his men in an open boat disturbed them, they plunged into the water, with danger of capsizal, for, as he quaintly remarks, "they were monstrous strong fishes." Walruses prefer a diet of mollusks, which they dig with their huge teeth, carefully discarding the shells. Nordenskjöld found an opened stomach like a dish of shelled oysters, though investigation disclosed, instead, clams and other shellfish. Marine worms and sea cucumbers are also relished, as are occasional bits of seaweed or even seal meat. Whether lolling on the ice or swimming among scattered floes, these ungainly animals are true lovers of the sea.

Another land animal also at home in the water is the polar bear, with the possible exception of the brown giants of Kodiak Island, largest of all land carnivora. Authentic weights of sixteen hundred pounds have been recorded, and much larger specimens reported. This great animal seems to prefer the sea, unless the cruel fin of the killer whale cuts the waves, when he scrambles for the nearest shore. He has been observed swimming more than twenty miles from land. Although his habitat is coldest and bleakest of all the bear tribe, he probably does not hibernate. Frozen ground and absence of natural caverns forbid. He devours fish or seals or caribou with equal zest and, when decrepit from age, seeks the shore to fill his stomach with moss and other vegetation. Laplanders call these expatriates "old land kings," and suspect they harbor the souls of fallen hunters. The white coat, by the way, is not so much to harmonize with the landscape as to conserve bodily heat in the bitter arctic winter.

Another land animal that readily takes to the water is the caribou, the reindeer of Santa Claus. These animals have been found swimming almost out of sight of land. There are herds on Spitsbergen in Latitude 80, hundreds of miles above North Cape. How did they get there? On floating ice, perhaps. Who knows? No wintry blizzard is too cold for them, so long as food is obtainable. They paw through snow to get at clumps of grass and will, when nothing better offers, seek the beaches to dine on seaweed.

Still more addicted to desolate landscapes are the musk oxen, which seem to have drifted from one uninhabitable island to another until in Ellesmere Land they have surpassed the caribous farthest north. Ruthlessly persecuted, a considerable herd still grazes along the sterile Greenland coast, whence they may have crossed long ago, on the ice, although Stefansson claims they never leave the land.

Far wider in range is the arctic fox. Nansen found one a hundred miles north of the desolate island of New Siberia, seeking new lands toward the Pole. He abounds in many islets widely separated from the continent, though how he reached them is a mystery.

Best known of all border dwellers are the seals. The sea elephant is the colossus of the family. Specimens twenty feet long and weighing several tons have been reported. With his ridiculous pendant proboscis, some eight inches long, he was once a familiar spectacle along remote shores where he has been all but exterminated. The leopard seal of the Antarctic is quite as savage as his namesake, the spotted terror of the jungle. But he is only one of many species. The common "hair seal" of the North Atlantic, though as much at home in the sea as the cod or salmon, loves to bask on the beach in the sunlight. Hunters slaughter him by the tens of thousands for his fat and hide. More valuable are the fur seals (really sea lions) of Bering Sea. Once threatened with extermination, they were long a theme of international dissension. Under governmental protection, they have so multiplied that millions now assemble at the summer rookeries on the Pribilof and Commander islands. There the roar of bulls fighting for their harems may be heard for miles above the loudest gales, while their companions frolic on the rocks or bask in the wan sunlight that filters through the fog. Then, after some months spent as landlubbers, Kipling tells us: "The great man-seal haul back to the sea and no man knows their path."

In few animals are the sexes more unequal. The female rarely weighs above eighty pounds, but her lord is a ponderous warrior who may tip the scales at nearly five hundred. From May until September he apparently neither eats nor drinks, an unparalleled exhibition of vitality. Mature at seven years, every male seeks a harem of his own, which may number over a hundred females. At fourteen, if not killed in battle with his fellows, or fallen prey to polar bears or killer whales, he becomes superannuated and rounds out a morose old age.

Other aquatic animals are the "sea cows," the dugongs, manatees, and others which subsist upon marine vegetation which they tear off through parted lips by the bushel. Bowing gravely while thus browsing, with head and shoulders out of the water, they were .the original mermaidens, an error all the more plausible since their body terminates in a leathery lobe like a fish's tail. Their legendary origin is preserved in their scientific name, Sirenia, from the sirens whose songs distracted Odysseus.

One species (Rhytina) that formerly inhabited Bering Sea, was named Steller's sea cow from the great naturalist who first observed it. On the desolate island where Bering died this strange animal had its home. Steller thought both milk and flesh superior to that of cattle and found the creatures so tame that while feeding one might put his hand upon them. The thick leathery hide was covered with hair, matted like an exterior skin, that swarmed with vermin and resembled the bark of an old oak. He mentions one specimen thirty-five feet long that weighed sixty-seven hundred pounds. When harpooned, its mates attempted rescue and seemed bewildered at man's ferocity. Yet within thirty years this harmless species had become extinct!

Reptiles have their representatives in the oceans. Huge sea turtles, which may tip the beam at half a ton, sleep upon the surface of tropic seas or lumber laboriously ashore to lay their eggs in the sand.

Less harmless are the sea snakes, which may reach a length of six feet or more. Some are black and yellow, others grass-green. Related to the cobra family, their venom is even deadlier. While anchored off Mombasa, I observed one crawl part way up a hawser. The native who killed it assured me in broken English, "If he bit me, I would swell up and die in twenty minutes." Evidently land forms that found the sea more congenial, they have become definitely marine and are often encountered in tropic seas. Coleridge's Ancient Mariner watched their antics about the ship as,

> Blue, glossy green and velvet black
> They coiled and swam; and every track
> Was a flash of golden fire.

Other animals, semiaquatic on land, take to the sea upon occasion. Hippos swim across the thirty-kilometer stretch that separates Zanzibar from the mainland. Crocodiles make even longer voyages. They have been observed twenty miles off the Malayan coast, while at least two individuals seem to have survived the voyage to the Cocos (Keeling) Islands in the Indian Ocean, more than six hundred miles from the nearest Sumatra shore. They also occur in the Palau Islands, nearly as far from Mindanao, and have been reported in the Fijis and Solomons.

CHAPTER XX

Feathered Migrants

I see my way as birds their trackless way.
ROBERT BROWNING
At length did cross an albatross—
Thorough the fog it came.
COLERIDGE

When once the storms had swept him off into so vast a sea—
a sea from which birds travel not within a year, so vast it is
and fearful.

HOMER

Wildest and freest of ocean's life are the birds. Some of
them seem as much a part of the dancing waves as flecks
of foam. They skim the surface or ride the billows more
trimly than any galleon or clipper ship; they plunge beneath
with dizzier speed than the pearl diver. And although they
nest on shore and frequent many a desolate crag or islet,
they are true children of the sea.

Naturalist and layman alike divide the birds into two
varieties—sea and land. The sea birds are usually unmistakable. Nature has waterproofed their vests and webbed their
feet for paddles. But even land types often raid the sea for
food, as the bald eagle does, or wade the shallows, as the
great blue heron does, or traverse wide stretches of water,
as our sweetest songsters do.

Most familiar of sea birds are the gulls. The personification of grace, they taught the Wright brothers how to soar

with the wind before they launched their first airplane from Kill Devil Hill in North Carolina. Of the fifty-odd species, the herring gulls are perhaps the best known. These flock about homing ships or greet the tide with shrill cries on many a sand bar. They are the "white wings" of the tide flats, and their office as public scavengers assures them governmental protection. At least one species, the Skua, has become a feathered highjacker, robbing other birds rather than fish himself.

Smaller and more quickly darting are the terns, which also number fifty species or more. While the gull flies with beak pointing straight ahead, the tern slants his beak downward like a mosquito. He is a famous diver and often reveals a school of fish by his frantic splashings. One species, the arctic tern, is our greatest wanderer, as we shall see when we discuss the mysterious migrations of the feathered world.

Friendly companions on many a voyage are Wilson's petrels, known to all sailors as "Mother Carey's chickens." Incessantly active, they skim low over the waves, exploring the trough and barely evading the crest. Although sometimes called stormy petrels, they are world-wide favorites.

More sea-loving than gulls or petrels are the albatross, immortalized by Coleridge in his *Rime of the Ancient Mariner*. Although there are some sixteen recognized species, the characteristic type is the great winged spirit of lonely southern seas. One followed us for days on a slow voyage across the South Atlantic. I often sprawled upon the deck to observe him as he hovered perhaps forty feet overhead, blinking at me with his solemn eyes. When anything edible was thrown overboard, he would throw up both wings like a drowning man and plop into the water. When taking off, he would run along the surface, gaining momentum like an airplane, but once aloft his matchless assurance was inspiring, so effortless were the infrequent movements of his wings as he seemed to glide through invisible channels in the air. When Table Mountain emerged from the mist he wheeled off toward the Antarctic, for land was not for this ocean waif. An albatross of another species followed us almost across the Pacific, but when the California coast appeared he too wheeled back into the open sea. Sailors, however, claim that an albatross will attack a man in the water, peck out his eyes, and even cleave his skull with his formidable beak. Not infrequently they catch the great birds with baited fishhooks.

Albatross may have a wingspread of eleven feet or more. Though heavy-bodied, they are the champions of sustained sea flights. Their closest rivals are perhaps the tropical birds and, even more, the frigate birds of warmer climes. These most graceful of all fliers, with long cloven tail like a swallow's, and scimitar wings seven and a half feet across, remain aloft hour after hour as though defying gravity. They are winged villains, however, as they often rob other birds, particularly gulls and terns.

At the opposite extreme is the pelican, most ungainly of fliers, "whose beak holds more than his belly can." There are ten species, the largest six feet long with a wingspread of ten feet or more, and a pouched bill eighteen inches long. They are capable fishermen and establish great rookeries. In 1932 on the tiny Chincha Islands off Peru there were observed from five to six million pelicans, cormorants, gannets, and other sea birds that had built up guano deposits a hundred feet thick! Their daily consumption of fish from the Humboldt Current was estimated at a thousand tons!

Perhaps the most skillful of fishermen are the cormorants, which number some thirty species. In the Far East they are sometimes trained to catch fish just as falcons are trained to attack game. A collar worn about the neck prevents the bird from swallowing the fish. The cormorant is a fearless diver; one was trapped in a crab pot a hundred and twenty feet below the surface. When swimming under water, they use both wings and feet, as do the scoters and the penguins. The fiercest of all bird fishers, however, is the savage sea eagle of the Pacific, a favorite study on embroidered Chinese screens.

Many species of shore birds also love the sea. Such are the sandpipers and their numerous relatives, which number over a hundred species. Familiar beach frequenters, these tiny racers embroider the scalloped edges of the surf with their footprints and punctuate the roar of the waves with their shrill cries. Their long beaks show unusual diversification. The curlews' beaks bend downward, the snipes' project straight ahead, while the avocets' seem to turn up their elongated noses at the world in general.

The ducks are a numerous family of more than a hundred and forty species, fully half of them marine. Much esteemed by sportsmen, many are table delicacies. Of similar build but larger size are the geese, which comprise some forty species. They love the marsh and tundra of the Far North and wing their way over vast areas of ocean.

Still larger are the swans, those ornaments of public gardens. Wild species are shyer than the geese; some have been reduced almost to extinction by man's rapacity. One of the most charming of childhood stories is Hans Andersen's "Ugly Duckling" which proved to be a swan.

Sea birds, emulating the Pilgrims of Plymouth, "suck the abundance of the seas." Fish is their staple diet, but mollusks are preferred by some. The ocean skimmers dine on sea butterflies or pteropods, the shore waders on mussels and the like. The oyster catcher has a specialized beak for prying open the shells of that obstinate bivalve. Many feed on the numberless worms and crustaceans of coastal waters.

The clown of marine birddom is the puffin, or sea parrot.

His squat body is snow-white in front, glossy black behind; his feet are vermilion, his grotesque beak striped with yellow, blue, and red. Perhaps it assists him in digging, for he is an adept burrower and also provides a pincer grip on a squirming fish.

The nesting habits of sea birds vary widely. The murres and guillemots of the Far North lay their eggs on the precarious verge of rocky clefts. The emperor penguin nests in the deep snows of the terrible antarctic winter. Gulls and terns often scoop out a hollow in the sand. Roam the beach grass glades which shelter these nests and the parents will swoop at you like angry hornets. Many species, including the petrels, either excavate burrows along seaward-looking cliffs or appropriate those of other birds. Eider ducks line their nests with down plucked from their own breasts. The osprey weaves a great clump of branches in the top of a dead tree. The sea swifts of Java construct their nests of seaweeds cemented with saliva; these furnish the famous bird's-nest soup of China.

Breeding grounds are often extensive. A vast area on Novaya Zemlya, which extends for six hundred miles into the Arctic, is called Gooseland. Favorite nesting places are the fringing tundra of Siberia and North America. Many a rocky islet is densely crowded with brooding sea birds which pre-empt almost every available inch of sand and rock.

In vivid contrast with the albatross and the frigate bird are the flightless penguins of the Far South. Their wings have become mere rubbery fins, enabling them to dart about under water as agilely as seals, while on shore they stand stiffly erect, like dignified old gentlemen. Penguins inhabit the Far Southern coasts of Africa, Australia, South America, and islands of that comparable latitude. They form almost the only land life on the frozen wastes of the antarctic continent. Fearless and friendly, they are, so Sir James Murray observes, "the civilized nations of those regions."

Pigafetta, encountering them in the Strait of Magellan, thought them a queer breed of geese and wrote, "These geese are black and have all their feathers alike both on body and wings. They do not fly and live on fish. They were so fat it was not necessary to pluck them but to skin them. Their beak is like that of a crow." Needless to say, Pigafetta was no naturalist.

Sir Francis Drake also had experiences with penguins off Tierra del Fuego and said of them, "We found great store of strange birds which could not fly at all nor yet run so fast that they could escape us. In body they were less than a goose and bigger than a mallard—such was the infinite resort of these birds that in the space of one day we killed no less than 3,000. They are a very good and wholesome victual."

Many a shipwrecked mariner has levied toll upon the penguins. John Neun, marooned for nearly three years on Kerguelen Island, found that the contents of three eggs of the king penguin filled a pint mug and were excellent fried in seal oil.

There are several species of penguins. Fossil specimens measure seven feet, but the king penguin was thought to be the largest living species until explorers in Antarctica discovered the somewhat larger emperor penguin. This magnificent bird may stand nearly four feet tall. Shackleton caught one that weighed eighty-five pounds. Though friendly, they resist aggression and, equipped with powerful wings and beaks, are no mean antagonists. When a visiting scientist tried to capture one, the outraged bird knocked him down and leaped on his chest. Penguins are the most human of birds. Social creatures, they congregate in great multitudes. They approach visiting ships bowing gravely, making long chattering speeches, evidently regarding human beings as another and possibly inferior kind of penguin. In their white shirt fronts and black coats, they assume always a quaint dignity. Anatole France wove about them his sardonic masterpiece, *Penguin Island*. Though true children of the sea, they seldom venture far from shore.

The auks are sometimes called northern penguins, for there is a resemblance. Living species, however, such as the razor-billed auk, can fly, as can the little auks, or dovekies, that wander from their native Greenland, appearing occasionally as far south as Hatteras. Eskimos catch these plump little birds in hand nets, preserve the bodies for the winter larder, and line their shirts with the downy skins.

The largest of the genus was the great auk, now only a memory. His resemblance to the penguins was more obvious, for he was flightless and stood quite thirty inches tall. He was the fastest swimmer and the most proficient diver of all North American birds. When Jacques Cartier visited an island off Newfoundland in 1534 the sailors killed two boatloads in half an hour. French cod fishers off Newfoundland depended upon the great auk for their food supply, while the eggs, more than five inches in length, were keenly relished. Then came the even more rapacious destroyers, who hunted them for their down and feathers, and the final act of the bloody tragedy. The last of the great auks was captured off Iceland in 1844. Some eighty specimens and perhaps as many eggs are preserved in various museums. But this splendid bird has gone to join the dodo of Mauritius and the moa, hugest of all birds, that was perhaps exterminated by the Maoris of New Zealand.

Man's bloodguiltiness is never more in evidence than when he has blotted out a species that can never be replaced. The Labrador duck was once abundant all along our northern coasts. A lone specimen was caught on Grand Manan in 1871 and another was thought to have perished on Long Island four years later. With his passing, the voice of the Labrador duck was stilled forever.

Among species driven to the verge of extinction is the trumpeter swan, one of the largest of all North American wild birds. Even where slaughter has stopped short of annihilation, it has been incredibly stupid and wanton. Coker found on the island of Lobos de Afuera a hundred thousand pelicans. Upon his next visit this immense rookery had been so disturbed by guano hunters that scarcely one of these harmless birds remained.

Still more indefensible was the raid of poachers on the great albatross rookery on Laysan Island in the Pacific. In 1909 these miscreants killed over three hundred thousand birds, strewing acres with broken eggs and mutilated bodies, and storing three carloads of wings for the milliner's trade. They would probably have exterminated the species had not the federal government dispatched a revenue cutter to bring the pirates to justice. Laysan is now one of those sanctuaries where birds are given a chance to recuperate.

Vast migrations are still one of the mysteries of the bird world. In some cases this is to escape winter's cold, in others to secure safe nesting places, in others to seek more abundant food supplies. But these do not explain in full the restless wanderlust which leads so many feathered adventurers to far countries.

The most landlubberly of birds are now and then migrants at sea. They have been sighted eight hundred miles from shore. Such extreme deviations from normal routes were due to gales, but the seasonal migrations of the tiniest of all, the hummingbirds, carry them half a thousand miles straight across the Gulf of Mexico.

Most spectacular of ocean flights, however, is that of the

golden plover. Nesting in Labrador, this shore bird flies to Nova Scotia, then takes off in an unbroken ocean hop of twenty-four hundred miles to South America, which probably consumes two days. Still more amazing is the flight of the golden plover from Alaska to Hawaii, also twenty-four hundred miles. What mysterious faculty guides them to those minute specks in the interminable Pacific no one knows.

The honking of migratory wild geese is a welcome note in Nature's minstrelsy. Their V formation, with some wise old gander in the lead, is a pattern for airplanes.

Bird banding has thrown much light on extensive migrations. Greatest of all is that of the arctic tern. In the Far North from June 15 to August 20 it nests and rears its young, then away to the islands which fringe the antarctic continents, eleven thousand miles distant, for another polar summer. Its round-trip journey covers twenty-two thousand miles, though deviations doubtless account for a much greater distance. More than any other created thing, it must love the light, for eight months of the year are spent in regions where the sun never sets, while the intervening months have far more than their normal share of sunlight.

Migrating birds travel rapidly, particularly when over the sea. Wild geese, though plump and heavy for their wingspread, are reputed to hit a pace of roughly a mile a minute. Ranging far into the upper air, they are sometimes brought to earth by moisture freezing to their wings. Oddly enough, though geese are noted for their long seasonal pilgrimages, one species, the emperor goose, never seems to leave the fog-cursed regions of Bering Sea. Its range is from Siberia to Alaska and the rocky chain of the Aleutians.

Many birds prefer night flying, as they must seek fresh feeding grounds on the morrow. They escape some perils from hawks and other predators but encounter another in lighthouses. Red or quickly flashing lights repel them, but a fixed white light seems as irresistible as the candle flame to the moth. The great white light on Fowey Rocks at the southern extremity of Florida is a notorious bird killer. Hundreds of birds are dashed against its flaring lenses or, seemingly hypnotized, circle about it until they drop exhausted on the rocks beneath.

Many migratory birds stop at halfway places to recuperate. The ponds and marshes of Cape Cod and Hatteras are favorite haunts. Individuals, pleased with the surroundings, go no farther, but alighting in coastal waters presents a new peril, the waste from oil-burning ships. When feathers become coated, flight is impossible and slow starvation ensues.

Only in the sea, with its annual pilgrimage of seals to the far-off Pribilofs, and the uncanny homing of the salmon and the elvers, can we find a parallel to these tides of bird life which stream back and forth across such imposing arcs of earth's circumference.

CHAPTER XXI

Farming the Sea

As your pearl in your foul oyster.
SHAKESPEARE

The wilderness ever recedes before the man with the hoe. He has felled the forests, drained the swamps, and irrigated the deserts until the riotous uplands have been restrained if not subdued; but he has paused upon the shore, for what could he hope to accomplish against the vast and untamable sea?

Nature's bounties from field and garden and vineyard are not wholly hers. A thousand Luther Burbanks have analyzed her soils and experimented with seeds and insecticides and fertilizers. Hence our grains are notable improvements upon the original wild grasses, while our apples and strawberries bear little resemblance to their pygmy progenitors.

Moreover, man has distributed his agricultural triumphs. The shapeless tubers the Incas nurtured with such patience have become the potato staples of Europe and North America. The Arabian coffee plant flourishes better in Brazil; the rubber tree from the Amazon thrives in Malaya. Animal husbandry shows equal strides in perfected strains of fowl and cattle and sheep and swine.

In contrast with such triumphs upon land, the sea remains unconquered and perhaps unconquerable. What man gleans there is largely natural and unchanged. He cannot alter the floating sargassum or the giant kelp or develop superior types of herring or great blue whales. And yet, baffled though he is by the sea's immensity and ungovernable power, he has made some forays beyond the tide marks.

His failure to utilize that rich and varied vegetation produced by the sea, however, has been indefensible. Only a few maritime countries have seemed to appreciate the wealth thus cast upon their beaches by the tens of thousands of tons.

Potash was originally obtained by thrifty Scotchmen by burning dried kelp. It really was pot ash. From it came our common element potassium, with its numerous compounds, and it is still a valued source of iodine, that powerful germicide and antidote for goiter. In the Hebrides and Orkneys, a hundred years ago, the gathering and burning of kelp was the chief industry. Scotland's production was worth two million dollars annually; that of Brittany at least a million. Manufacturers of glass and soap were large buyers of the product. Shore communities in Scandinavia, France, and Ireland harvested the crop at stated times by plucking it from the rocks at low tide or reaping it under water with rakes, hooks, and scythes attached to long poles.

Some of these sea cornstalks were burned but more were spread upon the land as fertilizer. Coastal soils, often impoverished or sterile, were enriched by such vegetation plowed under or placed in the individual hill. "Wrap seed potatoes in rockweed," says an agricultural authority, "and you will grow much larger tubers, free from rot or blight."

In France, two centuries ago, laws were enacted to share the available supply between those who wished to use it as "raw" fertilizer and those who preferred to burn it for its chemical ash. In the Channel islands definite times for harvesting were established. Meadowlands thus treated produced those blue-ribbon winners among the cows: the Jerseys, Guernseys, and Alderneys. Farmers in Rhode Island

and New Hampshire also plowed under rockweed to increase the clover yield.

That seaweed possesses considerable food value has long been known, but now that whole populations are reduced to hunger it might be more widely recognized. Improvident Americans commonly eat but two varieties of red algae, Irish moss (Chondrus crispus) and dulse. Collecting the former has furnished a minor industry to some rock-bound New England villages where the receding tides reveal clumps of this varicolored plant two or three inches high, which may be gathered by the bushel. From it comes a gelatinous pudding of the nature of junket. Dulse, obtainable in many coastal markets, is commonly chewed raw, though Scotchmen acclaim it delicious stewed in milk. A hardy pioneer in Provincetown, some years ago, experimented with various types of marine vegetation and actually made flour and bread from some of them.

While some European nations have far outstripped us in the use of seaweeds as food, only the Orient has shown any adequate appreciation of this vast food source. In native Philippine markets one may observe piles of seaweed resembling masses of maple sugar. Throughout the East Indies and along the coasts of China edible seaweeds are popular, but Japan, of all nations, has been most successful in farming the seas. Her long coast line, more than three times as extensive as that of the United States, is indented with innumerable coves and shallow bays where marine vegetation flourishes. Had she not utilized this both as fertilizer upon a worn-out soil and as food for an undernourished race, she could never have reached her recent prominence.

More than thirty types of marine vegetation are staple food products. Kombu, a universal favorite, is prepared from a brown-green kelp that may reach a length of a hundred feet or more. It is harvested in the fall, either by hand with long hooks or by dredging.

Agar-agar, prepared from a red seaweed, has proved its value in laboratory experiments, where disease germs thrive upon its gelatinous substance. The preparation seems to have originated in Ceylon, but the Japanese use it not only for scientific research but as an article of food. In fact they transform such marine growths into soup stock, vegetables, and even candy.

Seaweeds are the only vegetable known to the Eskimos of the Far North. The Hausch Indians of Tierra del Fuego were called kelp eaters by more aggressive tribes, as they subsisted largely upon the great beds of giant kelp in that region.

In Japan seaweed is frequently gathered by the women and spread upon the beaches to dry. Some is powdered for fertilizer, but much is heaped in long piles, covered to protect them from the rain, then burned slowly so as to avoid volatilizing the iodine content. The ash may yield as much as 18 per cent of potassium oxide and three fifths of 1 per cent of iodine.

A Japanese report, issued shortly before the war, listed a yield of 17,000,000 pounds of potassium oxide and 650,000 pounds of iodine from this source. The annual value of sea vegetation for fertilizer, chemicals, and food mounted high into the millions.

When our first war with Germany cut off the importation of phosphates, our government sought other sources of supply. None proved so promising as the great kelp beds of the Pacific, which stretch all the way to the Aleutian Islands. Dr. Marshall Howe, investigating these beds, found stalks growing to a length of more than two hundred feet. In favorable locations they were so rank as to impede navigation and form great natural breakwaters. A mowing machine was designed to be pushed by a launch through these marine jungles at a speed of some four miles per hour. The weed, turned up on an endless belt, was chopped into suitable lengths like a farmer's ensilage and piled in waiting scows. One machine could harvest twenty-five tons an hour. Arrived at the dock, huge forks pitched out the accumulated mass, to be dried and reduced to ash. Several companies were organized.

Such operations merely utilized natural growth. To plant or cultivate marine vegetation seems impossible, yet it is not. Along the Irish coast, where the bottom is firm and level, flat stones are laid down to catch the floating spores of marine vegetation. This is harvested the second year and the stones turned over for a new crop. In Japan thousands of acres of similar bottom have been devoted to the propagation of nori, a red alga known to us as laver. Instead of stones, bushes were placed so as to catch the spores and the resultant crop was harvested from January to March.

Sponges are cultivated in somewhat the same manner. Slabs of concrete, with bits of sponge attached, are placed in favorable waters and the mature crop sliced off to make way for a new one. The harvested sponges are placed in corrals of shallow water to slough off the animal tissue and prepare the skeletons for commerce. During this stage they must be protected against showers, like new-mown hay, or the texture will be injured. Although rubber substitutes are popular in bathtubs, sponges remain the best-known material for cleaning hot glass, hence are widely utilized in glass manufacture. They are graded according to quality from wire, grass, and yellow to the finest wool texture. Sponge fisheries have flourished for ages in the Mediterranean and are pictured on Inca pottery.

Oysters are far more intensively cultivated. The ground is chosen as carefully as the farmer selects black loam or river bottom. It must be firm, for mud smothers oysters, while shifting sand may bury them; it should also be free from rocks. Such "grants," usually given by the local township, are staked out like mining claims, and the "seed" strewn upon the bottom. This seed, or "spat," comprises the young oysters which have just graduated from the free-swimming stage, developed a shell, and are ready to settle down. Once attached to any firm surface, they stay put as definitely as any barnacle upon a rock. A single dead shell may be freckled with dozens of infant oysters. Favorable localities are chosen for collecting this spat, usually in coastal eddies or where two currents come together off a shallow point. Here are scattered by the thousands of bushels empty shells, preferably those of bay scallops, which are more brittle than most. When these have collected the young spat, they are dredged up and sold to oyster growers as seed. At some later date they are dredged up again so that the oysters may be separated and allowed elbow room, otherwise they may form "finger" oysters, long, narrow, unsightly, and difficult to open. This operation of dredging and sorting the oysters is repeated by growers who supply the fancy market. Oyster grants have their pests like the squash bugs and bean beetles of our victory gardens. One of these is the oyster drill (Urosalpinx), a beautifully fluted snail about an inch long. This creature, fastening upon a partly grown oyster, drills a tiny hole through one shell with a rasping tongue, rough as a file. Large oysters fall even easier victims to the starfish. Owners mop their grants by trailing great bunches of cotton waste which entangle the marauders. When drawn up on deck, they were formerly chopped into pieces, until experiment showed that a five-fingers divided might presently develop into five separate individuals, so they are now dipped into huge kettles of boiling water. In Connecticut, not a large producer, starfish, in one season, destroyed over six hundred thousand dollars' worth of oysters.

Nor are these the only enemies. The boring sponge is a terrible nuisance. Certain shore birds, particularly the oyster catcher, raid the beds, as do mangrove crabs in the tropics. Other shellfish, by more rapid growth and multiplication, smother the oysters or appropriate most of the available food supply. Mussels and the curious half deck (Crepidula) of our beaches are notorious offenders.

Severe storms may menace oyster beds quite as readily as ripening wheat or fruit crops, for drifting sand or silt is as destructive as rust or blight to upland harvests.

Some oyster growers cater to the select trade by cultivating oysters which they purchase full grown, to strew upon hard sand in cooler waters. Left there some months or even a year or more, they develop a more attractive shape with pearly valves, the "half-shell" aristocrats of oyster bars and grillrooms. Oysters, condemned by polluted waters, when thus transplanted, are soon purified and made marketable.

Oysters are sometimes harvested from rowboats by long-handled "tongs," but the common method is to dredge them from a power boat. Dumped on the deck, they are carefully sorted and the refuse thrown back into Davy Jones's Locker.

In France, Norway, and Japan bushes are preferred to shells for collecting the spat, which are suspended at certain depths and carefully tended. Parisians are fond of "green" oysters, so colored from the minute organisms upon which they feed; hence they are kept at the mouths of streams until they have acquired the desired tint.

Opening oysters for the market requires special tools and a deftness of wrist, as many an amateur has discovered.

Along the Gulf coast one may see piles of empty shells as big as houses, whence the "shucked" oysters have been shipped in iced containers like refrigerated fruit.

Maryland and Virginia are the great oyster states. In one season Maryland produced over ten million bushels, a record yield. A recent federal report lists the annual oyster harvest at some twelve and a half million dollars. Oysters are of world-wide distribution, where the waters are not too cold. There are excellent oysters in Australia and the East Indies, while the Romans sent all the way to Britain for specimens that probably owed their superior appeal to the expense of transportation. And yet distant "seeding" has been general. Chesapeake oysters have been liberally sprinkled along New England coasts, while carloads of Atlantic oysters have been transplanted to Puget Sound.

Although oysters have been most intensively cultivated, clams and quahogs have received some attention. The clam "set" may collect on the edges of channels along the sand bars, so that it can be scooped up in buckets. I have seen along Plum Island Sound in Massachusetts such windrows containing many millions of tiny "clamlets." Sprinkled over tidal shallows, in staked grants, they grow to marketable size. Quahog seed is also sometimes transplanted. In certain European and Far Eastern waters mussels are cultivated quite as extensively as oysters, and in somewhat the same manner.

That delectable morsel, the scallop, is merely the muscle which binds the two shells together, as the body parts are discarded. One bushel of scallops will produce between two and a half and three quarts of these "eyes." The bay scallop has the characteristic ridged shells; the larger "sea" scallop has smoother shells and is named, by the way, Magellanicus, from the great discoverer who first observed similar shellfish around Tierra del Fuego. They are dredged in waters up to fifty feet deep or more, and the eyes removed by skillful operators with special knives.

Other shellfish, though less popular, are gaining in public favor. That elusive elf of the flats, the razor clam, netted the diggers more than half a million dollars in a recent season, while the huge sea clam (Spisula), long a favorite in New England, has more recently invaded Western markets.

A valuable shrimp industry has developed in the Gulf of Mexico. I once spent some days at Biloxi, Mississippi, with the fishermen, a picturesque lot. From that port some eleven hundred boats, employing about forty-six hundred men, ranged up to a hundred miles from shore, sometimes remaining away for two weeks. Huge nets or trawls are suspended upon boards six feet long that distend the net to a width of forty feet. The lower edge is weighted, the upper made buoyant with corks. Rocks or sunken trees wreak havoc. Five barrels of shrimp are considered a fair day's catch. Speedy boats repair to the fishing fleet, pick up the catch, and return to the factories, where several thousand workers, mostly women, prepare the shrimp for canning. Government 'inspectors sometimes condemn a whole boatload. Recently a great bed of jumbo shrimp has been discovered in Gulf waters, where the patriarchs of this crustacean seemingly repair to spend their declining days. As these days are numbered, anyway, their capture does not materially interfere with the propagation of the species. According to a recent government report, the annual income from the shrimp industry exceeded five million dollars.

To grow lobsters for market seems hardly feasible, yet it has been attempted. Uneconomical because of the time involved, it also proved impracticable due to the cannibalism prevalent among young lobsters. Lobster eggs are still hatched, however, and the young fry protected until they are better fitted to cope with life's problems. Freshly liberated, little lobsters linger on the surface, a prey to sea birds and surface-feeding fish, so they are educated by sliding them down an inclined shoot to seek the bottom, where their chances of survival are much better.

Some fish eggs are also hatched and the young liberated. One species, the Alaska salmon, has thus been introduced into the waters of Chile and New Zealand.

Perhaps the strangest of farm projects in the sea is the growing of artificial pearls. This art was perfected in Japan, for it requires oriental patience. A bit of foreign substance is inserted between the valves, about which the irritated mollusk builds layer upon layer of lustrous nacre; thus pearls may be grown in various required shapes. Not only the pearl oyster, but the abalone and other shellfish have proved adaptable to this form of culture. There is something which savors of necromancy in thus copying Nature's one perfect gem—the pearl.

The federal government reports that some fifty species of fish and shellfish are commonly eaten in this country, but we lag far behind other lands in our appreciation of ocean's bounties. In London, in one year, three thousand tons of periwinkles were delivered at Billingsgate Market, while the Japanese were busy catching seventy million kilos of squid. Here neither are esteemed, while dozens of other edible varieties are quite ignored.

CHAPTER XXII

With Hook and Net

Third Fisherman: Master, I marvel how the fishes live in the sea.
First Fisherman: Why, as men do a-land; the great ones eat up
the little ones.

SHAKESPEARE

Primitive man first caught fish with his fingers, as I have
snatched whiting from the surf, or picked up flounders
lurking in eelgrass shallows. A Cape Cod neighbor even
dragged out a ninety-pound halibut flapping in shoaling
waters, while Indians pluck a dinner from salmon-glutted
streams.

Inventive skill, however, long ago added such fishing tools
as the spear, the hook, and the net. The spear, now unimportant, is still used by primitive peoples and survives elsewhere in the eel spear and the swordfisherman's harpoon.

The hand lines of cod and mackerel fishermen have been
superseded by more labor-saving devices. The hook is still
the favorite of the sportsman, with his expensive rod and
reel, but commercially is seldom used, except by tuna fishermen. Trawl or "long" lines are still set with baited hooks
every few feet, but most edible fishes are now caught by
various types of nets or seines. So diversified have these become that the federal government lists fourteen distinct
types, then lumps the remainder in a miscellaneous item—
fifteen. Basically, however, they are of two kinds: stationary
and movable. The stationary ones, embodying the principle

of the mousetrap, are nets draped upon poles and designed to lure the fish into an inner compartment, where they swim stupidly about until scooped up with dip nets. One sees many kinds in knocking about the world. The estuaries of Burma and the coast of Sumatra are dotted with them, as are more familiar shores. Streams are also partially diked off with nets to direct eels and herring through restricted narrows into convenient traps. All such inventions, however, suffer from one basic disadvantage—the fish must come to them.

Movable nets, on the other hand, seek the fish where they may be found. These, though diverse, are of three types. The purse seine is an American favorite. A net weighted at the bottom and suspended upon floats is circled about a school of fish, then drawn together at the bottom like a gigantic pocket. The gill net acts upon a different principle. Suspended from floats like a submerged curtain, it is an invisible barrier. The fish, thrusting their heads through the mesh, are held fast by the gills like ancient malefactors in the pillory. In England, power boats called drifters sometimes drag a hundred gill nets strung out for nearly two miles. At the height of the season ten thousand miles of net sieve the North Sea, or enough to span the Pacific at its widest point. Not only Great Britain, but France, Belgium, Holland, Germany, and the Scandinavian countries dip into this inexhaustible food bin which has been fished intensively for more than a thousand years.

Both the purse seine and gill net are designed for surface-feeding fishes. The ground feeders fall victim to the otter trawl, a huge baglike net, dragged along the bottom on wooden runners that keep the mouth widely extended. It scoops up cod, flounders, and an occasional lobster too big to crawl into the usual "pot." In America such boats that steam slowly back and forth across the fishing grounds are called draggers; in England they are known as trawlers.

A recent United States Government report shows that purse seines accounted for 1,500,000,000 pounds of fish; otter trawls for 625,000,000, and other devices in descending ratio. Professional fishermen number over 125,000 and employ 75,000 boats of all sizes.

A similar report from the United Kingdom lists over 60,-000 fishermen and over 3000 boats propelled by steam, roughly half of them trawlers, not counting innumerable smaller craft. Some fishing boats are of more than 300 tons burden, or three times the size of Columbus's flagship.

Smaller countries, in proportion to their population, are even more deeply involved. Norway, in a recent season, sent over 2200 boats from a single port in the Lofoten district not far from the scene of the famous maelstrom immortalized by Edgar Allan Poe. Out of a population of roughly 3,000,000, more than 100,000 were directly interested in fishing. If America were equally herring-minded, we would have nearly 5,000,000 fishermen and their assistants.

These men are of that iron breed in wooden ships that adventure stories feature. Listen to old salts discuss winter fishing on the Grand Banks and you will hear feats of hardihood—well authenticated, by the way—that stretch the very limits of human endurance. You may be told of the lone fisherman, separated from his schooner by driving snow squalls, who rowed his dory for five days until his fingers froze to the oars, yet survived; and of another, driven by gales clear across the Atlantic, who contrived to beach his craft on the broad side of Portugal. Gloucester has honored such unsung heroes by a statue of a fisherman in oilskins and sou'wester, steering his vessel through fog and treacherous seas.

Not a few cities have sprung up around the fishing industry: Yarmouth in England, Bergen in Norway, Gloucester in this country. Boston, a great fishing port, appropriately displays the model of a codfish in her statehouse, while those sandy shores beloved of summer tourists still bear the name Gosnold gave them—Cape Cod.

Needless to say, the sea exacts a gruesome toll from those who plow its furrows. In Cornwall, I visited a deserted village where every male member of the population had been lost in a winter gale. No wonder the surviving widows and fatherless children fled as from a pestilence.

Although many countries now tabulate fishing statistics, world figures are sketchy and inconclusive. Herring is king, the most widely distributed, the most eagerly caught. Unfortunately some governments list all varieties of this fish under a common head; others present such separate items as menhaden, sardines, pilchards, and whitebait. The annual catch, however, tops eleven billion mature fish, with many billions of lesser fry. At Great Yarmouth over a billion herring were landed in a single season. Though not prolific, as fish go, for the female herring commonly lays from thirty to forty-seven thousand eggs, the fish swarm in countless myriads. A school covering half a dozen square miles has been estimated to contain three billion individuals. Yet schools of twenty square miles are not uncommon. These are the source of the Englishman's breakfast of a "kipper," or Yarmouth bloater.

Young herring keep the canneries busy in Eastport and Lubeck, Maine, while more than half a million tons of sardines have been caught off California in a single season. Yet man, so Huxley estimated, caused little more than 5 per cent of the slaughter among the herring. Other fishes, sea birds, seals, whales, and lesser enemies combine with

the appalling hazards of the sea to account for the remainder.

Second in importance is the cod and his relatives, haddock, hake, pollock, cusk, et cetera. The cod makes up
roughly three quarters of an annual catch estimated at 4,-
500,000,000 pounds; the haddock about 15 per cent, and
less important varieties the balance. The cod, a ground
feeder, prefers cold waters ranging from 35 to 45 degrees.

Perhaps third in the list of world fishes are mackerel,
with an annual catch of over a billion pounds. They swim
north from the Virginia capes to New England and beyond.
Great schools twenty miles long and half a mile wide have
been observed. Moving leisurely, feeding upon the surface,
the fish fall prey to countless enemies. Predatory birds
glean a rich harvest, squid dart here and there biting furi-
ously with their parrotlike beaks, swordfish flail about with
their deadly swords, bluefish, already gorged, disgorge to
gorge anew, and yet the mottled legions advance by countless millions. If we include kindred species such as the Spanish mackerel and the giant tuna, this sky-blue member ranks
high among the finny tribes.

Of all fish save the herring, salmon are perhaps most
vital in the lives of many communities, particularly those of
the Indians of our Northwest coast. The annual catch exceeds half a billion pounds.

Other species, though much esteemed, are less abundant.
The world catch of halibut is scarcely ninety million pounds.
A great deal more of this chicken meat of the sea would
find a ready market; so, too, would swordfish, which yields
scarcely four million pounds, while other dwindling favorites are shad and sturgeon.

In the United States the annual catch of fish is well over
four billion pounds, or somewhere near 30 pounds per
capita. Consumption is higher in Great Britain, higher yet

in countries like Denmark and Norway. The value of our fish harvest, just prior to the war, totaled roughly $110,000,-000, but the finished product sold for more than $235,000,-000. Over half the catch came from coastal waters, the remainder from international fishing grounds. In the Pacific our boats ranged from the Galápagos Islands to Bering Sea; in the Atlantic from the Caribbean to Newfoundland.

In this country the six most valuable varieties were, in order: salmon, tuna, haddock, cod, flounder, and mackerel. The haddock, once little regarded, now outranks the cod in popular esteem. The two black lines down his sides, so fishermen aver, mark where the Devil gripped him, but failed to hold. With fingers cleansed, His Satanic Majesty then seized a cod, which also slipped away, leaving his flanks scarred with two white lines. Elsewhere the cod is more prized. Even little Norway catches more cod than here, while the catch in Great Britain exceeds our own at least fourfold.

Primitive man ate his fish raw. The custom still survives with dried and smoked varieties. Commercially, fish is of two kinds, dry and oily. The cod is readily dried, and in some localities piled like cordwood. Fishermen nail dried cod to barn walls, whence children cut strips like candy. Thoreau mentions cod so tough you could "split your kindling 'with' them." More oily fish may be smoked. Thus treated, the herring is popular, as are salmon and sturgeon.

Fish are best eaten fresh. Unfortunately they are highly perishable, so man's ingenuity has been taxed to develop preservatives. Probably the earliest methods were drying or smoking, but the value of salt was soon recognized. Strabo mentions the Sea of Azov in Russia, "where large quantities of fish are captured for the purpose of salting." The fisheries of Great Yarmouth require twenty thousand tons of salt a season.

Fish are not only dry-salted like cod, but packed in brine. Oily fish like mackerel may be thus preserved. The Japanese sometimes use sugar for that purpose. In Mediterranean countries olive oil has long been popular, while spices add that piquancy beloved in Scandinavian countries. Canning is a modern innovation, particularly successful with salmon, tuna, and sardines. Francis Bacon taught the world the value of refrigeration by his last experiment, when he immersed a freshly killed fowl in snow and thereby caught his death of cold. Refrigerating plants have become veritable factories of the sea, and frozen fish are shipped by truck from New England clear to St. Louis. More than three hundred thousand stores in this country are now equipped to handle frozen products and offer appraising customers the next best thing to fish still wet and glistening.

No fish would recognize some of the products into which modern ingenuity has metamorphosed him. Fish oil, of ancient manufacture, has lost none of its value, and is largely used in such enterprises as soapmaking, leather tanning, and in tempering steel. Fish bodies and bones, when ground into meal, are a valuable stock food, nor should this cause surprise, for reindeer eat stranded herring in Lapland, as do ponies in the Faeroe Islands.

Fish products not otherwise useful make excellent fertilizer. The Indian taught the Pilgrim that corn would thrive in sandy soil if a herring were placed in the hill. In many coastal villages menhaden are caught for no other purpose than to enrich impoverished soil.

Certain fish organs have specialized uses. The swimming bladder, an elementary lung, is often rendered into isinglass, while fish scales scintillate anew as artificial pearls.

The tough skin of the shark makes a durable leather that may possess ten times the tensile strength of oxhide. This tiger of the sea has also proved useful in other ways.

The quest for vitamins has opened up new horizons, and shark's-liver oil bids fair to become a more popular source than more familiar kinds. A fifteen-foot tiger shark yielded a liver weighing over two hundred pounds, from which was pressed sixteen gallons of prime oil. No wonder that shark fishing is thriving in California and Australia, nor should a foolish prejudice bar the use of the flesh, which is excellent in texture and flavor. The Chinese, with better judgment than ours, have long considered shark's fins a delicacy.

Man has done little for his fisheries except to ruin them by unwise exploitation and contaminated waters. The sturgeon has all but disappeared from coastal waters; the shad has alarmingly declined, while only governmental interference has preserved the Atlantic salmon from extinction.

Leading nations, finally awakened to the gravity of the situation, are now studying their fisheries. More than two hundred marine biological laboratories or experimental stations have been established in various parts of the world. Celluloid tags attached to tail or dorsal fin have revealed the wanderings of thousands of specimens. Much light has thus been shed, particularly upon salmon, haddock, and pollock.

Government hatcheries distribute fish eggs. In this manner the shad has been introduced into California waters and salmon into Chilean and New Zealand waters. Plaice, transferred from one side of the Dogger Bank in the North Sea to the other, have grown twice as rapidly because of improved food supply.

The contamination of rivers and streams has greatly restricted the breeding grounds of certain species, while dams have proven impassable barriers to salmon and are now provided with sluiceways up which the fish may fight his desperate way. Governments have shown an increasing interest in the discovery of new fishing grounds. The supply of halibut in the Pacific has been notably increased, while similar explorations have opened widening prospects in Australia.

America ranks third among the nations in the volume and value of its fisheries. The United Kingdom excels it in both respects, while Japan has long led the world. Prior to the war, in spite of cheap labor and depreciated currency, Japan's fisheries were at least 50 per cent more valuable than our own. Had that nation not turned to the sea for a good part of her sustenance, her teeming population would have starved on the produce from meager and depleted farmlands.

The combined value of the world's fisheries has been estimated at eight hundred million dollars, which is almost certainly too low. Moreover, as the industry, disrupted by war, feels the impetus of inflation, it will doubtless boom far beyond the billion mark.

Most romantic of all fisheries is whaling. To be sure, the whale is not a fish, but methods of capture are quite analogous. The days of long, sleepy voyages to the Pacific, of a wild chase through blinding spray, of darting harpoon and lance, have gone forever. Whales are now shot by bomb guns and dragged by the tail either to shore factories or mother ships which are floating factories themselves. Whale oil, once the prime illuminant, is now used for soap, synthetic butter, and many other products. Fishing grounds have shifted from Baffin Bay, Java Head, and the Solander Rock off New Zealand to the bleak Antarctic, and the pugnacious sperm whale has yielded place to the giant sulphur-bottom. Whale ships, like the *Tirze Viken*, of thirty thousand tons, are accompanied by ten smaller whaling boats that comb the seas for this most gigantic of all prey. Nor can one fail to be saddened by statistics which show that, since 1900, seven hundred and fifty thousand whales have thus been slaughtered.

Innumerable other industries are linked with fisheries in our complicated economy. Boat building is a respectable industry of its own, as are repairing and equipping from the varied stores of the ship's chandler. Coal and oil mining, transportation, distribution, and lesser business ventures all receive an impetus from the lowly fish.

When our then Secretary of State purchased Alaska with $7,200,000 of public money, that vast empire of fog and ice was called Seward's Folly. But in the season of 1940, twenty-seven thousand people were employed in her fisheries, while the value of their product exceeded $63,000,000.

John Cabot, with his crew of eighteen men, returning to report the discovery of Newfoundland, was rewarded by Henry VII with ten pounds sterling, or about fifty dollars. In its fisheries alone, that investment has yielded more riches than Aladdin's cave!

CHAPTER XXIII

Mining the Sea

Methought I saw a thousand fearful wrecks;
Ten thousand men that fishes gnaw'd upon;
Wedges of gold, great anchors, heaps of pearl,
Inestimable stones, unvalued jewels,
All scatter'd in the bottom of the sea.

SHAKESPEARE

Mining somehow suggests digging. In popular fancy the miner burrows like a human mole in Pennsylvania's coal seams or South Africa's underground ledges of golden quartz. To mine water seems absurd, yet all the mineral wealth obtainable by delving in the earth is but a fraction of that dissolved in the sea. Beyond the tide marks lies the last and far the richest of our undeveloped resources.

Salt was the first product of ocean's mines. The Neolithic hunter who scraped the white residue from tidal rocks to season his aurochs steak set the pace which mankind has followed but haltingly ever since. The blood still retains something of the salt it contained when all life swam in the sea; hence salt hunger is well-nigh universal among all higher animals.

In the low-lying outskirts of Cadiz in Spain one may inspect those shallow reservoirs that admit the sea. Evaporation leaves a mineral content which is heaped in gray pyramids to leach in the rains and bleach in the sun. This simplest of ocean-mining operations is an ancient industry which lingered in New England until fairly recent times. Travelers in Muscovy wrote in the early 1500s: "At Astrakhan salt is made naturally by the sea water which casteth it up into great hills"; they also mention "great store of salt wells about 250 versts from the sea." For such wells spring from reservoirs of concentrated brine deep in the earth, the remnants of buried seas. Oil for the lamps of China is less vital than salt for the rice of China; hence at Tzeliuching in western Szechwan such a reservoir has been tapped for more than two thousand years. The brine, pumped from depths of three thousand feet, is conveyed in bamboo pipes to vats where the salt is extracted by heat evaporation. These venerable wells still produce some two hundred and fifty thousand tons of salt annually.

More modern methods tap deposits of saline crystals left in caverns when imprisoned seas dried up. There are such deposits in Germany three thousand feet in thickness, where the glistening crystals are mined like coal and underground chapels are carved in solid salt. Into some of these deposits, which are widely scattered over the world, water is introduced until, becoming heavily charged with mineral substance, it is pumped out again to be evaporated and the contents purified.

Although gold was the magnet which led the conquistadors to ravage Mexico and Peru, their galleons sailed over richer treasures than ever gleamed in Aztec or Inca temples. There is enough yellow metal in the sea to make every inhabitant of the globe a millionaire. True, the dilution is enormous, some two parts to a billion, yet even that infinitesimal amount would yield eleven tons of gold for every cubic mile. And there are more than three hundred million cubic miles of water in the sea!

Blackmore, who spent five thousand dollars to extract five dollars' worth of gold and silver from the sea, calculated

that a cubic mile contained ninety-three million dollars
worth of gold. He also found that a million gallons of sea
water yielded somewhat better than an ounce of silver.
But whatever the exact figure, and estimates vary, they
mount into totals that would wipe out all national debts
without noticeably diminishing the supply.

So far analysis of sea water has revealed over fifty of the
ninety-odd known elements. All are probably present in
minute amounts, even that fiery malcontent—radium. For
water is the universal solvent, and it has been dissolving
mineral matter for a long, long time. How to extract that
mineral matter is the problem which confronts experiment-
ers in the future.

Some progress has already been made in this fascinating
field. The Germans were pioneers before the war, while in
this country the Dow Chemical Company had long been
tapping a great subterranean reservoir of concentrated brine
at Midland, Michigan. As needs multiplied, they went
directly to the ocean off Texas and North Carolina. Here
mountains of oyster shells gathered from the sea were
crushed and passed through limekilns to huge settling
tanks, where sea water was pumped in. The lime from the
shells combined with certain elements in the water to form
milk of magnesia, which, mixed with hydrochloric acid,
precipitated magnesium chloride. Electrolysis was then
invoked to open up far-reaching and still uncharted possibilities in chemical research.

The most spectacular result was the recovery from sea
water of magnesium, that silvery metal one third lighter
than aluminum, which has so stimulated airplane construction. Here lightness combined with strength is vital. Nature
long ago demonstrated that truism, for the frigate bird,
most tireless and graceful of fliers, has a lighter bone
structure than any other bird. There is about one part of

magnesium to every thousand parts of sea water—a meager trace, we might suppose; yet, stated differently, each cubic mile holds in solution no less than four and a half million tons. No wonder this useful mineral, from the greatest of all mines, has been hailed as the metal of the future! The Age of Iron, which eclipsed the Age of Bronze, may yield in turn to the Age of Magnesium!

War put to baser uses this magic metal which seems destined to revolutionize industry. In certain preparations it bursts into flame, to kindle obstinate conflagrations. The Germans first showered English cities with such fiery missiles, to have their own destroyed by deadlier bombings. It was magnesium which reduced so much of Osaka and Tokyo to ashes before the advent of the more terrific atomic bomb. Let us hope that in the better world of the future man will direct the fruits of earth and sea to worthier ends.

Another bulky product of ocean mining is calcium chloride, sprinkled by the ton on our highways to lay the dust. Other substances are used in cement and plastics, the building materials of the future, as well as in synthetic rubber. More volatile products enter into soap and various solvents and dry cleansers, as well as insecticides, germicides, and fungicides.

Blackmore estimated that the iodine in the sea was worth nearly as much as the gold. Bromine has even more uses. Twenty-five hundred gallons of sea water yield a pound of this potent red liquid, which reappears in photographic supplies and helps to silence the knock in auto motors. Bromine is also an ingredient of many drugs.

By a variety of operations at once simple yet exceedingly complex, the Dow Company combines and rearranges the elements in ocean's minerals in more than five hundred trade preparations.

Petroleum is another product of the sea. Occasionally it seeps out upon the surface, while some shales are saturated with it. But the great reservoirs, like oceanic brine, are hidden in the bowels of the earth. There drills, piercing ever deeper, uncover fresh deposits which so far have kept pace with an ever expanding demand. From these recesses petroleum may burst forth in geysers expelled by liberated gases; in others it must be pumped to the surface. Geologists are still uncertain about its origin, but they believe it is the residue of countless organisms that once flourished in the sea. Many diatoms have tiny droplets of oil within their glass cases. Oil and water do not mix, so oil from decaying life has accumulated to be imprisoned under sediments that turned to rock. Such an explanation is suggested by minute shell formations that prospectors find in petroleum-bearing areas.

When Marco Polo returned from his wanderings in the realms of Kublai Khan, he mentioned springs of oil on the banks of the Caspian which was "good for camels that have the mange." This tale was greeted with guffaws of mirth as merely one more of those tall stories which branded the Venetian as the champion liar of the Middle Ages. And yet poor Marco, though anything but a scientist, was doing his best to describe the "liquid black gold" which has lubricated the wheels of progress and become the life-blood of international commerce, and the springs he spoke of bubbled from the site of the great Russian oil wells at Baku.

Coal beds, though remains of vegetation which flourished in carboniferous swamps and jungles, owe both form and preservation to rock coverings laid down in the beds of shallow seas. Here again Marco Polo's story of the "black stones" which the Chinese burned for fuel was greeted with the contempt which revolutionary statements usually encounter. The peat beds of Ireland and Germany show a parallel formation of fuel, though palmlike ferns and other primitive trees are, of course, lacking. In any case our coal, if not a marine product, has been preserved by the sea, which is quite as important.

Limestone and its more refined derivative, marble, are definitely marine, for they are but the skeletal remains of countless sea organisms pressed into solid rock. Chalk, as we have already observed, is solidified globigerina ooze which covers so much of ocean's floor.

Slate, to tile our roofs, is only clay ground fine by erosion and solidified by pressure under water, while the gritty rock formed by the shells of marine diatoms and radiolarians, when pulverized, is used by jewelers to cut and polish gems.

Our driest deserts, those alkali beds of the Southwest, are but the bleached bones of shallow seas that once ebbed and flowed where water is now more precious than gold. The famous twenty-mule-team borax wagons freighted the crystalline residue from such evaporation, while similar deposits formed the nitrate fields of the Chilean coast which have fertilized gardens all over the world.

Not a few mines encroach upon the sea. Ancient tin mines in Cornwall have galleries extending some distance from shore so that workers, in stormy weather, so I was told, could hear the muffled sound of waves above their heads. The oil derricks of California have waded out like metallic giants into the Pacific, to tap deposits far beyond the tide line and invade that ill-defined region where sovereignty, state or federal, seems in doubt. Sulphur domes, those vast deposits of acrid yellow powder, have also been preserved by accumulated sediment, and are even sought under shallow seas.

In many shore localities beach sand, ground into convenient sizes by the waves, is shipped in scows for building purposes. How much of the material that went into the skyscrapers of New York was first prepared by the sea no builder could even guess, yet the total must be stupendous. Our roads and sidewalks may often be traced to the same origin.

Mollusk shells, particularly those of oysters, are a valued product. Almost pure lime, they are appropriated by the hen as substance for her eggshells, nor will she readily be satisfied with a substitute. Many a shore road has been made passable by surfacing with oyster shells.

Even where they are not the direct source of minerals, the seas have long been sorting out and rearranging and preserving them. True, this took place when much dry land was still submerged, but they remain vast reservoirs of undeveloped wealth. And now that the weighted piano wire and the fathometer have plumbed their greatest depths, chemical research is beginning to reveal something of their inexhaustible riches.

CHAPTER XXIV

Ships

Like a stately ship
Of Tarsus, bound for the isles
Of Javan or Gadire,
With all her bravery on, and tackle trim
Sails filled, and streamers waving.

MILTON

Raising the pine wood mast, they set it in the hollow socket, binding it firm with forestays, and tightening the white sail with twisted ox-hide thongs. The wind swelled out the belly of the sail and round the stern loudly the rippling waves roared.

HOMER

Water is a natural barrier. And yet the first apelike man who floated upon a log embarked on that adventurous quest which has transformed the once impassable seas into the highways of the world.

Advanced cavemen lashed several logs together. Peruvian Indians make rafts of balsa reeds, while natives of Madras and Manchuria venture into rough waters on makeshifts quite as crude. Abraham Lincoln took his one long voyage down the Mississippi on a raft.

The next improvement shaped and hollowed out a log into a rough canoe. One may observe such pirogues along muddy African rivers, in South America, in the Far East. The Indians of our Northwest carved out impressive craft from giant cedars. In Ceylon, I once rode in a canoe only eight inches wide. Outriggers gave that broad base which prevented capsizal. In similar, though larger, canoes lashed together for cargo space, South Sea Islanders made voyages that would have shamed Columbus.

But dugout canoes are heavy. Hence North American Indians, shaping birchbark over light wooden frames, created craft of grace and elegance. Eskimos used hides for their unsinkable kayaks, while clumsy tubs of leather swirled across the Euphrates when Babylon was but a village.

And then, as workmanship improved with better tools, boards were sawed and fitted to build the punts and skiffs and dinghys, the dorys, whaleboats, and gondolas, and all the countless species in the great order of boats.

Ships are only a larger edition. The first recorded specimen appears upon the wall of an Egyptian tomb more than six thousand years old. With its half-moon hull, its single mast, and rowers seated in the waist, it differs little from craft that sail the Nile today.

The Phoenicians were the first nation, except perhaps the Cretans, to gain supremacy by seamanship. Their long galleys were dependent partly upon sail, but more upon oars, for with the muscles in his shoulders has man conquered the sea. Perhaps these hardy Argonauts never rounded the Cape of Good Hope as Herodotus hints, but they did explore the sinister African coast beyond the Equator, and braved the boisterous North Atlantic perhaps to the shores of the Baltic. Unfortunately their priceless heritage of sea lore has been lost. The most graphic account of a Phoenician voyage survives in the Book of Jonah, which bequeathed to all seafaring men that personification of bad luck, a sky pilot!

Greek records are more complete. Homer's demigods drew up their long galleys upon the shores of Troy. Many craft of the period were reinforced by ropes. Some had a dozen wound about them or stretched lengthwise through the hull, just as Arab dhows still sail the Indian Ocean bound together with coir ropes of palm fiber.

Most illustrious of Grecian ships was the trireme, which gave Athens mastery of the Aegean and might have made her mistress of the world. This ship carried three rows, or "banks," of oars on each side, one above the other, which provided greater motive power. Unless scudding before the wind, the mast, with its single sail, was shipped to make room. A typical trireme had a complement of 170 rowers, 17 sailors, and 10 soldiers or marines.

The famous quinqueremes of Carthage had five banks of oars manned by 300 rowers, nor did that end the race for larger vessels. Galleys with ten banks of oars were not uncommon among the Macedonians, the Syrians, the later Carthaginians, and the Romans.

The peak of such superships was reached under Ptolemy Philopater of Egypt. According to Athenaeus, his state galley was 420 feet long by 57 broad; the hull towered 80 feet above the waves; 4000 rowers manned her 40 banks, the highest oars being 57 feet long. She also carried 400 sailors and supernumeraries and 2850 soldiers. If her dimensions are not greatly exaggerated, she must have been a marine monstrosity.

Merchant ships of the period, however, were of impressive size. That which bore the Apostle Paul to his shipwreck on Malta carried "two hundred, three score, and sixteen souls," a number much above the capacity of the Middle Ages.

Many Roman merchantmen were of two hundred and fifty tons burden; some even more commodious transported elephants from Asia Minor. One of these ships brought the Vatican Obelisk from Egypt, no mean engineering feat, as the huge column weighs five hundred tons. In addition she carried eight hundred tons of lentils, a cargo that would have taxed the trading ship of even a century ago.

Ancient galleys had some points of superiority over sailing craft of a later date. They could turn more readily and even reverse their direction, nor were their voyages interrupted by calms. But they were ill equipped for stormy waters and compelled to land every two or three days to replenish a meager water supply. Navigation was by daylight from headland to headland.

Speed averaged perhaps seven miles an hour. For a brief period this might be doubled—a speed beyond the limits of many a tramp steamer of the present. Thucydides mentions an Athenian galley that sailed in one day under forced draught from the Piraeus to Mytilene. The direct distance, 186 miles, was probably exceeded by the crude navigation of the times.

Merchant ships often voyaged in convoys. Strabo, visiting the Egyptian port of Myos-Hormos on the Red Sea, was surprised to learn that a hundred and twenty ships sailed thence to India on the favoring monsoon.

War always stimulates invention. War galleys were the first specialized ships. The terrors of ancient sea fights can scarcely be exaggerated. The primary method of attack was by ramming. The heavily timbered prow, tipped with bronze, originally in the form of a ram's head, was driven, with crushing force, against the side of an opposing galley. Seamanship maneuvered to execute or avoid this fatal thrust. Later the ram became a submerged prong below the water line, a device copied in the hull of steel warships until recent times. So-called crows were also introduced: huge derricks that grappled an enemy ship with hooks.

The Romans, forced to battle the Carthaginians on the unfamiliar sea, introduced the tactics of land fighting. They constructed bridges to board an enemy galley, held fast by grappling hooks. Boarding parties long remained a familiar spectacle. In the Battle of Lepanto, which broke the sea power of Turkey, the five hundred janissaries who defended the great galley of the Pasha of Egypt were cut down to the last man by armored Spanish infantry. Even the Battle of Trafalgar found Magon, the French admiral, mortally wounded while leading his crew to the deck of a British frigate.

Fire from balls of blazing tow, dripping with olive oil, was a deadly menace. Hannibal, fleeing the wrath of Rome to Asia Minor, is reported to have won a sea fight by substituting jars of poisonous serpents.

Galleys that could not be reached by ram or boarding bridge were put out of commission by sideswiping them to smash their oars. Julius Caesar complained, of the maritime tribes of Gaul, that their "ships were made wholly of oak —and secured by iron chains instead of cables." Too stout to be rammed, they were also too high-sided for boarding, so the ingenious Roman dismasted them by ripping out their rigging.

Naval battles of antiquity sometimes involved hundreds of units. The Athenians, trusting to "their wooden walls," led 385 war galleys against a superior Persian navy in the decisive victory of Salamis. No wonder Aristophanes thrilled at "their azure prows." More than 600 galleys clashed in the final conflict that saw Rome wrest the mastery of the seas from Carthage.

Xerxes, according to Herodotus, transported his forces into Europe in 1207 triremes and 3000 lighter vessels, with a total complement of 81,400 sailors and rowers, and 36,210 Persian soldiers.

The elegance of Roman streamlining was diverted into ugly channels through the Middle Ages. Then speed was sacrificed to safety, and grace to clumsiness. The Kogge of the Hanseatic League was a slightly elongated tub. To complete the comparison, she bore tublike platforms at every masthead as lookouts and fighting tops.

The Vikings introduced a pleasing innovation, for their ships not only approached the Grecian model but were more seaworthy. Several specimens, in fair preservation, have come down to us. The Gogstad ship was 79 feet 4 inches long, 16 feet 6 inches wide, and 6 feet deep. Of 30 tons burden, she carried 32 rowers. A larger ship, 130 feet long, dating from the ninth century, has been unearthed in the Orkneys.

The Vikings called their longer craft serpent ships, those less pretentious sea dragons. They bore the distinguishing figurehead, for builders of all ages have adorned their cutwaters with shapes pleasing or frightful, from siren to Medusa. Chinese even now provide their junks with grotesque eyes to "see their way about."

Viking ships were of oak and could be dragged ashore. Though undecked and carrying neither chart nor compass, they were better provisioned than Greek galleys, and often transported living cattle for food. Although provided with a mast and sail, the savage sea kings hung their shields along the bulwarks, bent their shoulders to the oar, and ventured out into the Atlantic even in winter. They rounded North Cape, colonized Iceland and Greenland, and explored Labrador and Nova Scotia five centuries before John Cabot viewed those forbidding coasts. With little shelter from the elements, drenched with icy spray, singing songs of blood and pillage, steering by sun or stars or by blind instinct, they issued their ringing challenge to the sea.

For centuries oars were the only reliable motive power. At first they were wielded by free men who sought livelihoods from commerce or were prepared to defend their homes. But wars and conquests inaugurated a bloodstained chapter in which the central figure was that very nadir of human misery, the galley slave. His presence made most galleys floating hells. Chained to the oar, naked and half starved, lashed to superhuman exertion, he sometimes survived for twenty years! Both Moslem corsairs and miscalled Christians strove for maritime supremacy on the cringing backs of shackled oarsmen. Cervantes, the Spanish Shakespeare, was once a galley slave.

Slowly man learned to chain the winds instead of his hapless fellows. Though sails had been employed for thousands of years, they were useless except when "scudding free." Then some unknown genius introduced three masts in place of one, increased the yardage, and improved the rigging and tackle. As navigators learned to sail ever nearer to the wind, the galley slave faded from the picture to become only another memory of man's inhumanity to man.

An early type of sailing ship was the caravel, a three-masted, squat affair that flaunted long pennons to conceal her ugliness. Yet such potbellied craft bore Columbus and Da Gama and Magellan upon their momentous voyagings. Caravels had meager accommodations for the crew, who usually slept on deck, cooking their meals on brick ovens with metal covers. Driven below by cold or boarding seas, they shared cramped quarters with rats and vermin, among ballast just above the smelly bilge water.

In their long struggle for dominion of the seas, English and Spanish shipbuilders followed divergent trends. The English favored lightness and speed, the Spanish sheer bulk. The galleon *Madre de Dios*, captured in 1592, was the largest ship afloat. She drew 26 feet of water and displaced 1600 tons. Her mainmast towered 121 feet above the sea, while her stern rose grandly in a profusion of gilded and carved woodwork. These conflicting theories, the ponderous vs. the agile, met in mortal combat when the Invincible

Armada, buffeted by the mariners of Queen Elizabeth, was shattered by storm and shipwreck.

The glorious Age of Sail dawned with the packet and clipper ships of the early 1800s. The East India Company first designed them for passengers. The cabin class, who paid from ninety-five to two hundred and fifty pounds sterling for the long passage from England to India, provided their own furniture and bedding. Even a century ago steerage passengers on the transatlantic run brought their provisions and faced starvation on protracted voyages. Crews called "packet rats" were the sweepings of the gutters, while the captains, perhaps from necessity, frequently acquired the surname "Bully." All were fearless and able mariners.

The packet ship *Red Jacket* made the voyage from New York to Liverpool in thirteen days, eleven and a half hours— better time than many a steam freighter logs today. But it was the clipper ships rather than the packets which flung their topsails to the breeze and sacrificed comfort and even safety to sheer speed. For the China trade had opened to these fleet carriers a vision of fabulous profits in competition that grew ever keener.

Peter the Great of Russia was doubtless the most illustrious of shipbuilders, for he wielded adze and mallet with his own hands in the docks of Holland. But the outstanding genius of clipper ships was Donald McKay.

His triumphs have become almost legendary. Upon narrow hulls he set towering masts alive with billowing canvas. Though buried in spray, awash in boarding seas, wet and uncomfortable, his creations made record time in every ocean. The ship *Lightning*, of 2090 tons burden, on her maiden voyage to Liverpool in 1854, reeled off 436 knots in twenty-four hours, a mark unequaled in sailing annals. A larger ship, the *James Baines*, of 2515 tons, made Liverpool in twelve days and six hours; thence she sailed to Melbourne, around the Cape of Good Hope, and back to Boston via Cape Horn, girdling the globe in a hundred and thirty-two days. Once in the roaring forties her log read "ship going 21 knots," a sailing speed unmatched before or since.

McKay's masterpiece was the *Great Republic*, built in 1853. Largest of all clippers, with a tonnage of 4553, her mainmast, fashioned from a giant tree, was 44 inches in diameter and 131 feet long. Above it towered lesser additions until the tip of the royal mast spired grandly 200 feet above the water line. But a blazing warehouse set fire to the great ship while she lay in her New York berth. Though scuttled to save her hull, her loss brought financial ruin to McKay. Raised and equipped with smaller masts and yards, she yet gave some indication of what she might have done had the master builder's dream been realized. She still holds the sailing record from Sandy Hook to the Equator, a flat sixteen days, and once she logged 413 knots in twenty-four hours. Remaining in commission until 1872, she found the only grave appropriate to clipper ships, in a furious gale off Bermuda.

The full-rigged ship was the queen of the seas, a sight beloved by every old salt, as she scudded like a cloud before the wind. Modifications of masts and rigging introduced the whole race of barks and barkentines, brigs and brigantines, and even sloops. Unfortunately square-riggers have gone out of fashion. Only a few still linger as grain carriers from Australia around the Horn. Square yards provided a certain balance, and ships could remain more closely bunched in convoys. But economy and ease of management evolved that more familiar type, the schooner. Her sails could be hoisted from deck and reefed with comparative ease. There was no going aloft to hang like flies on a swaying yardarm in howling gales; hence a smaller crew was required.

The first schooner seems to have been built by Andrew

Robinson, of Gloucester, in 1745. She had two masts, the familiar yachting rig, and was destined to become the model fishing vessel of the future. Schooners with three masts were built to carry freight, then gradually enlarged until the peak was reached in the seven-masted *Thomas W. Lawson*, which registered 10,000 tons. She too came to rest in Davy Jones's Locker, off the Scilly Islands, in a gale in 1907.

Disreputable pursuits played no little part in ship design. The first "clipper" seems to have been built for the opium trade of China, where speed above all else was a requisite Malay craft with rakish three-cornered sails, light of draught and swift, could sail far closer to the wind than the average square-rigger. From coverts in Borneo they darted forth like killer whales to prey upon some great merchantman becalmed in Macassar Strait. Nor were the white man's hands less dyed with blood. No ships were of more evil repute than the slavers which eluded waiting gunboats by superior speed and seamanship, leaving their trail of manacled corpses cast to the sharks.

The genius of China created the junk, high fore and aft, her sails of bamboo strips. Yet in such ships the great Admiral Cheng Ho, long before Columbus, made voyages that totaled seventy-five thousand miles, to spread throughout the Orient the superior culture of the Ming emperors.

Arab art centered in the dhow, with forward-slanting masts and three-cornered sails. One may still observe them, clumsy but seaworthy, in Mombasa, or Ceylon, whence they have voyaged across the Indian Ocean. Moored in harbor, and surrounded by lesser craft, they awaken memories of Sindbad the Sailor and *The Arabian Nights*.

The first iron ship of record was launched in Yorkshire, England, in 1777. Though scoffed at, the superiority of iron began to win recognition in Great Britain about 1829. These experiments in shipbuilding were the forerunners of a new era, the Age of Steel.

Meanwhile a new motive power had been discovered, far greater than that of groaning galley slaves, less capricious than the winds. Steam, the Hercules that slumbers in every drop of water, had been dimly glimpsed from the days of Archimedes but, like the more appalling power of the atom, mankind had not yet harnessed it to useful work. There are shadowy references to one Blasco de Garay, of Barcelona, who is credited with propelling a boat by steam in 1543. More authentic records antedate that of Robert Fulton, in both Europe and America, but he first built a steamer capable of a sustained voyage when in 1807 his *Clermont*, 133 feet long and 18 wide, sailed up the Hudson 150 miles in 32 hours.

Steam long remained coupled with the wind, for even the *Great Eastern*, launched in 1858, carried six masts. Her inefficient engines turned both paddle wheels and a screw. Nearly 700 feet in length with a beam exceeding 82, she was handbilled as the largest craft since Noah's Ark. But she marked too abrupt an advance for the scientific knowledge of the day and was useful mainly in laying the transatlantic cable. Nevertheless, in size she remained unexcelled until the launching of the White Star liner *Baltic* in 1905.

Yet steam has not exterminated sail. In fact the world's registry of sailing ships, which totaled 7,701,885 tons in 1850, had risen to 9,167,620 in 1900. A motorboat, for all its silver and mahogany, can never rival the grace or beauty of the sailing yacht, nor yield the thrill of hand upon the tiller, with a fresh breeze bulging her canvas.

Recent decades have witnessed an international rivalry for maritime supremacy in size and speed and luxury. German efforts that culminated in the huge *Vaterland*, later operated by the federal government as the *Leviathan*, were resumed after World War I in the *Bremen* and *Europa*. Italy entered the lists with the *Rex*; France with the *Normandie*; England with the *Queen Mary* and *Queen Elizabeth*. These marine giants (the *Queen Mary* is 1018 feet long by 119 broad with a tonnage of 80,773) are really floating townships, equipped with hospitals, theaters, restaurants, and shops. Their spacious decks even permit a variety of outdoor sports. On a single voyage the *Queen Elizabeth* brought back from Europe over fourteen thousand American soldiers.

Meanwhile motive power has undergone still more momentous changes. For a time the Age of Steam shackled a new galley slave, the grimy stoker, to an inferno of dust and heat below the water line. Oil has proved cleaner, easier to handle, requires fewer workmen, less cargo space. Triple expansion engines now utilize to the last pound steam once wasted. Diesel engines offer alluring possibilities. Electricity may yet prove the most efficient of power. Mankind, though momentarily stunned by the demoniac frenzy of the atomic bomb, already dreams of a day when a spoonful of matter may drive a great liner across the Atlantic.

That these floating communities will ever be surpassed is doubtful, for man has now embarked in earnest upon the conquest of the air. But ships will long survive, in spite of darting airplanes; and their memory will linger in salty tales and resonant chanteys and timeworn sagas of peril and adventure.

Meanwhile, from the "Quinquereme of Nineveh" to the dingy tramp, ships have played their part in the spread of that commerce and culture which have created our civilization. And all deserve mention, whether fishing schooners or clipper ships, tanks, tugs, or icebreakers; yes, even the battle wagons bristling with 16-inch guns, and the more ponderous airplane carriers.

Their glamor also invests fringing occupations—the ship-yards, sail lofts, tar works, ship chandlers, and the villainous crimp with his shanghaied victims. For over all hangs that aura of adventure expressed in Longfellow's lines: ". . . the beauty and mystery of the ships, And the magic of the sea."

CHAPTER XXV

Argonauts, Ancient and Modern

Come, my friends,
'Tis not too late to seek a newer world.
Push off, and sitting well in order, smite
The sounding furrows, for my purpose holds
To sail beyond the sunset.
                    TENNYSON
While the hollow oak our palace is,
Our heritage the sea.
            ALLAN CUNNINGHAM

Jason's quest for the Golden Fleece and the exploits of Odysseus doubtless flowered about a central stem of fact. But the oldest travelogue purporting to be true is the Periplus of Hanno, who, somewhere about the year 570 B.C., led a Carthaginian colonizing expedition down the western coast of Africa. Only mutilated fragments have been preserved in a Greek translation which recounts how "he sailed . . . with sixty ships of fifty oars each and . . . men and women to the number of thirty thousand and provisions and other necessaries." Founding settlements as he went along, he voyaged possibly as far as the Equator before being forced to turn back. Among other marvels, he observed "elephants feeding . . . streams full of crocodiles and river horses," and listened to the weird rhythm of the Dark Continent, "the sound of drums and confused shouts." Most amazing of all were the "strange people . . . whose bodies were hairy and whom the interpreter called Gorillae [probably chimpanzees] . . . three women were overtaken but they attacked their conductors with their teeth and hands and could not be prevailed upon to accompany us. Having killed them we flayed them and brought their skins with us to Carthage." There one was hung up in the Temple of Moloch, the earliest historic reference to the giant jungle ape.

Still earlier, about the year 610 B.C., occurred the fabulous voyage of Phoenician galleys at the command of Pharaoh Necho of Egypt. According to Herodotus, they sailed down the Red Sea and reappeared three years later through the Pillars of Hercules, having circumnavigated Africa. He says, "They declared—I for one do not believe them—that in sailing around Libya [Africa] they had the sun on their right hand." This, of course, was one bit of evidence that might really have occurred on the voyage.

An atmosphere of romance has always invested those Tyrian galleys which every three years brought to King Solomon "ivory and apes and peacocks"; nor have geographers ceased to puzzle over the location of that Ophir which supplied the gold that adorned Jehovah's Temple in Jerusalem.

Somewhere about 600 B.C., according to Pliny's terse comment, "Midacritus [a Greek] was the first to import white lead [tin] from the 'tin' isle." In the museum at Penzance are stone weights and other mementos of what must have been an active commerce in this metal with the Phoenicians.

Another Greek, named Pytheas, sailed about 320 B.C. from what is now Marseille on a more ambitious expedition. He seems to have circumnavigated the British Isles, noting the shortness of summer nights, then proceeded northward.

He described a strange phenomenon as "neither earth, water nor air separately," but a sort of combination of all three, which he likened to "sea lung" in which "the earth, the seas and all things were suspended—it could neither be travelled over nor sailed through." Just what he meant by "sea lung" is conjectural. Perhaps he had in mind some Mediterranean sea jelly. In any case, Stefansson calls his crude effort an apt description of the mingled fog and water and floe ice of the Arctic.

Pytheas mentions a mysterious Ultima Thule which may have been the Faeroe Islands, or some part of Norway, or possibly Iceland. Unfortunately the record of his voyage survives only in a few quotations from his critics. For Pytheas suffered the fate of Marco Polo, the comic figure of Italian burlesque. Strabo thus curtly dismisses him, "Pytheas, who has given us the history of Thule, is known to be a man upon whom no reliance can be placed."

Turning to another part of the world, Strabo strikes a more modernistic note when he complains, "Generally speaking, the men who hitherto have written on the affairs of India are a set of liars." He accepts, however, the tales of a blithe adventurer named Artemidorus, who "mentions serpents of thirty cubits in length which can master elephants and bulls. In this he does not exaggerate. But the Indian and African serpents are of a more fabulous size and are said to have grass growing on their backs." Perhaps "moss" would have been more accurate, nor can we help but wonder what Artemidorus may have been drinking.

When Nearchus, the admiral of Alexander the Great, coasted from northern India to the Persian Gulf, he followed the prevalent merchant routes to the Far East. His mariners were dismayed by the tidal bore at the mouth of the Indus. During the first century Hippalus calculated the periodic monsoons so that ships thereafter plunged boldly out across the Indian Ocean, escaping inshore currents and other hazards. In the far offing lay those exotic Spice Islands which Strabo dimly visualized as "the cinnamon country— the commencement of the habitable earth on the south," though he may have had in mind the remoter coasts of Africa.

Unfortunately the records of explorations in the Indian Ocean, quite as perilous and brilliant as those in the Atlantic, are even more meager. Somewhere about 510 B.C., Darius Hystapsis of Persia ordered a Greek, Scylax of Caryanda, to locate the mouth of the Indus River. Sailing down this turbulent stream and skirting the coast, Scylax circumnavigated Arabia and eventually reached Arsinoë near Suez, at the head of the Red Sea. Avoiding the Persian Gulf, already charted, and pausing to trade with shore communities, he spent nearly two years and a half on this voyage of some twenty-five hundred miles.

In the reign of Hadrian, Greek navigators had rounded the southern point of Hindustan and explored the Bay of Bengal. A certain Alexander, who seems to have been one of history's most daring adventurers, sailed boldly across this huge indentation to follow the shores of Burma and Siam. Rounding the Malay Peninsula, known as the Golden Chersonese, he crossed the Gulf of Siam to Cambodia and thence north to Cochin China, where he at length came in contact with the Chinese. Other voyagers, following his lead, in vessels provisioned for three years, even proceeded some distance up the coasts of China; nor did the streams of commerce flow only in one direction, for in A.D. 97 a Chinese named Kan Ying visited the Persian Gulf and meditated a trip to Egypt; while Chinese records also mention the visit to their emperor of Roman ambassadors with presents from Marcus Aurelius in the year 166.

The Vikings left few records. According to a fragment

preserved by Richard Hakluyt, "Othere," about the year 820, told his lord, King Alfred, that "he dwelt northmost of all the Norsemen," and "said he was desirous to try once on a time, how far that country extended due north." His voyage around North Cape to the shores of the White Sea made him perhaps the first of arctic explorers.

Brief sagas recount the voyages of Northmen to America. One hardy sea king, Bjarni, sailed from Norway about 986 to visit his father in Iceland. His restless parent had gone to Greenland, whither Bjarni followed. Driven far to the west, he sighted what is probably Labrador, but did not land. Turning back to Greenland, he found his father and related his adventures to Leif, the son of Eric the Red. The latter purchased Bjarni's ship and, sailing in 1002 with thirty-five men, landed in the country of Flat Stones, perhaps Labrador, but was driven south by storms to a land "where grapes grew." As wild grapes do not flourish north of Passamaquoddy Bay this nature note fixes the northern limit of his shadowy "Vineland." Leif had never seen grapes before, but a German sailor taught him how to make wine. He journeyed still farther south, to Cape Cod, perhaps to Chesapeake Bay. Somewhere he built huts as winter quarters. Loading his craft with wine and lumber, he returned home in 1004. Possibly other Norsemen followed his trail to the New World, but all records have disappeared.

In the Middle Ages, when Mohammedan powers blocked approaches to the Far East, commerce between western Europe and the Orient was monopolized by Venice and Genoa. Portugal, fronting the Atlantic, sought a new sea route around the formidable bulk of Africa. Madeira was rediscovered in 1412, for the Phoenicians had been there. The Cape Verde Islands, sighted long before by Hanno, were relocated in 1443. Urged on by the energy of Prince Henry the Navigator (1394–1460), Portuguese explorers crept down thousands of miles of coast line flanked by deserts or jungles. One after another they erected markers to commemorate their "farthest south." They crossed the Equator in 1471 and observed the mouth of the Congo a few years later. In the museum at Capetown is a twelve-foot stone cross left some distance north of that city by Diego Cao in 1484. Then, in 1487, Bartholomew Diaz was blown by gales entirely around the southern tip of Africa.

Yet Columbus had blundered upon the Western Hemisphere in 1492, before the Portuguese exploited this discovery. Finally Vasco da Gama was commissioned to sail to India, with three ships, the *San Gabriel*, the *San Raphael*, the *Berrio*, and a supply ship. From the Cape Verde Islands he struck out boldly across the Gulf of Guinea, avoiding adverse currents and other shore hazards, until near the latitude of the cape. Proceeding up the eastern coast, he picked up an Arab pilot who had been to India and arrived at Calicut in 1498. His men, visiting a Hindu temple, thought it a Christian church, but were perplexed by figures of the saints with grotesque faces and six arms. Da Gama lost thirty men from scurvy while recrossing the Indian Ocean and was forced to burn the *San Raphael* in Africa. But he returned safely after an absence of a little over two years.

This memorable voyage sounded the death knell of Venetian and Genoese prosperity and opened up a vast empire to Portuguese enterprise. In 1500 Cabral, with thirteen ships, sailing far westward and blown out of his course, touched Brazil. He, rather than Columbus, might have discovered the New World, an interesting speculation on the erratic course of history. He did bequeath Portuguese supremacy and its native tongue to that vast country which may someday rival the United States in the Western Hemisphere.

Meanwhile England had caught the enthusiasm. John Cabot, in 1497, sailing almost due west, rediscovered the

Iron Coast the Northmen sighted and gave to England Newfoundland, the cornerstone of her colonial empire. British archives still preserve a brief note in the handwriting of King Henry VII, "to him who found the new ile 10 pounds." Later the monarch added a modest pension.

Vasco Nuñez de Balboa, a penniless adventurer from Hispaniola, learning from a native chief on the Isthmus of Panama of a vast water to the westward, set out on September 1, 1513, with 194 Spaniards and 1000 natives to thread the deadly jungle. On the twenty-fifth day he caught a glimpse of the Pacific which he named the "Great South Sea." Some days later, wading into the water, with a world-embracing gesture, he took possession of all its coasts in the name of the King of Spain.

Ferdinand Magellan, a Portuguese at odds with his own government, sold the King of Spain the idea of sailing west to the Indies as Columbus had done. For Spain, indeed, there was no alternative, since Portugal guarded all African trade routes. Magellan had already visited the Indies via Good Hope and burned with enthusiasm to girdle the globe. And so, on September 20, 1519, he set sail on the most ambitious voyage of history. He had five ships, the largest the *Trinidad* of 120 tons, the *San Antonio*, the *Santiago*, the *Conception*, and the *Vittoria*. His inventory comprised a long list of trade goods for the natives, as well as live cows, pigs, and chickens for the Argonauts. Crossing the Atlantic, he arrived on the bleak Patagonian coast, where he spent the winter. Discovering the strait which bears his name, he blundered through to the Pacific. I once knew a sea captain of fifty years' experience, whose crowning achievement was a passage through these straits without a pilot. But he had charts and a wealth of information. Magellan's fleet, now reduced to three by shipwreck and desertion, skirted the coast until he reached the belt of trade winds, then plunged straight out into the heart of the Pacific. There disease and starvation proved almost impassable barriers. Pigafetta, the Italian scribe, has left a vivid word picture: "We were three months and twenty days without getting any kind of fresh food. We ate biscuit which was no longer biscuit but powder of biscuit swarming with worms, for they had eaten the good. It stank strongly of the urine of rats. We drank yellow water that had been putrid for many days. We also ate some ox hides that covered the top of the mainyard. We left them in the sea for four or five days and then placed them on top of the embers and so ate them, and often we ate sawdust from boards. Rats were sold for one-half ducado apiece. We held our noses as we drank water for the stench of it." That scourge of all early explorers, scurvy, now sapped waning vitality. Pigafetta wrote, "The gums of both the upper and lower teeth, of some of our men, swelled so that they could not eat under any circumstances and therefore died. Nineteen men died from that sickness. Had not God given us good weather, we would all have died in that exceedingly vast sea."

In the Far East, Pigafetta mentions "bats as large as eagles," "trees which produce leaves that are alive," i.e., leaf insects; while of the Bataks of Sumatra he remarks, "They eat human hearts in the juice of oranges and lemons."

Meanwhile, in the hour of triumph, the great commander was killed in a native brawl on the little island of Mactan, in the Philippines. The date was April 27, 1521. A marble shaft marks the supposed site. I once spent an unforgettable moonlight evening in its shadow, trying to reconstruct, in fancy, the savage scene from four centuries ago.

Sebastian del Cano, a mutineer whom Magellan pardoned, returned to Spain with thirty-one men of the original complement of two hundred and eighty, in the little *Vit-*

toria, the sole surviving ship, after an absence of three years. Magellan's memory lingers in the perilous strait, in the vast ocean that he rechristened the Pacific, and in two blurry swarms of stars called the Magellanic Clouds. Pigafetta thus describes them: "The Antarctic is not so starry as the Arctic. Many small stars clustered together are seen which have the appearance of two clouds of mist."

Sir Francis Drake, adventuring in Panama in 1573, caught his first glimpse of the Pacific from the branches of a lofty tree. In his own words, he "besought God to give him life and leave to sail an English ship in those seas." Slaver, freebooter, sea robber, as judged by present standards, he stood upon the outer fringe of recognition by the Crown, for England and Spain were still nominally at peace; but on December 13, 1577, he finally wore out of Plymouth harbor with five vessels to "plough a furrow around the world."

They were a motley assortment. His flagship, the *Pelican*, later renamed the *Golden Hind*, was of 100 tons burden and carried 18 cannon. With him sailed the *Elizabeth* of 80 tons, the store ship *Swan* of 50, the bark *Marigold* of 30, and the tiny pinnace *Benedict* of 15. In such cockleshells did this doughty sea king set out to circumnavigate the globe.

True to his acquisitive instincts, he captured a Portuguese ship which he rechristened the *Mary* and, better still, a Portuguese pilot, Da Silva, whose presence proved invaluable. At the Strait of Magellan, Drake broke up the *Mary*, which was leaking badly. Encountering true Cape Horn weather, his cable parted while he lay at anchor and he was blown out to sea, in a gale the "like of which no traveler hath felt." The *Elizabeth* waited a month, then returned to England; the little *Marigold* was swallowed up by Cape Horn graybeards. Reduced to a single ship, Drake proceeded up the coast, taking rich prizes. Off Valparaiso natives came out bringing "hennes and a fat hogge." Fearing to return by the strait, for he knew the enraged Spaniards would string him up to the nearest gibbet, he skirted the coast of California as far north as Vancouver, then struck out across the Pacific, reaching the coast of Mindanao about October 1, 1579. On an uninhabited islet off Celebes, he tarried for a month, enjoying a tropic paradise, where he observed "an infinite swarm of fiery worms flying through the air . . . no bigger than common English flies . . . wonderful store of bats as large as hennes . . . crayfishes of exceeding bigness [the robber crab] . . . that climbed trees . . . sufficient for four hungry stomachs," and many other marvels. Escaping shipwreck by a narrow margin, he visited Java but dared pause nowhere else until he reached the Guinea coast, where he took on "oysters, fruit and water," arriving at Plymouth September 26, 1580.

Drake's own log of this remarkable voyage, which he may have given to Queen Elizabeth, has been lost. He was not immediately received at court, for his position was equivocal to say the least. When the Spanish Ambassador Mendoza clamored loudly for his head as a common pirate, Elizabeth demurred, for she had helped finance the undertaking, and Drake had prudently shared with her thousands of pounds' worth of valuable cargo. The English sovereign, now flirting with France instead of Spain, finally visited the Deptford Docks, where the *Golden Hind* lay moored, and on its deck knighted the commander, whereupon the exasperated Mendoza wrote to Philip of Spain, "The woman is occupied by forty thousand devils," an unchivalrous but perhaps justifiable estimate, from his viewpoint. A chair made from the wood of the *Golden Hind* was later presented to Oxford University.

The hardships that beset these early explorers find expression in the terrible experiences of John Davis, one of England's most intrepid navigators. Separated from his commander, Sir Thomas Cavendish, Davis lingered about the Strait of Magellan until, blown far off his course, he discovered the Falkland Islands. Returning to the strait and short of provisions, he took on fourteen thousand penguins, improperly dried to preserve them. On the South American coast, where he paused for water, several of his men were ambushed by the Portuguese. After putting to sea shorthanded and in all haste, he found the penguins beginning to decay, breeding vermin that Davis aptly called "the worms of Hell." "There was nothing," he wrote, "that they did not devour, iron only excepted. They destroyed stores, clothing and then began to eat the ship's timbers, threatening to gnaw through the sides." He added grimly, "They would eat our flesh." From such ghoulish rations, a strange malady broke out among the crew, with painful swellings, so that "divers grew raging for some died in loathsome and furious pain." Davis finally blundered into an Irish port with sixteen men of an original complement of seventy-six, only five of whom could stand upon their feet, while the stench of the polluted ship filled the harbor like a blasted whale.

Quite as intrepid were Dutch navigators, quite as brilliant their discoveries. William Barents sailed north from Amsterdam on May 10, 1596. In the Arctic his ship passed a dead whale that "stouncke monsterously." Landing in Spitsbergen, he killed a white bear whose skin was "thirteen feet long." Caught in the ice off Novaya Zemlya, he erected a hut where his company spent the interminable months till spring, the first white men who ever wintered in the Arctic. But the sagas of those who suffered and died in those grim seas embrace many nationalities.

The Dutchman Schouten was the first navigator to round Cape Horn, the date January 29, 1616. It was the Dutch vessel *Duyfken* that sighted Australia in March 1606, and it was Dirck Hartog, of Amsterdam, who first visited western Australia in October 1616; for a long time that isolated continent was called New Holland. And it was Abel Tasman who sighted Tasmania and New Zealand.

Last of all the continents, Antarctica seems to have been first visited by Nathaniel Palmer, an American whaler, in 1820, although Captain Bransfield, in an English ship, observed those sinister coasts at about the same time.

Nor should we omit some mention of lesser-known explorers. The Arabs, in their leaky dhows, were the great voyagers in the western Indian Ocean. Unknown navigators from southern India, from Malaya and China, vied with their exploits, while for sheer daring nothing can surpass the voyages of South Sea Islanders in outrigger canoes. It was thus, so tradition states, that a starving remnant reached New Zealand to people that country with sturdy Maori stock.

Many volumes could be written about the picturesque sea characters whose daring and resolution clarified our geography. Sailing on impossible quests, in craft ill manned and often unseaworthy, battling storms, scurvy, and starvation alike, in unknown seas, their hardships were truly incredible. Long after Da Gama set the course for India, the death rate among voyagers to the Spice Islands was six out of seven, but every adventurer thought himself the lucky seventh.

Wasted by tropical diseases, decimated by warlike natives, they charted the seacoasts and routed the commerce lanes of the world. The humble sailors who suffered most have passed from the scene without a trace, but even their leaders, whose names survive, were wretchedly rewarded. Here are a few illustrious names gleaned from a far longer list:

The brother of Leif Ericson fell fighting the savages in the New World.

Columbus, sent home in fetters from Hispaniola, died broken by disappointment at Valladolid in 1506.

Balboa was executed for treason by his envious country-men, in the public square of Darien, four years after he had discovered the Pacific.

Magellan waded ashore in full armor only to fall beneath the spears and bludgeons of Philippine savages in 1521.

Vasco da Gama fared better than most, for he became one of the richest men in Portugal and Viceroy of India. But he was wounded by a native assagai in Africa and died of a tropical fever in the Far East at the age of sixty-four.

Sir Francis Drake, seeking to retrieve his shattered fortunes, succumbed to dysentery at fifty-six, off the coast of Central America, and was buried at sea.

Davis, whose incredible hardships we have briefly noted, perished in a fight with Malay pirates off Molucca.

Verrazano was hanged as a pirate by the Spaniards at Cadiz.

Barents perished of cold and exposure in an open boat in the sea which bears his name.

Sir Hugh Willoughby and all his crew died of cold and hunger somewhere in Lapland.

Sir John Franklin and his entire party were lost trying to force the Northwest Passage.

Bering succumbed to scurvy and disappointment on a frozen island in Bering Sea.

Henry Hudson was set adrift in a boat by his mutinous followers, to die amid the floating ice of Hudson Bay.

Captain Cook was killed in a scrimmage with Hawaiian natives.

And so the tragic tale might be prolonged for many pages. Hard, ruthless, sometimes cruel, but always indomitable were these men, conquerors in the truest sense, for theirs was the conquest of the unknown.

CHAPTER XXVI

Mutineers and Piracy

But ships are but boards, sailors but men: there be land-rats and
water-rats, water-thieves and land-thieves.

SHAKESPEARE

. . . dreams he of cutting foreign throats,
Of breaches, ambuscadoes, Spanish blades,
Of healths five-fathom deep.

SHAKESPEARE

Class cleavage was never sharper than between cabin and
fo'c'sle. A ship was an isolated hamlet shut off from the
world. In a crisis one man decided; others obeyed. The captain's aides were his officers, hard-fisted, with harder hearts;
they alone were armed. Orders were enforced by sea boots
and belaying pins, while hostile factions forward—tough old
salts, drunken derelicts, sweepings from the gutter—mut-
tered sullenly. Only iron men, tempered in an iron discipline, could hope to brave that "old devil, the sea."

On ancient galleys oarsmen were definitely slaves, of less
value than beasts of burden, whose hardships cast a somber
pall on the progress of navigation. Their passing left men
free, at least in name, for the victim of knockout drops
ashore, when roused from stupor by the kick of some brutal
mate, and belabored into cringing submission, might have
echoed that word "freedom" with bitter sarcasm. The elemental savagery of the sea was often reflected in those who

sought to cope with it. The English press gangs, which tore landsmen from their families, or, boarding incoming ships, condemned men to further service, differed little from the Roman centurions who scourged captives into the galley hold. Yet maritime law has curbed abuses, bettered the treatment of sailors at sea, defined their rations and living quarters, and greatly increased their wages.

Gruff old Sam Johnson said that a ship was little better than a jail with an added element of danger. Sailors, on some windjammer off the Horn, ordered aloft to take in sail in screaming gusts, clawing at the salt-roughened canvas until their fingers split to the bone, smothered in freezing seas, half dead from lack of sleep and meager rations, would have endorsed that statement.

No wonder mutiny has imperiled almost every great voyage of discovery. The leader, engrossed by some grand vision, has held tenaciously to his course. His men could sense little of all this. They thought him mad. Ignorant, split into cliques, fearful for their lives, they became as tractable as wolves. Columbus filled his crews with jailbirds liberated for that purpose. What could such men realize of their admiral's lofty plans? As they roamed the weird meadows of the Sargasso Sea, found the compass no longer pointing to the north, and beheld strange constellations in the sky, they blustered and threatened. But that voyage was a brief one in tropic weather.

Magellan, wintering on the sterile Patagonian coast, found even fellow captains conspiring against him. Ruin faced the project in its beginning. Outnumbered, he boldly seized the initiative. Mendoza, the king's treasurer, was stabbed by his orders and a ship captain, De Cartagena, beheaded. Both were then quartered and impaled on stakes as a grim warning that discipline must be maintained. Six men, according to one account, were hanged from the yardarm and forty mutineers ironed between decks. By such bold measures was the insurrection crushed.

Sir Francis Drake, following Magellan's route some half a century later, also faced incipient revolt. John Doughty, former friend and ally, was convicted, by a jury, of fomenting mutiny. He had previously been deprived of his command of one of Drake's ships for an alleged misuse of stores. Another officer, Captain Winter, offered to go surety for Doughty, whose guilt was at least questionable. Yet he was beheaded under the very gibbet erected by Magellan, from which a Spanish skeleton still swung. When, fast upon a reef off Celebes, the *Golden Hind* faced shipwreck, Drake's chaplain hinted this might be punishment for Doughty's execution; the truculent Devon sea king thereupon had him ironed and threatened with harsher treatment. But Doughty's English kin branded Drake "the greatest rogue in Christendom."

Magellan's act was certainly more excusable, for the Emperor Charles V had given him power of "rope and knife" over every man in the expedition. His course, though bloody, was dictated by necessity. Yet we can scarcely wonder that men should rebel on that wild coast, with only hardship and probable death in the offing.

Less fortunate than Magellan or Drake was Bartholomew Diaz, who should have borne the flag of Portugal to India. In 1487 he reached the goal long anticipated by Prince Henry the Navigator, when he rounded southern Africa. Proceeding eastward to what is now Port Elizabeth, his men rose en masse and compelled him to return. Although he did accompany the later voyage, the name of Vasco da Gama has long eclipsed his own. That commander, more resolute and brutal, might have crushed the mutiny just as he subsequently forced a taciturn Arab to talk by spraying him with molten lead!

Less fortunate still was Henry Hudson, whose name survives in the noble river which he explored in the *Half Moon*, and in the icy bay where he met his death. Cast adrift with a few loyal followers in an open boat, he was never heard of again.

To hold such lawless crews in check was the role of superior force; the disorderly brutes forward were overawed by the better armed and more intelligent brutes aft. This is evident in the sea rules laid down by Sir William Monson, a British authority of the period: "A captain is allowed to punish according to the offense committed, . . . to put men in the bilbows [an iron bar with sliding shackles], . . . to keep them fasting, . . . to haul them from yardarm to yardarm under the ship's keel, . . . make them fast to the capstan and whip them, . . . hang weights about their necks till their hearts and backs be ready to break, . . . gag and scrape their tongues." He sagely adds—"This will tame the most rude and savage people in the world." Such was the stern law by which Britannia ruled the waves!

Other nations were even more barbaric. A luckless wight under the Dutch Commodore Jacob Roggeveen, when a failing water supply made the crew half desperate with thirst, pierced a cask in the hold which contained brandy instead of water, and, maddened by drink, attacked the cook with a knife. Overpowered by other members of the crew and roughly manhandled, he was twice keelhauled by command of the commodore—that is, dragged on a rope from yardarm to yardarm under the keel, where the barnacles cut him to ribbons and left him half drowned. Shackled for some days, until partially recuperated, he was given three hundred lashes. As these cut to the bone, salt was·rubbed into the wounds. He was then chained to the forecastle deck on a diet of bread and water, where he expired after some days' exposure to the broiling sun.

It was Roggeveen who discovered Easter Island with its strange stone faces, and massacred dozens of natives who supplicated him on their knees with palm branches.

Russian records are even more revolting. In 1712 the Cossack Mercurius Wagin set out from the mouth of the Yana River to explore the islands in the Arctic. When provisions failed, he returned to the mainland, where his men first robbed birds' nests, then subsisted upon field mice. In dread of further expeditions they finally murdered the leader and three others who sided with him.

Another Cossack, Basil Poyarkov, pushed down the valley of the Amur, a fearful three years' journey, whence he sailed to the Okhotsk Sea, first of all Russians to venture out upon the Pacific. When provisions failed, he resorted to cannibalism. His party actually devoured some fifty hapless natives. As the residue fled for their lives, he sacrificed certain of his own men and eliminated the sick by setting fire to the tall grass which surrounded them. Though considered well educated, for he could read and write, he out-Heroded Herod, and was too brutal even for those lawless times. Arrested, he was carried to Irkutsk and thence to Moscow, where he "disappeared." His ghoulish deeds throw into shadow his inflexible courage and resolution.

The classic of all mutinies is that of the *Bounty*. Captain Bligh, an able navigator but a stern disciplinarian of the old school, was overpowered off Tahiti by his men, led by the mate Christian, and set adrift in a boat with twenty-odd followers. How he navigated this craft to the Dutch island of Timor, more than three thousand miles through uncharted seas, is an ocean classic. But the story of his mutinous crew is still more adventurous. Some scattered about and were later brought to stern justice, as interpreted by the British Admiralty. But Christian and the leading spirits, knowing that the gibbet awaited them, sought out a lonely island, Pitcairn, where they severed all ties with the world by burning their vessel. There they lived with a group of islanders who had accompanied them. But strong drink was the serpent in this Eden. Several were murdered by the long-suffering natives, until finally but one survived, Adams, who, repenting, taught his flock from the Bible and lived out his turbulent life in patriarchal calm. The story of the mutineers is common knowledge. Upon my desk, as I write, is a skeleton leaf, gathered by a descendant of these same mutineers, from a curious plant that grows on Pitcairn Island.

Mutinous uprisings have had more modern settings. A grim tragedy occurred in 1875 on the ship *Lennie* out of Antwerp. The seeds of discord lay in her cosmopolitan crew: four Greeks, three Turks, one Austrian, one Dane, one Italian, and one Englishman. She was scarcely out of sight of land when the captain was stabbed by one of the Greeks. The murder of both mates followed by a ferocious necessity. The steward, a Belgian, was the only man left on board with any knowledge of navigation. Craftily he stalled the ship off the French coast and by messages in bottles managed to notify the authorities. French armed patrols came on board and four members of the crew were duly hanged.

On the other hand, ships have sometimes put to sea in an ultrareligious aura. Sir Hugh Willoughby, among other instructions, carried the following: "that no blaspheming of God nor detestable swearing be used in any ship nor communication of ribaldries, filthy tales, nor using unGodly talk—neither dicing, tabling or other devilish games." Among the requirements were, "morning and evening prayers—and the Bible or paraphrases to be read devoutly and Christianly."

Such piety has sometimes been assumed as with the Cape Cod skipper, noted for his regular attendance at church, who burst forth in a torrent of profanity soon after the anchor was shipped. To a dismayed greenhorn on board he explained, "We set Jesus Christ ashore at Highland Light and pick him up on our way back."

Punishment for mutiny was not always swinging at the yardarm but occasionally that doubtful alternative, marooning. Magellan executed only a few mutineers. Two of them, one a priest, he abandoned on the Patagonian coast, where they doubtless died of privation.

Alexander Selkirk, left on the Juan Fernández Islands, off Chile, spent more than four years in a solitude that gained for him immortality as the original Robinson Crusoe.

Nor did discord always break out in the forecastle. It was his officers who outvoted Bering, incapacitated from scurvy and malaria, allowing his vessel to drive ashore on the frozen island of the Commander group, where he met his death.

Accompanying scientists have also proved troublesome. Steller often clashed with Bering, while Captain Cook called some of his savants "damned disturbers of the peace," and threatened to maroon them. These men were interested in collecting strange species, while the captain thought only of perilous navigation in uncharted waters. Both were right.

Most arresting of crimes is murder on the high seas, particularly when guilt is in doubt. A famous instance was the brutal killing of the captain of the bark *Emma*, his wife and second officer. The mate, Bram, convicted on circumstantial evidence and sentenced to life imprisonment, was pardoned some years later by President Wilson.

Less advertised was a revolting incident that befell an English trading steamer bound for the Orient. She turned back to New York when her Eurasian oilers and stokers crammed the chief engineer head foremost into one of his own furnaces. The courts failed to determine the guilty persons.

A still more gruesome episode occurred on another British ship in Manchuria. When the mate, something of a slave driver, disappeared, the captain concluded he had been detained by some shore debauch, and sailed without him. But at Hamburg his lifeless body was found bound, gagged, and walled up in a living tomb behind piled-up sacks of soybeans. Lingering starvation in the gloom had certainly revenged his pitiless subordinates.

Successful mutiny has often led to piracy. Men outside the pale of the law have welcomed the sinister freedom of the seas. Sometimes the officers, even the captain himself, have turned robber, to lead a band of cutthroats on a career of pillage.

Piracy is of ancient origin. Phoenician merchants suffered, as did those of Greece. In the days of the Roman Empire pirates became so audacious that Pompey the Great won his laurels by ridding the Aegean Sea of them. Julius Caesar was the most illustrious of their captives. Held for ransom by a group of sea robbers, he later avenged himself by crucifying them all.

The Vikings, who long ravaged western Europe, baffled even Charlemagne. Like migrant gulls, they pounced upon the coast, then fled in the smoke of blazing villages. No wonder the liturgy of the English Church added the prayer, "from the fury of the Northmen, Good Lord, deliver us." But these marauders sought homes as well as plunder, and became the Normans of history.

The corsairs of the Middle Ages were even more barbaric. Their deeds had religious sanction, for they were the advance guard of Mohammed in a ceaseless warfare with the infidel. America's first intrusion into Mediterranean affairs was Decatur's expedition against the Bey of Algiers.

English buccaneers were little better. They pillaged the shores of New Spain, even though their respective countries were nominally at peace. Such was Morgan, who burned the city of Panama and was rewarded by being made English governor of Jamaica! Such was Sir Francis Drake himself, who preyed upon Latin shipping with no legal warrant, to win his Spanish nickname, "The Dragon."

From such semilawlessness to a brazen disregard of all law is but a step; thus arose the race of Blackbeard and those other hairy and bewhiskered gentry who sailed under the Jolly Roger. Their forcing of innocent victims to walk the plank, their drunken orgies on coral beaches, their flouting of every regulation, human and divine, have furnished a lurid background for thrilling sea tales.

Morbid fancy has even invested some of these swashbucklers with an uncouth dignity. Through a fog of oaths and clashing cutlasses, a few emerge as historic figures. Such a one was John Avery, born in Plymouth, England, in 1665. He rose to the rank of mate, headed a successful mutiny, and turned pirate. Operating in the Indian Ocean, he captured the treasure ship of the Great Mogul, bearing the emperor's lovely daughter and laden with a hundred thousand pieces of eight. He retired to Madagascar, a favorite rendezvous, where he ruled as a native monarch. Homesick for England, he finally returned, to be tricked out of his ill-gotten wealth and die in poverty at Bideford. The bluff pirate was no match for the financial sharks of Bristol!

Still more imposing was Bartholomew Roberts, a Welshman, long recognized as the King of the Pirates. He was a teetotaler who allowed neither gambling nor women on board his ships. Strict attention to business is said to have netted him over four hundred prizes, but he was cut down in action at the age of forty.

At least two women pirates, Anne Bonny and Mary Read, rose to eminence in their rather dubious profession. The famous Captain Kidd, however, who was hanged on insufficient evidence, may have been a victim of political intrigue. Prospectors still search beach sands from Nova Scotia to Florida for his buried treasure!

Piracy rose to the rank of big business in the Orient. Malays in proas with lateen sails lurked in sheltered coves to dash out upon Western shipping, in a mad clash of kris and cutlass, of boarding pike and smoking blunderbuss. Worst of all were Chinese and Japanese pirates, whose leaders sometimes became recognized powers and wielded much authority. Asiatic cruelty and disregard of human life were never more flagrantly displayed than by these miscreants. Nor has the advance of civilization obliterated the evil, for piracy still lingers along the southern coast of China.

In wartime, privateers have been sanctioned by governments. Though sailing under letters of marque, some were as lawless as freebooters. In fact Admiral Nelson claimed that all privateers were no better than pirates. That picturesque hero of our schoolbooks, John Paul Jones, would certainly have been hanged by the English could they have laid hands on him. Nor should we forget that the notorious pirate, Lafitte, of Louisiana bayous, was a stout ally of Andrew Jackson's in the defense of New Orleans.

Smuggling has always been a breeding ground for lawlessness at sea. Human life was cheap, compared with rich merchandise on which no duties were paid to the king's excise men. Such questionable pursuits, which flourished particularly on the coasts of Cornwall, have been immortalized in Gilbert and Sullivan's extravaganza, *The Pirates of Penzance.*

A darker blot was spilled on history's page by those who dealt in human freight, the slavers. In the Indian Ocean this industry, if it could be called such, was in the hands of Arabs who practiced none of the merciful teachings of the Koran. But so-called Christian nations are in no position to cast stones. Sir Francis Drake accompanied a slaving expedition to western Africa in a ship ironically named the *Jesus.* Storming a native village where many women and children were slaughtered, the marauders captured several hundred blacks, who were taken to the West Indies to be sold to Spanish planters. Hawkins, a relative of Drake's, who commanded, was later knighted by the English Crown and chose as his coat of arms a slave in fetters!

To her credit, be it said, Great Britain outlawed slavery long before it was abolished in this country, and by arbitrary but righteous decree branded all slavers as pirates, to be hanged when captured on the high seas.

Poachers have been quite as lawless as pirates. Kipling voiced their slogan in his *Rhyme of the Three Sealers:* ". . . there's never a law of God or man runs north of Fifty-Three." Few evidences of ruthlessness are more appalling than the slaughter of wild life. The year the Pribilof Islands were discovered, five thousand sea otters were taken. Even then a prime skin brought a thousand dollars from Chinese mandarins. Five years later this interesting creature had disappeared.

In six years sixty thousand walruses were slaughtered, largely for their teeth. Ivory and fur have proven almost as potent magnets for man's greed as spices and gold.

Russia has dealt harshly with seal poachers, but perhaps a life sentence chained in the salt mines of Siberia is none too severe for these brigands of the sea.

CHAPTER XXVII

Shipwreck

He sinks into thy depths with bubbling groan,
Without a grave, unknelled, uncoffined, and unknown.
BYRON

My earliest vivid recollection of the sea was of watching a huge wave curl over the iron ship *Jason*, from Calcutta, as she lay broken in two off Cape Cod. Only one member of her crew survived, riding the breakers to safety on a bale of jute!

Years later, on a leisurely hike from Provincetown to Highland Light, I counted fifteen great masses of wreckage, varying from a ship's foredeck to an entire hull, for in the offing lurked Peaked Hill Bars, one of the graveyards of the sea. Often I listened to tales of shipwreck in beach shanties tapestried with lobster buoys and tarred twine, while in later years I observed wrecks in various latitudes; for the good ships hove to in Davy Jones's Locker far outnumber all the sails and funnels now afloat.

Thumbing a pilot book of the South Pacific, I stumbled on the terse notation: "Helen Reef . . . 35 miles east of Tobi Island . . . the sea breaks violently. On the southwestern side of the reef are the remains of a wreck." The wreck of what? Could any of her crew survive in that lonely ocean? No one knows. A nameless wreck—a saga of the storm, as brief but eloquent as the inscription on a tombstone obscured by brambles and "silver oaks" I recently deciphered in a Cape Cod cemetery—a name, scarcely legible, a date, and the one comment, "Lost at sea."

Shipwreck, the shrieking wind, the crash of timbers, the roar of breakers—how futile then appear man's utmost efforts to conquer the unconquerable sea.

Two classic pictures of such elemental anarchy illuminate the Scriptures. The Book of Jonah relates, "there was a mighty tempest in the sea, so that the ship was like to be broken. Then the mariners were afraid and cried every man unto his god, and cast forth the wares that were in the ship into the sea, to lighten it. . . ." Again: ". . . the men rowed hard to bring it to the land; but they could not: for the sea wrought, and was tempestuous. . . ."

Paul's shipwreck, as related in the Book of Acts, describes how, "falling into a place where two seas met, they ran the ship aground; and the forepart stuck fast, and remained unmoveable, but the hinder part was broken with the violence of the waves . . . and they which could swim . . . cast themselves first into the sea . . .: And the rest, some on boards and some on broken pieces of the ship. And so it came to pass, that they escaped all safe to land."

Men have met the raging sea in varied moods. Xerxes ordered the waves to be whipped for wrecking his bridge of boats across the Hellespont; Canute, the Danish conqueror, seated on the beach, commanded the tide to cease its advance; Julius Caesar, borne across the stormy Adriatic in a frail boat, reassured the captain with the words, "Thou bearest Caesar and his fortunes." The Duke of Wellington, just turning in on a stormy night, when informed, "The ship is about to sink," stoutly replied, "Then I shall not trouble to remove my boots," but most men, in such a pass, have followed the shipmates of Jonah and "cried every man unto his God."

Greek literature recounts many incidents of Poseidon

shaking his formidable trident. A fragment from the geographer Posidonius relates a gripping tale of the Red Sea: "It chanced that a certain Indian was brought to the king [Ptolemy VII] by the [coast] guard of the Arabian Gulf. They reported that they had found him in a ship alone and half dead . . . he spoke a language they could not understand." Recovered, he finally mastered Greek sufficiently to explain how "all his companions had perished from hunger." Thereupon a certain Greek named Eudoxus accompanied the exile on his return voyage to India only to fall a victim to shipwreck himself on the African coast. There he discovered, half buried in the sands, "the end of a prow with a horse carved upon it," the figurehead of some nameless wreck. "The pilots in Alexandria" recognized this trophy as having come from Gades on the far Atlantic, suggesting that the unknown ship must have circumnavigated Africa. Eudoxus, impressed by this evidence, determined to follow that route himself. Sailing south from the Pillars of Hercules, he again met shipwreck, but, constructing a boat from the wreckage, he managed to find his way back to a settled community. There the fragment of Posidonius terminates, regrettably, for we would know more of the enterprising Eudoxus.

More than once shipwrecks have changed the course of history. Herodotus relates how the invading navies of the great king crashed upon the promontory of Athos, while thousands of bodies washed ashore. Japan was spared invasion by invincible Mongol warriors when hundreds of ships in Kublai Khan's vast navy were destroyed by a typhoon; nor was it so much Admiral Howard or Sir Francis Drake who crushed the Invincible Armada as the tempests, which strewed wreckage along the iron Scottish coast to break forever the maritime supremacy of Spain.

Drake himself came within an ace of losing his ship, his

life, and subsequent immortality when the *Golden Hind* drove full speed before the trade winds on a sunken rock off Celebes. The date was January 9, 1580. For twenty hours the ship hung upon that precarious pinnacle surrounded by deep water. Drake's narrator relates, "We lighted our ship . . . of three tunne of cloves, 8 peeces of ordinance and certain meale and beanes." Preparing for death, all hands partook of the Sacrament while in the quaint language of one voyager, "each theefe reconciled himself unto his fello theefe." When all hope had been abandoned, a shifting wind slid the ship into deep water; Drake paused for twelve days on the southern coast of Java for repairs.

When Leif Ericson voyaged from Iceland to Greenland twenty-one of his thirty-five ships foundered at sea. Suppose the future explorer of North America had been in one of them?

The *Wanderer*, last of the New Bedford whalers, was outfitting for a year's cruise when I spent some hours on deck breathing the atmosphere of Herman Melville and Moby Dick. With the tryworks, the harpoons and blubber spades all about, one caught himself involuntarily listening for the lookout's hail from aloft, "Thar she blows." Yet only two days later a hurricane that laid the great steamer *Arabic* on her beam-ends off Nantucket drove the *Wanderer* on the rocks at Cuttyhunk to smash to kindling wood almost within sight of her home port.

Such episodes might be multiplied by thousands. There was the stout ship *Duncan Dunbar*, en route from Plymouth, England, to Australia, in 1857. Her owners had lavished a fortune upon her cabin fittings. All down the African coast and across the Indian ocean she flew literally upon the wings of the wind. There was feasting and wine and music as she approached Sydney, after a speedy voyage. The harbor entrance lay dead ahead. But somehow she missed the channel and drove, with the full force of her fourteen-knot impetus, against the cliff. None could survive those climbing seas, least of all Seaman Johnstone, who was a poor swimmer. But a huge wave bore him aloft, to leave him clinging like a limpet to a cleft in the rock. From that perilous eyrie mountain climbers rescued him late the next day by letting ropes down the sheer wall, the only bit of human flotsam from 59 officers and men and 63 passengers. But more amazing yet, this was the third shipwreck from which Seaman Johnstone had emerged as the sole survivor! If the sea has its Jonahs, as superstitious sailors maintain, it also has its pampered favorites, the Seaman Johnstones who cannot drown!

Human conduct in shipwreck runs the gamut from the heights of heroism to a selfish cowardice beneath contempt. Perhaps the most appalling of marine disasters was the wreck, in 1816, of the French frigate *Medusa* on Arguin Bank, sixty miles off the African coast. Of her complement of over four hundred, one hundred and forty-seven were left to their own devices on a crowded raft submerged two feet or more. Here conditions soon became indescribable. Some, drunk from casks of wine brought along, fought like wild beasts; the wounded and dying were thrown overboard. Many were driven mad. Cannibalism was the inevitable last resort. After thirteen days fifteen half-crazed survivors, all that remained alive, were picked up by another French ship. The incapacity and worse which induced the ship's officers to abandon these unfortunates plumbs the lowest depths of heartlessness.

In bright contrast was the wreck of the iron troopship *Birkenhead* on an uncharted rock two miles off the South African shore. The date is one to be remembered in the British Army, February 26, 1852, the hour about 1:30 A.M. Two of the boats, old and leaky at best, were smashed by falling masts or capsized at once. Colonel Sexton, in command of the troops, ordered them to assume drill formation while sailors placed the thirty women and children on board the first boat. The horses were released in the hope that they might swim to shore, but their screams from the darkness spoke eloquently of sharks. The soldiers remained at their stations while the ship gradually broke up. As she slid into deep water, some fifty clung to the main topmast, which still protruded above water. Those who ·did not die at their posts or find room in the few remaining boats attempted to swim ashore, though much impeded by beds of giant kelp; sixty-eight succeeded, four hundred and fifty-five failed. Dr. Culbane, sent ashore in the boat with the women, found a horse at a tiny shore settlement and rode all night through savage country, a hundred miles, to Capetown to summon help. This arrived in time to rescue some of the human flies who still clung to the topmast. A marble shaft was placed by Queen Victoria in the colonnade of Chelsea Hospital in memory of the brave men who died in the wreck of the *Birkenhead*.

The climax of all shipwrecks, however, was the sinking of the *Titanic* about 2:20 A.M., April 15, 1912. Most superb of ocean liners, made "unsinkable" by her steel compartments and double bottom, on this, her maiden voyage, she carried one of the most distinguished passenger lists on record. There were 1348 in that list, besides the ship's complement of 860. The night was calm, the sea oily-smooth, and therein lay its danger, for no white fringe of surf outlined the sinister iceberg which waited in the dark. Too late the lookout saw it; the great ship swerved, but not in time. The ice tore through her bottom from compartment to compartment, and she settled ominously. There were not enough lifeboats to accommodate her huge personnel. Her SOS was caught by the steamship *Carpathia*, fifty-eight miles distant, which speeded at once to the rescue. Women and children first was the unquestioned rule. Upon the deck the band played until the end. An hour later the *Carpathia* arrived, but 1503 persons had perished. Few were drowned, for life belts would support them, but in those icy waters death was a merciful release.

Not always are shoals or cliffs or floating ice required to send a good ship to the bottom. The sea, in one of its demoniac rages, can tear it literally to pieces. Such a fate doubtless befell the steamship *Portland* in the great November gale of 1898. Sailing out of Boston with crew and passengers numbering about a hundred, she foundered some fifteen miles off Race Point on Cape Cod. Her wreckage, together with many dead bodies, strewed the beaches for weeks. Recently divers have located her hull and further explorations are promised.

The loss of the ships of La Pérouse is one of the grisly tales of the sea. These fine French frigates, *Boussole* and *Astrolabe*, sailed from France in 1785 to chart the shores and islands of the Pacific and bear the gifts of civilization to the natives. Louis XVI of France instructed them to supply primitive peoples with "vegetables, fruit and useful trees of Europe," adding, "his Majesty would consider it one of the happiest triumphs of the enterprise were it to be concluded without costing the life of a single man." The ships cruised about for two years; sighted Mount St. Elias in Alaska; lost one captain and ten men to the savage natives of Samoa. Last heard from in Sydney, Australia, they disappeared.

In 1791 the French sent out three ships under D'Entrecasteaux to search for them. During the two years' voyage the leader died, the ships were detained during the Napoleonic Wars, nothing was accomplished. Dillon, the mate of a sandalwood trader, finally traced the missing ships to

Vanikoro Island, where they were evidently wrecked. No survivor of the expedition ever returned, but among the relics preserved by the natives in their "spirit house" were sixty human skulls!

More gruesome than those which crashed on shoal or reef or even disappeared in the classic German phrase, "sunk without a trace," are the dead ships that remain unburied, the derelicts that drift about, a menace to navigation. Some of these have supported human life for an incredible period. Outstanding was the strange fate of the brig *Polly*, which sailed from Boston in December 1911. On board were the captain, mate, four sailors, a cook, and two passengers. One of the latter was swept overboard in the terrific gale which dismasted the craft; the other, a mere girl, died soon after. And now the survivors found themselves in the unenviable position of Coleridge's Ancient Mariner: "Water, water, everywhere, Nor any drop to drink."

The captain, with Yankee ingenuity, rigged a clumsy still from pistol barrels and teakettle, but the ultimate product was a miserable pittance. One after another the members of the little party succumbed to hunger and thirst. For six months the hulk drifted about the Atlantic. Only the captain and one sailor, mere hairy skeletons, survived to be picked up by an English ship off the African coast.

Darker rumors cluster about ships that were sunk deliberately by those on board. World War I was followed by an epidemic of such occurrences. As the chief value of many an ancient hulk lay in her marine insurance, if this could be collected without arousing too much suspicion, the lure was attractive. To be sure, a certain finesse was required, such as Byron visualized when he wrote: "He was the mildest mannered man That ever scuttled ship or cut a throat."

But deeds of this type were discouraged by severe penalties in courts of justice.

Most intriguing of sea mysteries are those which remain unsolved. Such a fate overtook the fishing schooner *Commerce* in September 1849. Returned from a successful cruise on the Banks, she anchored half a mile off the sand dunes of Truro on Cape Cod, while her captain, eight men, and a boy put off in the longboat. Yet not a soul among them, seafarers all, ever reached the shore alive. The boat, with a stove plank, drifted into the shallows, to be followed by the bodies one by one. There was no storm, the sea was relatively calm, several of the crew were known to be exceptional swimmers, those who were not could have clung to the oars or the still floating boat. What actually happened will never be known.

Still darker is the mystery that shrouds the American brig *Mary Celeste*. Found drifting off the African coast in 1872 by the brig *Dei Gratia*, she yawed clumsily and answered no hail. Investigation failed to disclose anyone on board. Breakfast dishes remained on the cabin table, the captain's wife had evidently been interrupted while at work on a child's dress, neither money nor effects were disturbed. The longboat, only, was missing. Apparently the ship had been abandoned in breathless haste, but why? Many theories have been woven about this incident, and it has reappeared thinly veiled in more than one romance. But it remains perhaps the most baffling mystery of the sea.

Superstition has created those phantom ships which haunt lonely coasts. Most famous is the celebrated *Flying Dutchman* which cruises endlessly about the Cape of Good Hope. Many an honest seafaring man has caught glimpses of some "spectral bark" or heard voices hailing from the darkness. There is so much that is wonderful and unexplained about the sea that credulous natures may be pardoned for such fancies, but the scientist knows that the sea is mysterious enough without introducing the supernatural.

One of the most touching of religious observances is the sunrise service on Easter morn held at Chatham, Gloucester, and some other ports. Worshipers, with bowed heads, there strew flowers upon the waves in the hope that they may drift above the resting places of those whose sleep will remain unbroken until "the sea gives up its dead."

CHAPTER XXVIII

The Romance of Charts

He does smile his face into more lines than is in the new map
with the augmentation of the Indies.

SHAKESPEARE

Charts are marine maps. Where the latter give elevations
above sea level, the former reveal depths below. Designed
for navigators, they have become bewilderingly complex, as
we shall presently observe.

The very name, derived from the Latin *charta*, a papyrus
or parchment, conjures up visions of a bearded Phoenician
poring over some rude sketch, off an unfamiliar coast. In
those days maps and charts were identical, for they traced
only the outlines of land masses and seas, and so they remain interwoven in that history of cartography which reflects our ever widening knowledge of the earth.

The oldest maps in existence are supposed to be two bits
of Egyptian papyrus, in the museum at Turin, which locate gold mines in Nubia. They date from the thirteenth
century B.C. But there are in the British Museum clay tab-
lets from Babylonia, which are cadastral maps, or plots of
real estate holdings, for the benefit of tax collectors, which
date from 2300 to 2100 B.C. At least one of these gives a
crude outline of the head of the Persian Gulf. Sargon of

Akkad, in 3800 B.C., is known to have had similar maps.

Strabo spoke disparagingly of "the old charts." In 560 B.C., Anaximander, with buoyant audacity, had made a map of the whole world. Of such cartographers Herodotus wrote, "I laugh when I see many who have drawn the circuits of the earth without any right understanding," adding as a clincher, "They make Asia equal to Europe!"

At least two centuries before Christ the Greeks were making maps with fair accuracy, considering their crude instruments. They knew the earth was spherical, for Pytheas, about 326 B.C., had taken the latitude of Marseille, while Eratosthenes, who died about 196 B.C., had actually measured the circumference and found it to be about twenty-five thousand miles! Democritus, who seems to have visited India, drew a map of the world he knew as a parallelogram, much longer than its height, thereby bequeathing us our word "longitude." Strabo, borrowing the idea from the Babylonians, proposed to "cut the grand circuit of the earth into 360 divisions," our modern degrees.

But Greek measurements were vague, hence often misleading. They had no compasses to give direction, no clocks to record longitude. Their unit of land measurement was the *stadion*, which seems to have been 606 feet, 9 inches. But at sea they recorded distances as "so many days sail."

Ptolemy, who wrote extensively from A.D. 127 to 151, was the great geographer of antiquity. He preserved the fragmentary information of his time, but with it incorporated personal errors of judgment. Rejecting Eratosthenes's accurate measurements for a smaller circuit of the globe, he branded Pytheas a liar and imposed his own mistakes upon posterity. Then fell the prolonged night of ecclesiasticism, when geography became a monkish interpretation of the Scriptures, and the earth was flattened once more, with four corners and Jerusalem at the center!

Fortunately the Renaissance recovered much of the ancient knowledge forgotten during ages of vandalism and ignorance. Columbus knew that the earth was spherical, for a fellow Italian, Toscanelli, with a globe which gave the circumference as eighteen thousand miles, advised the voyage. Had not the Great Navigator reasoned that the Indies were so near, he might never have set sail from Palos. For Strabo had written, "If the extent of the Atlantic Ocean were not an obstacle, we might easily pass by sea from Iberia [Spain] to India still keeping the same parallel." There is also a copy of Marco Polo, with marginal notes thought to be in Columbus's handwriting. And so an error in cartography led to the discovery of the New World!

Maps owe much to Richard Hakluyt, the Welshman whose life spanned the glorious Age of Exploration between 1553 and 1616. As a young man this Master of Arts from Oxford and future Dean of Westminster was shown by an older cousin "certain bookes of Cosmographie [and] an universall mappe" which fired his zeal to "prosecute that knowledge and kind of literature." He lectured on "both the old imperfectly composed, and the new lately reformed mappes, globes, and spheres." To him, it has been said, "England is more indebted for its American possessions than to any other man."

The ancient Greeks had globes. Strabo even suggested one ten feet in diameter to allow for all known countries. Hipparchus had said, "No one could tell whether Alexandria were north or south of Babylon, nor yet the intervening distance without observing the latitudes." But longitude stumped him. He complained that "the only means we possess of becoming acquainted with the longitudes of certain places is afforded by the eclipses of the Sun or Moon." Latitude, the distance north or south of the Equator, is determined by the altitude of the sun or some fixed star above the horizon. But longitude—the east or west—can only be measured from some artificial point, and is best revealed by accurate timekeepers. In 1740 Great Britain appointed commissioners for the discovery of longitude at sea, and offered prizes for more dependable chronometers.

At Greenwich Observatory, near London, a point of reference was also established which has become Longitude Zero. Patriotic fervor, however, induced France to prefer a similar starting point at Paris; and Portugal at Lisbon. Even America, in the Coastal Survey of 1844, reckoned longitude from City Hall in New York.

Mariners of the eleventh century were familiar with the compass. Though credited to the Chinese, it may have originated independently in western Europe. It was only a magnetized needle, floating upon cork or reed, which pointed roughly north. Unfortunately earth's centers of magnetic force are far removed from the true poles, nor do they remain stationary. Columbus seems to have been the first to discover this discrepancy, which terrified his associates as evidence of divine displeasure. The first map to allow for such variations appeared in 1532.

At London the compass in 1580 pointed 11 degrees east of north; in 1812 it had swung 24 degrees west of north. Now it is veering to the east once more. In Maine compass readings are 22 degrees west of north; in Washington State they are 25 degrees east!

Nor is our earth a true sphere. The polar regions are flattened by about twenty-six miles, a distortion that seems to have been first revealed by the strange antics of Jean Richer's clock. This sensitive mechanism, carried from Paris to Cayenne, lost two and a half minutes in twenty-four hours, because the pendulum swing was affected by the greater distance from earth's center. Sir Isaac Newton unraveled that riddle.

The only accurate map is a globe. But it would require one of satellite dimensions to record a city lot. Hence, for convenience, mathematicians are forever striving to reduce a spherical to a flat surface, an attempt as impossible as the squaring of the circle. Still a number of roughly satisfactory makeshifts have been devised. The earliest was that of Gerhard Kremer, known as Mercator. In 1569 he published his map of the world in which he "projected" a sphere upon a cylinder which could be rolled out flat. This necessitated monstrous distortions, for Greenland appears as large as all South America. But his projection is useful to navigators, for a so-called rhumb line, the course of a ship at sea, always appears straight, and the angles where it crosses the meridians remain unchanged.

Another projection, useful to mariners, is the gnomonic, which presents the surface of the earth as it would look to an observer at the center. All great circles then become straight lines. More familiar to the layman are polyconic projections, which transfer a spherical surface to cones, while maps of small areas simply ignore all curvature.

When Peter the Great of Russia wished to learn what seas might separate his Far Eastern dominions from the Americas, he wrote with his own hand to Vitus Bering, "You are to ask what the coast is called, note it down, make a landing, obtain reliable information, and, having charted the coast, return." By such an imperial sweep of the pen he brushed aside all difficulties. Bering's infrequent observations, while groping through dense fogs, were commended by Captain Cook, sailing the same seas, when he wrote, "He delineated the coast very well." Yet the Russian court preferred the sketches of the Cossack Shestakoff, who could neither read nor write. No wonder early maps were a jumble of fact and fancy.

Charts are specialized maps for mariners. In the crude

form visualized by Peter the Great, they merely record coast lines. Yet bottom configurations in shallow waters are no less essential, for navigators must also know depths, shoals, rocks, and other details of an ever changing and capricious sea.

Our first glimpse of such notations are from Scylax of Caryanda, who lived perhaps five centuries B.C. He wrote, "The Pillars of Hercules are opposite from one another and distant from each other by one day's sail." Of the desert island Pharos, he remarked, "good harborage but no drinking water." He also warned, "The parts beyond the Isle of Cerne are no longer navigable because of shoals and seaweed." Even at that early date those shifting sea contours were recognized, which make chart revision a never ending task.

When Captain Pet set sail from London in 1580 to explore the Northeast Passage, his instructions read, "In syght of any coast or land . . . set the same with your sailing compass, how it beares off you, drawing also the form of it in your book . . . draw the manner of biting in of every bay, and entrance of every harborrow, note the slake or still water . . . how much water it hieth and what force the tide hath to drive the ship in one hour." As if sailing the thousands of miles of bleak Siberian coast line were not enough for a 40-ton ship, he was further instructed, "If you arrive at Cambaluc [capital of China] bring thence the mappe of that country . . . take with you the map of England set out in fair colours . . . also the map of London," and (sage propaganda) "let the river be drawn full of ships to make the more show."

Many are the advances and retreats in the ceaseless battle between sea and shore. Off Cape Cod, the island of Billingsgate, which once supported a thriving village, has disappeared, while scores of acres have been added to Chatham's barrier beaches. Rivers are particularly savage agents of both building and erosion. Sand Island, at the mouth of the Columbia, moved two miles in fifty years. In the same interval Cubits Gap in the Mississippi Delta has increased the area of Louisiana by more than fifty square miles.

Even rocky coasts are continuously remodeled by the sea. Within the memory of man several of the Faeroe Islands have been reduced to rocky pinnacles. The vaster convulsions of nature add complications. Earthquakes have elevated sections of the Alaska coast forty-seven feet. The slow oscillations of continents and oceans cause some coast lines like those of Maine or Norway to subside, while others as gradually emerge.

Until recent years charts were made entirely by triangulation. Given one side and the adjacent angles, the investigator may fathom space beyond the farther planets to the fixed stars. Establishing at sea the necessary side called the base line offers special difficulties. Captain Fitzroy of the *Beagle*, when charting the wild Cape Horn coast, from a measured base line on shore sighted distant headlands from both directions, then moved on to a new base line. When offshore buoys are used, which have been anchored by hundred-pound weights in depths of nearly two miles, sound has been enlisted as a measuring device. The intervening time between the flash and report of a gun at one extremity have given the distance to the other.

Mechanical improvements have facilitated chart making. On shore theodolites, which are specialized surveyors' transits, give the heights of distant cliffs and hills. From the sea such elevations would be revealed by the sextant. Range finders—small telescopes with the lens divided by fine lines—measure distances. Shore parties carry pocket compasses for direction and aneroids, which register heights above the sea. Heliostats—mirrors mounted on poles—reflect a sunbeam to distant observers from any direction. Artificial horizons assist in taking latitudes.

Fine pen-and-ink sketches accompany the charts of many coasts and islands. Pilot books are often illustrated with drawings of striking configurations, easily recognized by approaching mariners. The bearings of such objects are given from several positions—that is, the angle between the direction of sailing and the true north-and-south line. Pilot books frequently offer the assurance that "these bearings are true."

The field work of chart making has sometimes proved dangerous. The work must be pursued in all weathers, or it would never be completed. On the ill-fated expedition of La Pérouse in 1786, twenty-one men were drowned in the surf while making soundings off the Alaska coast. Nor have modern improvements eliminated such perils. Lieutenant Commander Bond, while on a launch surveying the Sulu Sea, had his leg badly lacerated by a crocodile.

Where soundings were once laboriously made by letting down weights, fathometers now rapidly record the depth by echoes from the bottom. But since it is also necessary to know the precise position of such soundings, acoustic buoys have been devised. These are equipped with underwater hydrophones and out-of-water radio flashes. About every ten minutes the survey ship explodes a bomb under water. The hydrophone on the distant buoy picks up the sound, which it flashes back by radio, thus establishing the distance.

Though the value of accurate charts has long been recognized, it was not until 1795 that the British Admiralty founded the Hydrographical Department under Earl Spencer, with a personnel of one hydrographer, one assistant, and one draftsman.

A cartographer had been appointed by the States General of Holland in 1633 to correct charts from ships' logs, but it was not until 1720 that the King of France established a central chart office in Paris. In 1807 Congress authorized a survey of the coast of the United States. This was the origin of the United States Coast and Geodetic Survey. A hydrographic office, based on the British model, was established in connection with the Bureau of Navigation at Washington, in 1866. At least eighteen nations now publish navigation charts.

Unfortunately they do not all employ the same units of measurement. The English fathom of six good feet is also current in America and Japan. Most other nations prefer the more scientific meter, while the Russians have employed a unit of their own. Nor, as we have observed, do all agree upon Greenwich longitude.

Charts now give an impressive array of information: numerous soundings, rocks visible and rocks awash, shoals and channels, currents, beacons, buoys, and lighthouses, as well as shore heights and even buildings. Although apparently the last word in ultrarefinement, they are continually being improved.

All maps are drawn to scale. This is sometimes expressed in miles per inch; more technically in actual ratios. Thus the map of Asia produced by the National Geographic Society is drawn to a scale of 1:17,500,000. Charts are usually drawn to scales varying from 1:1,200,000 to 1:10,000. The latter enlargement is standard in negotiating harbor entrances.

Early maps were not only rough in workmanship but roughly reproduced. The Aztecs had maps on cloth, the Incas portrayed their mountainous empire in the first relief maps on record. The voyage of Columbus was recorded by Juan da Cosa on a tanned bull's hide. South Sea Islanders made crude but serviceable charts of sticks. Now even the fine paper of modern charts sometimes suffers a perilous distortion by shrinkage.

Printing revolutionized cartography. The first printed chart appeared in 1477, the first map engraved on copper in 1560. Colored maps are often lithographs from originals drawn on stone. Finely engraved maps are reproduced from etchings on copper plates which will warrant about three thousand impressions. Governments usually sell maps and charts at cost. Prior to the war Great Britain issued 3725 different charts and published some 600,000 copies annually.

A chart of large scale serves well in mid-ocean, but harbor entrances require more careful delineation. Ships have been lost because charts were not of the required scale, and court actions have resulted. Such actions have also hinged upon obsolete charts, which may be worse than none at all. Nearly 85 per cent of all charts issued in the United States replace older ones. Requirements become more exacting as ships of deeper draught test channels, once considered ample, by revealing unsuspected obstructions. Buzzards Bay in Massachusetts was thought to be thoroughly charted by ninety-one thousand soundings made at intervals of from fifty to one hundred yards. Yet the cruiser *Brooklyn* struck a rock submerged but eighteen feet where the chart read thirty-one. Such lurking perils are detected by dragging a wire from five hundred to fourteen hundred feet in length at the required depth through channels and harbors.

The British Admiralty, in a recent season, received from captains of the Merchant Marine 367 reports of newly discovered hazards to navigation. Eleven were of actual collison with sunken rocks or shoals. Frequently, however, such tips prove erroneous. Tide rips or schools of fish may be mistaken for shoals, dead whales for rocks. Latitudes and longitudes may also be inexact, so that the surveying ship must explore many square miles of sea in the suspected area. At such times it is discouraging to find a thousand fathoms over a supposed reef.

The recent global conflict has revolutionized the making of maps and charts. A soaring eagle observes the wilderness in one comprehending glance. Airplanes now fly much higher and travel at a swifter pace, while cameras equipped with lenses many inches in diameter see far more clearly than the eagle's penetrating gaze.

Our air forces in various parts of the world have mapped areas more than twice as extensive as the United States. They employed a Tri-metrogon camera which is really three in one. One lens points downward, two at oblique angles. In combination they photograph from one horizon to the other. At a height of twenty thousand feet, they cover an area nine by thirty miles. The camera snaps automatically at intervals so that photographs widely overlap. As the pilot returns along a parallel course, he could, in three hours and a half, photograph the state of Rhode Island!

Accurate maps, repeatedly corrected, have recorded in seven days an area of ninety thousand square miles, or more than the state of Minnesota. Such work would once have required years of laborious triangulation. Military maps have been shot from airplanes speeding nearly four hundred miles an hour from heights of six miles or more. In the famous stratosphere balloon flight of November 11, 1935, photographs reproduced the curvature of the earth from an elevation of 72,395 feet, or nearly fourteen miles. Photographic plates sensitized to infrared light, thus recorded in lasting form details invisible to the human eye.

Aerial photographers commonly snap five hundred pictures on a trip covering several hundred square miles. In a single morning they have covered an area equal to the state of Vermont. From such photographs, which commonly overlap 60 per cent, distinguishing features may be fitted together like a jigsaw puzzle, and the combined rearrangement photographed as a unit.

Stereoscopes which give three dimensions are now equipped with devices that reveal both the altitude of cliffs and the depth of ravines. Like the physician's X-ray pictures, however, they must be interpreted by trained observers. In such pictures paved roads and plowed lands are light, meadows and swamps are dark, and forests fuzzy.

Peering down from great heights, the camera readily gazes through shallow waters, thus discovering in a few moments sunken obstructions that dragging wires might not make known after weeks of patient toil. Nine-lens aerial cameras now trace coast lines which Magellan rudely sketched from shipboard. Such charts, compared with future impressions, will show changing contours far more accurately than has ever been possible before. Survey ships now measure bottom configurations to the edges of the continental shelves, which may be more than a hundred miles from shore. In years to come the library at Washington, which now houses some seven hundred thousand maps in cylindrical cases for immediate reference, may require extensive additions.

The magnitude of the cartographic assignment may be glimpsed when it is noted that in 1943 trained draftsmen made by hand nearly five million corrections on marine charts. Particularly in the Pacific region, islands and coral reefs had to be entirely redrawn, for previous charts were frequently miles out of the way. In that one year over two million nautical and sixteen million aeronautical charts were produced. Such mass production dwarfs all previous operations. In a little over three years the Eastman Kodak Company turned out enough film for military maps to make a strip reaching four and one half times around the globe.

Printing operations acquired a similar tempo. Within

three months expeditionary forces in Africa received over ten million maps. Printed on a single sheet, these would have stretched five thousand miles and weighed over five hundred tons. Nor are governments the only large producers. In three years the National Geographic Society issued over twenty million maps! And yet with all this fabulous activity great areas of sea and shore have never been charted at all!

Perhaps the next grand adventure of the cartographer will be the mapping of the upper air and the abysmal sea. For both now lie beyond the range of his investigations.

The Romance of Charts is a phrase at which America should thrill. For the very name was selected not by explorers nor even governments, but by a map maker. It was Martin Waldseemüller, professor of cosmography at the University of St. Die in Lorraine, who decided that the New World should be called after Amerigo Vespucci, because "he had discovered it." Whether that Florentine adventurer deserved such an honor has always been challenged, though he rose to eminence and became chief pilot of Spain. But error or otherwise, the choice of an obscure cartographer is written for all time across the two great continents of the Western world.

CHAPTER XXIX

Lighting the Sea

Aloft the lighthouse sent its warning wide
Fed by their faithful hands.
CELIA THAXTER

Darkness magnifies the perils of sea travel. When night fell, ancient galleys drew up on the beach, Portuguese caravels lay to. Beacons were few indeed, yet, seacoasts even in those primitive times were not wholly dark. Greek poets mention a beacon at Sigeum in the Hellespont as early as 660 B.C. Of the stone watch towers built by the Phoenicians and Romans, seventeen have been identified as crude lighthouses.

The Pharos of Alexandria guided shipping into that great port three centuries before Christ. One of the seven wonders of the ancient world, its marble tower, cemented by molten lead, was variously reported at from four to six hundred feet high. The Arabian geographer, Edrisi, who lived from 1099 to 1170, wrote, "It is visible the distance of a day's sail. During the night it shines like a star; by day you may distinguish its smoke." Evidently the watch fires burned continuously. This splendid edifice seems to have disappeared about the year 1300. Overthrown by an earthquake, it was doubtless used for building materials, as were the outer layers of the Great Pyramid.

The oldest lighthouse in the world stands near Corunna, in Spain. It was probably built by the Phoenicians as a guidepost on their hazardous voyages to Cornwall, although it has also been credited to the Emperor Hadrian. Remodeled and modernized, it is still in use.

Italian city-states helped a little to illuminate the Dark Ages. Pisa had a beacon in 1157; Leghorn in 1163. A tower erected by Genoa in 1139 was not in use until long afterward; Venice first lighted a similar tower in 1312.

Boston Light, erected in 1716, is the oldest in America. There were then probably no more than seventy lighthouses in the whole world.

To warn shipping from dangerous rocks or shoals has often taxed man's ingenuity. Many of these remain unconquered and are perhaps unconquerable. Most illustrious of lighthouse builders was the Stevenson family, whose talents ran through several generations. Robert Louis Stevenson, though trained as a construction engineer, preferred literature.

Off the pitiless coast of Finisterre in Brittany is an indentation fretted with reefs, called the Bay of the Dead. The French decided to erect a lighthouse upon one of these reefs known as Ar'men Rock. It rose scarcely five feet above low water, tough, worn smooth, yet pitted like a decayed tooth. Submerged at high water, it was buried almost continuously in boiling foam. Engineers waited an entire year before they could even set foot upon the rock for a preliminary examination. During the next two years builders landed twenty-two times for a total of twenty-six hours' work. After fourteen years this monument to courage and tenacity was at last completed.

Even elevated sites present a problem. Tillamook Rock off the Oregon coast is 112 feet high, yet engineers waited for six exasperating months before they could set foot upon its steep sides. Even then an English engineer lost his footing and was drowned in the swirling currents.

North of the Shetland Islands towers North Unst Rock, 196 feet above the sea. On its highest crest workmen felt secure in their temporary barracks, until a climbing wave burst open the door to deluge them in three feet of water, while another nearly wrenched off the roof. When the lighthouse was completed, a wave, vaulting up the steep sides, stove in a door weighing nearly half a ton.

Sand bars may be as deadly and are more treacherous than rocks. A classic example is Rothersand at the mouth of the Weser. To warn ships from this evil spot, German engineers constructed a steel caisson 70 feet high. Tilting ominously, it was forced down until its cutting edge was buried forty feet and its top, repeatedly extended, was 107½ feet high. Much of the interior sand was replaced by thousands of tons of cement and rubble. The steel cylinder became the base of the present lighthouse.

Quite different methods were employed on One Fathom Bank in the Strait of Malacca. This playground of breakers, swept by powerful tides, was fourteen miles from shore. Hollow steel piles, driven through twenty-eight feet of sand to firm bottom, were filled with cement. Upon the platform thus erected a lighthouse was built to guide commerce through one of the busiest sea lanes in the world.

Nor were the elements the only hazards. Malay and Chinese wreckers, alarmed at this threat to their gruesome calling, repeatedly attacked the laborers. But one need not voyage halfway round the world to find such opposition, born of poverty and greed. Wolf Rock, five miles off Land's End, England, gained its sinister name from a hollow formation which reverberated to the waves like the howl of a wolf. Fearing this might warn away shipping, hardy Cornish men ferried out several boatloads of stone to fill the cavity and stifle the howl. One may imagine their annoyance at the graceful tower which now crowns that grisly rock.

Wreckers also protested when the Lizard Light was built upon the Cornish coast. As the builder recorded, "They affirme I take away God's grace from them," an odd theological slant, to say the least. Stevenson wrote that when a lighthouse was proposed upon the Isle of Sanday, in the Orkneys, the inhabitants remonstrated, "If wrecks were to happen they might as well be sent to the poor island of Sanday as anywhere else."

America has also had its "moon cussers" and their ghoulish toll of the sea. Ralph Waldo Emerson related how the keeper at Nauset Light on Cape Cod was criticized by neighbor wreckers, while Chatham men were once called "brick in the stockings," because some legendary forebear was accused of tapping shipwrecked seamen on the head. A horse, led along the beach with a lantern bobbing from its neck to lure passing ships, bequeathed its name, so folklore has it, to Nag's Head on the Carolina coast; while it is a matter of historic record that no fewer than fifty wrecking boats once put out from Key West to glean a rich harvest from West Indies merchantmen.

But there is a brighter side to such somber recitals. When French warships, swooping down on the Eddystone Rock, carried away English workmen, Louis XIV ordered their return, with the apology, "I am at war with England, not with humanity."

Lighthouse keepers are among the most courageous guardians of civilization's far frontiers. In the fourteenth century, when Edward, the Black Prince, rebuilt the beacon on Cordouan Rocks at the mouth of the Gironde, he commissioned a holy hermit to tend the flame. When that worthy man died, the light died with him; but since that day innumerable other watchers have kept the faith in the face of much hardship and danger.

Henry Winstanley, who built the first Eddystone tower,

perhaps the most famous lighthouse in the world, rashly hoped that he might be present in a severe storm. As if in answer to that challenge one of the heaviest gales that ever swept the English Channel tore the structure from its foundations and bore him, with five companions, to his death. The present structure is the third to be erected upon that formidable rock.

The first lighthouse on Minots Ledge, south of Boston, was also demolished. In a lull of the storm, pale watchers from shore heard the last signal of the doomed keepers, the ringing of the lighthouse bell, just before it crashed into the sea. Workmen then attacked this menace to navigation in earnest, but they toiled three years before the rock, almost always awash, could be leveled sufficiently to lay the first foundation stone for the present tower.

The first keeper of Boston Light, George Worthylake, was drowned, with his wife and daughter. Benjamin Franklin, then but thirteen, wrote a poem on the tragedy, which he peddled about the streets of Boston. A furious hurricane in 1906 destroyed Sand Island Light in Mobile Gulf and Horn Island Light, near the mouth of the Mississippi. All the inmates lost their lives. But such fatalities might be indefinitely multiplied.

Nor is death the only peril that lurks in the shadows. Isolated towers like those on Bishops Rock thrum to a tempest like gigantic tuning forks, while the roar of wind and waves is stupefying. No wonder watchers grow taciturn and morose. Gruesome tales of insane keepers by Wilbur Daniel Steele and Rudyard Kipling have been drawn from stark reality.

In such stations the keeper is given an assistant for mutual help and companionship. But that safeguard has proved inadequate. On an exposed rock in the Bristol Channel one keeper suddenly died. His companion, fearing a possible charge of foul play, dared not commit the body to the sea. Instead he placed it in a rude cage on the gallery outside. Days passed before he was relieved. Meanwhile he kept the light aflame, but nightly vigils with his silent companion left him a shattered wreck.

Even three keepers may not suffice, as was proven by a mysterious occurrence on the Flannan Rocks, off the lonely Hebrides, in 1900. The relief boat found the lighthouse tenantless, with no trace of the missing inmates. It was conjectured that one of the men, venturing out upon the rock, was swept away by a wave, while his two companions perished in attempting a rescue. But no one knows.

A humane rule now requires that keepers in isolated stations be relieved at monthly intervals and allowed two weeks' liberty. But although relief keepers are on call on the neighboring shore, the transfer cannot always be effected. The keepers in Longships Light, less than two miles off Land's End, were once marooned nearly three months by winter gales. Relief, too, has its perils. In 1899, while attempting to take off the keeper of the light near East Cape, New Zealand, the boat capsized, drowning the chief and three other men.

Physical discomforts are many. In the Red Sea, one of the hottest places in the world, Sanganeb Light marks a dangerous coral reef. Its skeleton steel tower rises 180 feet. How its keepers must swelter on a broiling summer's day may be faintly imagined. In vivid contrast are lighthouses which winter storms surround with ice thirty feet thick.

Loneliness and sheer monotony may be more than mere discomforts. The most isolated light in America is at Cape Sarichef, Alaska, overlooking the dreary reaches of Bering Sea. In former years the keeper's nearest neighbor was a trapper ten miles away. Once he waited nearly ten months for his mail. No wonder he began to hear, in howling blasts, the voices of islanders murdered long before by Russian sealers. Now radios and airplanes make life endurable, although the present keepers sometimes complain when giant Kodiak bears break down the outer doors of their storehouse.

Sabine Bank Light is fifteen miles off the Texas coast, but Stannard Rock in Lake Superior is even more isolated, for the nearest land is twenty-four miles away. And yet the keeper's life is considered a healthy one. As a young man, I boarded many days at Monomoy Light, amid Nantucket Shoals, absorbing something of the loneliness and the eerie night shadows. The jovial keeper often boasted of the abundant fresh air.

On the upper Hudson a keeper died at ninety-three, after fifty-two years of continuous service, bequeathing the job to his son, who was sixty-five. But shore stations may prove dangerous. At least so thought the keeper at Trinidad Head, near the mouth of the Columbia, when, during a furious storm in 1913, he beheld a huge wave curl over a 175-foot cliff to wash level with his eyes. The impact deranged the machinery and all but wrecked the edifice.

In some shore stations the keeper's wife may have a flower garden or even raise a few vegetables. The original deed to Navesink, at the entrance to New York Harbor, provided that the keeper might pasture two cows in a neighboring field. The keeper of a coastal light on the Gulf of Mexico was greatly annoyed when the sea, raging eight feet above high-water mark, carried away a fatted pig, but his emotions were even more intense when some weeks later the pig returned of his own volition, none the worse for his adventures.

But we can sympathize with the keeper at Gay Head, Martha's Vineyard, who in 1805 petitioned Secretary Gallatin of the federal Treasury, "I humbly pray you to think of me and (if it shall be consistent with your wisdom) increase my salary." President Jefferson decided that a fifty-dollar raise was not unreasonable and upped the annual stipend from two hundred to two hundred and fifty.

Lighthouse keepers frequently exceed the course of duty in preserving human life. Twice during hurricanes the keeper at Bolivar Point, Texas, intervened to prevent appalling disaster. In 1900, one hundred and twenty-five persons found shelter in the tower, and again in 1915, fifty refugees shivered for two long nights on the spiral stairway as the seas demolished every neighboring building.

A shining page recounts the exploits of Grace Darling. She was alone with her aged father in Longstone Light on the desolate Farne Islands near the Scottish Border, when the steamer Forfarshire crashed on the outer rocks. Most of the crew perished, but Grace, then twenty-one, helped to row the wretched coble to the wreck to take off four men and one woman. Although she died shortly afterward, her memory will linger until the last lighthouse is darkened.

Originally lighthouses were only glorified bonfires, as wood in iron grates or baskets sent forth a fitful glare. Later charcoal and coal were used, but economy and efficiency have determined the illuminant in more recent times.

Oil remains the favorite, although the olive oil of antiquity has yielded in turn to lard oil, whale oil, and petroleum products. Gas has been found serviceable in stationary beacons, but electricity, though excelling in brilliancy, has seldom been employed because of its greater cost.

The oil burner is only a large lamp whose radiance elaborate lenses magnify many thousandfold.

Most lights were once stationary; now most of them fit

into an intricate pattern of flashes and occultations. Grim Minots Ledge sends forth a solitary flash, followed by four others and then three more. This means, to sentimental couples on the rocks at Scituate, "I love you."

White is the prevalent color, but harbor lights may flash the danger signal red or sometimes green or blue. Certain lights even alternate from white to red to green, for every one must have characteristics to distinguish it at sea. Colored lights, however, suffer from restricted range, since red lenses cut down light rays by one half, green lenses nearly 75 per cent.

Revolving lights require a costly mechanism, for the lenses may weigh several tons. To minimize friction, they often float upon a bed of liquid mercury.

Lights of the first order command wide stretches of seacoast, while harbor approaches are marked by numerous beacons of lesser range. The unit is the candle power. Until 1811 the Eddystone was illuminated by twenty-four candles of standard size. As calculations vary, however, the comparative power of prominent lights is not only the theme of endless argument, but also subject to frequent changes.

Along the outward approaches to Great Britain, Fastnet Rock Light shines with the radiance of 750,000 candles; Bishops Rock with 622,500; the Eddystone with 300,000. Boston Light has a white flash of 100,000.

Electric lights are immeasurably the most powerful. While lenses can go only so far with an oil lamp, an arc that dazzles the eye is capable of much greater magnification. The Lizard Light has 3,000,000 candle power; St. Catherines on the Isle of Wight 5,000,000; and the Isle of May in the Firth of Forth over 6,000,000.

The French, who pioneered with electricity and elaborate lenses, have made their coast perhaps the best lighted in the world. There one superlight guides shipping well within the range of the next superlight. Cape Hève Light is of 25,000,000 candle power; Point of Creac'h 30,000,000, but the most powerful lighthouse in the world was installed by the Germans on Helgoland to illuminate a broad segment of the North Sea. From the lantern 272 feet above the waves three great shafts, which revolved at intervals of 120 degrees with the power of 43,000,000 candles, could be plainly seen at Büsun, thirty-five miles away.

The most powerful lighthouse in the United States was established at Navesink on the New Jersey coast, where its costly French lenses, equipped to generate 25,000,000 candle power, proved so annoying to shore dwellers that landward-facing panels were darkened. Though directly visible only twenty-two miles, the flashes have been detected seventy miles at sea. Such superlights are really too powerful. Were it not for the curvature of the earth, they could be seen for hundreds of miles. But why send expensive light rays wandering off into space? So thought the department at Washington when they substituted at Navesink the more moderate but still excessive illumination of 9,000,000 candles.

Even this reduced brilliance proved superfluous in the maze of oceanic guideposts that mark the approaches to New York Harbor. These include 46 lighthouses, 2 lightships, 60 light beacons, 77 fog signals, and sundry assorted buoys. Hence, during the recent war the Navesink mammoth was still further reduced to a beggarly 5000 candle power, and this almost total eclipse, so Coast Guard headquarters asserts, is scheduled to continue.

With the passing of Navesink's former glory, the most powerful light in this country, 5,500,000 candle power, is now at Hillsborough Inlet, Florida, while Liston Range in Delaware Bay is a close second with 5,000,000. Cape Cod Light, whose lenses magnify a 1000-watt light bulb to

4,000,000 candle power, remains the dominant beacon on this shore of the North Atlantic.

Cubits Gap at the outlet of the Mississippi with 2,000,000 candle power is the most brilliant on the Gulf of Mexico, and Farallon, California, with 2,200,000, the brightest on our Pacific coast. Molokai in Hawaii, however, has a radiance of 2,500,000, while among interior waters White Shoal Light guides shipping through the Strait of Mackinac with an illumination of 3,000,000 candles.

Altogether there are in this country, including Alaska and Hawaii, no fewer than twenty lighthouses of 1,000,000 candle power or better.

Notable lighthouses mark other coasts. Japan, before the war, had many, as did China. Towers in the Philippines were built to withstand a hurricane pressure of 120 miles per hour. Twelve hundred lighthouses dot the long and perilous coast line of Norway. From Cape Columbine, South Africa, a powerful electric arc flashes beams of 9,000,000 candle power to guide ships to that continent, as they reach southward for the Cape of Good Hope.

Even secondary lights are welcome gleams through the darkness. I recall how cheery seemed a firefly glow from the gloomy Haitian coast, and another from Borneo, and another from Mombasa—but world travelers learn to welcome those friendly signals everywhere.

Height is needed to overcome the "thick rotundity of the world." The typical shaft marks a twin conquest over distance and wave action gleaned from costly experience. Hatteras, our loftiest shaft, is approximately two hundred feet high. The French tower on Ile de Vierge, 262 feet, is probably the loftiest in the world. Natural heights are sometimes excessive. Navassa, on a turtle-backed islet in the West Indies, is 402 feet high; Makapua Point, near Pearl Harbor, 420, while the Point Loma Light, near San

Diego, is 462. Such elevated beacons may be hidden by low-lying fog.

Lightships have partially solved the problem of unconquerable shoals. The first of these floating lighthouses was the Nore, which anchored at the mouth of the Thames in 1732. In candle power such ships usually range from 2500 to 20,000, but the *Royal Sovereign* in Dover Straits excels many a first-class lighthouse with 750,000. Swinging idly in the tide rips is a test for sea legs, while the deadly monotony is little relieved by a spice of danger. Some lightships are equipped with engines, but many are quite helpless when mooring lines part. Hatteras Light has broken loose several times. Once it escaped Diamond Shoals by a miracle, to run hard aground on the cape itself. Winter ice drifting down from Labrador has dragged many a lightship from its anchorage. One would think such ships safe from collision, yet the steamship *Olympic* once cut the Nantucket Shoals lightship nearly in two. In the hurricane of 1944 a lightship off Martha's Vineyard foundered with the loss of all on board.

Light buoys are a more recent invention. The most powerful are 60-foot giants that weigh 17 tons and stand 28 feet out of water. One of the largest, generating 392 candle power, is stationed off Peaked Hill Bars, Cape Cod. It burned continuously a year and a half on a single charge of compressed acetylene gas. A combination light and whistling buoy, its eerie wail is familiar to summer tourists.

A light buoy on Florida Keys blundered far to sea, still flickering its erratic warning. Another buoy, breaking loose from its anchorage near New York Harbor, appeared six weeks later on the coast of Ireland, a more rapid passage than that of many an archaic windjammer.

Light, unfortunately, has one grave defect. Fog, most dreaded of sea hazards, can obscure even the rays of

Helgoland. Hence navigators have enlisted the aid of less satisfactory sound. The bell on Inchcape Rock has been immortalized by Southey, while Kipling has rendered bell buoys an even better tribute in verse, but at best they are local warnings of limited range. The whistling buoy may carry for miles, but foghorns, still more impressive, are now a part of most lighthouse equipment. The foghorn at Ushant, with a roar like an enraged lion, seems to rip the very fog to shreds. The forerunner of all such stentorian devices, in America at least, was a cannon installed at Boston Light which was fired only in answer to similar signals from sea. Unfortunately sound waves, which are only ripples in the air, may be diffused or even deflected by winds.

Less important, but still indispensable, are those silent, lightless beacons, the buoys, spar, can, and otherwise, that set off the shallows and fringe the channels of every great port of the world. These must be overhauled and painted at least once a year.

Lighthouses were once private enterprises. In 1514, Henry VIII of England granted a charter to a guild of mariners to assist shipping. Queen Elizabeth broadened the charter powers to include the erection of beacons and other sea marks. A noble benefaction is Jument Light, off a dangerous bit of French coast. For its erection the world traveler Jean Potron left a bequest of four hundred thousand francs. But lighthouses now are government property and maintained by special departments. To maintain them tolls are levied on shipping; hence a course at sea is sometimes altered by thrifty sea captains to avoid such expense.

When the federal government was established in 1789, there were only 12 lighthouses in operation on our coasts. George Washington several times gave additional building operations his presidential sanction, while Alexander Hamilton wrote a special request to Congress for a light at Cape Hatteras. Recent government reports list 14,947 lighthouses, beacons, and other aids to navigation.

And now modern researches into what would have seemed black art to our elders has introduced a more potent agent in the radio beam. This mysterious ray penetrates the densest fog and is manifest beyond the range of the most brilliant light. First-class stations have radio equipment to flash information to ships while far at sea. In combination with a simple but ingenious apparatus on shipboard, this beam enables the officer on the bridge to plot his position on the chart and even to correct his chronometers.

Such wizardly devices threaten to curtail the usefulness of more simple beacons, although the latter will be maintained for a long time to come. Great areas of seacoast are still poorly lighted or entirely dark. There is not a single lighthouse on the whole continent of Antarctica!

A further factor in the eclipse of the lighthouse lies in the exploration of the ocean of the air. Progressive countries are now dotted with beacons to guide airplanes through the darkness. Some of these generate 1,000,000 candle power. But however much methods of transportation may change, lighthouses and their numerous kindred, beacons and buoys and foghorns, have written an inspiring chapter in man's conquest of the sea.

CHAPTER XXX

On the Bridge of a Great Liner

Any one can told the helm when the sea is calm.
                    PUBLILIUS SYRUS
        . . . though the yesty waves
    Confound and swallow navigation up.
                    SHAKESPEARE
Now in the surging sea an island lies—Pharos they call it—
distant as far from the Egyptian stream as a hollow ship runs
in a day when a whistling wind blows after. By it there lies a
bay with good anchorage, from whence they send the trim
ships off to sea after supplying them with drinking water.
                    HOMER

When the *Majestic* was the most luxurious liner afloat,
I was frequently the guest of her staff captain as she lay
berthed on the Manhattan water front. On such visits I
never failed to marvel at her bewildering equipment of aids
to navigation. Landsmen may know that the bridge is the
nerve center of the ship, a corridor stretching from side to
side, commanding a view of bow and forward deck. The
brain of the ship is the officer in charge, while at hand are
all the mechanisms to control a moving mass of thousands
of tons "sky-hooting through the brine."

A more picturesque sea life vanished with the passing of
the clipper ship, when old salts, their forearms tattooed

with anchors or mermaids, foregathered in the dogwatch to smoke their pipes and swap lurid tales of adventure. But the sea still has a language and customs all its own. Each four-hour watch is terminated by the sounding of "eight bells," varied only on New Year's Eve, when the boatswain rings sixteen to salute the New Year. Distances are still reckoned in knots, a cable's length is one hundred fathoms, and position on board is located by port or starboard, bow or stern.

Ancient galleys hugged the shores and sailed by daylight, while coastal voyages are still conducted by "dog-barking" navigators, guided, according to cynical report, by the baying of familiar dogs. Far different was the bold man who first turned the prow of his ship straight out into the open sea.

And yet South Sea Islanders made long voyages in outrigger canoes. Matchless navigators, they calculated the drift of wind and current and were guided by the stars. With only the rudest charts of sticks to give direction, they located distant islets that are the veriest pinpricks on modern maps, gambling, meanwhile, with death by thirst or starvation. The Norseman, though in more seaworthy craft, were quite as daring. Their helmsmen had acquired the wisdom of the salmon and the seal and steered, apparently, by instinct. Nor should we ignore the seamanship of those Greek or Arab adventurers who first pushed boldly across the Indian Ocean, even though the monsoon gave them their direction and their goal was the broad seaboard of Hindustan.

Such navigation requires uncanny skill in deciphering the hieroglyphics of sea and sky: the clouds which herald changing winds and threatening storms; the colors of the water fretted by a breeze still miles away, or disclosing tide rips or nearer shoals. Grizzled veterans still grope their way through the fogs of the Grand Banks with only their knowledge of drifts and currents and what the "dipsey" lead can reveal of water depth and bottom, while in mid-ocean navigators often sail for days by "dead reckonin'."

The position of a ship at sea is determined by its latitude north or south of the Equator, and by its longitude east or west of some chosen point, usually Greenwich, England. As we have already observed, Pytheas of Marseille, about the year 326 B.C., took the first latitude by observing the elevation of the sun at noon on the longest day of the year. The principle has never varied, although mechanical equipment has greatly improved. In the Middle Ages a clumsy contrivance called the cross-staff gave the approximate angle of elevation. A refinement was the astrolabe, a metal circle with numbered degrees and a central pointer. Columbus and Vasco da Gama used the astrolabe. Unfortunately it required two men to manipulate it and the readings were faulty at best. The more accurate sextant was not invented until 1731. One man takes its reading, usually on the bridge at noon. Star charts have also been perfected for night observations or when the noonday sun is overcast; artificial horizons establish sea levels in thick weather and lesser refinements and improvements have been added.

Longitude was long a problem. It demanded an artificial fixed point of departure which, even now, has not been universally recognized. The ancients could think of no method except comparing the times of eclipses from different locations. Sir Isaac Newton advocated observing the position of the moon. Unfortunately this demanded an unwarranted amount of calculation by the officer at sea. In 1598, Philip III of Spain offered a thousand crowns for a workable method. This prize was topped by the States General of Holland with an offer of ten thousand florins. The chief difficulty was an accurate timepiece. The sundials, hourglasses, and clumsy water clocks of the ancients had given way to metallic timekeepers, but these still were unreliable. In 1714 Parliament, fully roused to the needs of the occasion, established and endowed a commission with ample funds. How crude were existing methods is revealed when this commission offered twenty thousand pounds sterling for any method of taking longitude at sea within an error limit of thirty miles!

This princely sum was claimed in 1761 by John Harrison, who had constructed a chronometer of compensating metals that allowed for temperature changes. Greenwich Observatory, however, was still wrestling with lunar observations, so it was some years before Harrison received all the promised prize money.

Since his day chronometers have approached a perfection which can never be attained. However, their variations of but a few seconds over considerable periods may be measured and allowed for. Great ocean liners now carry at least three chronometers and deck or hack watches almost as accurate. Moreover, as a final touch, the corrected time can now be flashed to ships at sea by radio.

The helmsman, however, cannot steer by latitude and longitude, for he needs something before his eyes to hold the course. That miracle is performed by the compass. Just who discovered this magic finger will never be known. Authentic Chinese records mention one in 1279, although it was used at a much earlier date. Some form of compass appeared during the Third Crusade, 1190–92. Roger Bacon understood the principle involved. A magnetized needle, floating upon pith or cork, it revolutionized navigation, although Francis Bacon was in error when he wrote, "The immense regions of the West Indies had never been discovered if the use of the compass had not been known." No pointer guided Leif Ericson to Vineland or the Arabs on their voyages to India.

Housed in its binnacle, the compass is now a marine necessity. But it has defects. Not only do shifting magnetic poles cause variations, but the steelwork of a great liner agitates the needle. Hence a new mechanical wizard has been devised to supplement the older and still useful original—a gyrocompass that operates independently of magnetism. This compass is a delicate top that spins with a velocity of 8600 revolutions a minute. Such whirling objects maintain a fixed position so long as they continue to whirl. The gyrocompass also points due north and never deviates unless—and herein lies its only defect—the motor which operates it fails to function. Hence it must be watched.

The ancients judged position at sea by the distance traversed since the preceding day—instructive if one knows the rate of motion. The Dutch log was perhaps the first crude recorder—a block of wood thrown overboard from the bow and the time interval checked at the stern. As this involved loss of the log, the latter was attached by a rope, and the "run-out" time measured. Such makeshifts have given the name "log" to the accurate speedometer. This is a metal cylinder trailing from the stern or from one side of the bridge. The water, pouring through this cylinder, turns a mechanical spinner whose revolutions per minute give the rate of progress. Another mechanism on the bridge is a tachometer, which records the revolutions of the ship's propeller per minute.

An altogether different log is the daily record of events. This is less important now than formerly, but the "log" of an old whaler, blundering for years about the Pacific, is a veritable treasury of sea lore, terse, ungrammatical, its novel spelling interspersed with sketches of whale flukes and unknown headlands drawn in India ink. One can almost hear the topsails flapping with each conventional conclusion: "So ends this day." Magellan left no log, but Pigafetta's chronicle is invaluable. Drake probably kept one, but it has disappeared—an irreparable loss.

Weather is never more vital than at sea. Sailors become adept at reading the portents of mare's-tails and mackerel skies. But a more accurate informant is the barometer—called the "glass." Mere height of mercury is less instructive than a changing trend, a rising or a falling barometer. Admiral Beaufort devised a wind chart for navigators. This he divided into twelve divisions, ranging from a gentle breeze to a hurricane. Numbers 8 and 9 on the chart recorded a gale with velocities from 34 to 47 miles per hour. Higher still was a storm—divisions 10 and 11 respectively, which ranged from 48 to 65 miles. Number 12 was the ominous cage of winds, from 65 miles to velocities that defied all measurement.

By a similar method the Douglas chart analyzes waves. This is divided into nine sections. Number 5, or "very rough," shows waves from 5 to 8 feet high; numbers 6, 7, and 8 carry that height progressively to 40 feet, labeled a "heavy swell"; number 9 is a "confused swell," such erratic spoutings as seamen encounter in typhoons.

Sounding lines, perhaps the earliest of all aids to navigation, are still retained, although they have yielded to the fathometer. This measures echoes from the bottom and is really a combination of three instruments. One, the transmitter, sends a sound straight downward from the ship's keel; another, the hydrophone, picks up the returning echo; while the third, or receiver, makes it audible. Geared to this apparatus is a knob or pointer which automatically records the depth. As a great ship approaches the harbor, fathometers keep the bridge in almost continuous contact with the bottom. Changing depths, when coupled with readings from the chart, also help determine the ship's position in thick weather.

The hull of a great liner is divided into compartments by steel divisions. Suppose a fire, one of the deadliest hazards of ocean travel, breaks out in any compartment. The bridge is instantly notified by mechanical informers that never sleep. One of these resembles the board in a hotel which summons the bellboy to a particular room. A light instantly flashes the identification of the threatened compartment. Another recorder, connected by tubes, shows a thin wisp of smoke. It is so delicate that it reports a workman puffing a cigarette far below the water line. Night and day a member of the crew is stationed before these recorders. Steel doors, that can be operated from the bridge, immediately shut off the threatened compartment, while the trained fire-fighting force proceeds to combat the conflagration. One advantage is a never failing water supply.

The hull is not only divided into compartments within, but in the steel shell one overlaps another. No thousand-foot hull could withstand wave action without yielding. Each compartment allows for considerable "play." Hence in stormy waters the officer on the bridge peers anxiously into a weird gridiron that traces in neon lights a rough outline of the hull. When the great ship racks and strains, the amount of "give" is instantly recorded. As the danger limit nears, the engine room is directed to cut down the speed, otherwise the huge hull might break in two when lifted upon a rolling hill of water. Sailing ships often lay to—that is, faced into the wind to ride out the storm. Steamships usually cut down speed to avoid too great a strain upon the hull. But even the largest of them are sometimes compelled to give over, turning bow into the waves to await better weather.

Off the bridge is the chartroom, with its elaborate equipment, where the course of the ship is plotted day by day, an operation requiring great mechanical skill.

Speaking a ship at sea is always interesting. Small ships may approach so closely that the officers converse through megaphones. The most common signal is by whistle. Big liners seldom sound that resonant note that echoes for miles, save when leaving or approaching their berths, or warning smaller shipping out of the way. Fogs make the sirens play their weird symphony of confusion and fear and warning, for collision is always a possibility.

The semaphore is a favorite device for transmitting messages. In its crudest form it is an upright with crossbars that may be arranged to represent every letter of the alphabet. Signalmen with a flag in each hand use the same alphabet in wigwagging. Flags of various patterns and colors convey messages by international code. A flag upside down is the signal of distress; a yellow flag, the ominous warning that death lurks near in the form of smallpox, cholera, or perhaps bubonic plague.

At night ships converse by Morsing—flashing the letters of that well-known code. For distant hails the radio is unrivaled. Every big steamship has its radio room and its "Sparks" who presides there. And when peril does loom, swift and appalling, the radio's SOS may sweep all other programs off the air, even presidential addresses, as a nation listens to the call for help from a great ship foundering somewhere out there in the dark!

A complicated system of speaking tubes and telephone wires connects the bridge with every department. The crew are quite as integrated and well oiled as the machinery. Supreme, below decks, is the chief engineer, who acknowledges no superior but the captain. Few municipal plants have engines half so powerful as those under his supervision; the Queen Mary's generate two hundred thousand horsepower.

Every member of the ship's personnel, from the oiler to the steward, knows his duties.

Over all are the officers, whose rank is disclosed by the number of gold stripes upon their sleeves. In primitive ships the captain was the only officer. On sailing craft he was assisted by a first and second mate, while third mate was added on larger ships. Nowadays a superliner not only has a long list but carries two captains, who bear four gold stripes upon their sleeves. One is the staff captain, who directs all ordinary proceedings, the other, according to prevalent opinion, merely entertains his guests. But no matter how carefree his lot may seem, he is burdened with a perpetual responsibility, which a crisis brings into stark relief.

It is to be hoped that passengers upon a great liner, who have submitted to the customary irksome boat drill while draped in bulging life preservers, may never be disturbed by the five or six sharp blasts upon the whistle which spell danger! Then indeed the captain, mounting the bridge, becomes a dictator who may shoot to kill anyone who disregards his orders. In that hour he rises above all thought of personal safety, prepared to go down with his ship. This solemn obligation, an unwritten law of the sea, is not a senseless sacrifice of his life upon the altar of custom or tradition but a recognition of a greater responsibility; he, whose duty it is to protect his passengers and crew, must take no thought of himself. Only by assuming so detached a position can he remain calmly efficient.

Such an office is attained only after a lifetime of hard work and stern experience. For the youthful apprentice, promotion comes slowly, step by step, after mastering innumerable duties, further delayed until a vacancy appears in the ranks above. Yet in spite of exacting requirements, inadequate pay, and unavoidable danger, the life continues to attract an eager body of young men, enthused by the traditions of their forebears and the never failing lure of the sea.

The captain of a great liner is now furnished with all possible mechanical devices. His powerful binoculars bring far-off objects near; his range finders approximate their distance; he is surrounded by capable assistants. Familiar though he is with the flashes of guiding lighthouses, the location of channel-marking buoys, a pilot will presently stand beside him whose knowledge of harbor approaches is more detailed than his own. But he remains the captain who can, if he chooses, brush aside that pilot's orders. For with all the refinements of science, the personal equation can not safely be ignored. Navigation can be learned, but seamanship never. It was inborn in the Phoenicians and the Norsemen and the Kanakas of the Pacific, and remains that one indispensable talent in those who tread the bridge of a great liner.

CHAPTER XXXI

How the Sea Controls Our Climate

The gaudy, blabbing and remorseful day
Is crept into the bosom of the sea.
SHAKESPEARE
The low'ring element
Scowls o'er the darken'd landscape.
MILTON

We think of weather in terms of atmosphere. High pressure is a synonym for "fair"; low pressure, for unsettlement and storm. But investigation shows that climate is quite as much a product of the oceans, which exert a perpetual check upon extremes of temperature and are the ultimate source of that moisture which makes life livable.

Climate is, first of all, a matter of temperature. Humidity is perhaps the next consideration, although winds may play a decisive role. Sunlight is also a factor. Unalaska is not particularly cold, but only five days of the year are free from fog. In desert regions those fogs would offer a welcome shade in almost unbroken sunlight.

Parmenides, in the fifth century B.C., proposed a division of the global surface into the five great zones which appear in our geographies today. These, two polar and two temperate, separated by a broad tropic belt, are determined by latitude alone.

Since that time other divisions have been suggested, for latitude is by no means the sole consideration. Aristotle thought there should be ten zones, while a recent study, based upon more exact information, would divide land areas into three: coastal, continental, and mountain. Here the determining factor is often altitude, but even more is the relationship to the surrounding sea.

To begin with, our global climate is nearly three quarters "oceanic." Overflowing the coastal areas, bringing cool springtimes and warm autumns, this oceanic climate penetrates far into the great land masses with their wider fluctuations in temperature and moisture. In continental areas altitude enters the picture, with its fall of one degree in temperature for every three hundred feet of elevation. In lofty mountains this factor becomes predominant—hence we find snow-capped peaks in Africa under the very shadow of the Equator. Yet even there the influence of the seas remains, for whence came the snows?

The oceans are the great stabilizers, which have been called a bank where deposits of radiant energy are paid out gradually. Where one unit of that radiant energy will heat a given volume of air, no less than three thousand units are required to heat an equal volume of sea water. The temperature of mid-ocean surfaces, as we have observed in a previous chapter, probably fluctuates less than one degree in twenty-four hours. In the Sahara the daily range may exceed a hundred. Hence oceans are cooler in summer, warmer in winter than the land, where coastal cities appreciate in July the salt breeze which may turn January snowstorms into rain.

Ocean currents and the winds they warm or chill are among the great regulators of temperature. Because of the Gulf Stream with its companion winds, northwestern Europe is thirty-five degrees warmer than mere latitude would warrant. The Japanese Current, raising the temperature of the Gulf of Alaska at least twenty degrees, sends its chinook winds through the passes of the Rockies to melt Alberta snows.

Cold currents may be quite as effective. Smith has calculated that melting ice in the North Atlantic offsets one half the summer sunshine. Yet the waters of the Labrador Current bear a chill at least ten times as great as that of the dissolving ice they carry.

The influence of fringing or landlocked seas is often paramount. O. Pettersson has linked the water temperatures of the North Sea and the Baltic with thermometer height and barometric pressure over Scandinavian and other neighboring territories. The Mediterranean exerts a similar influence on the surrounding terrain, while the Red Sea, though too narrow to dominate adjacent land masses, is cooler than African and Arabian deserts.

More important, however, than their regulation of temperatures, is the ocean's gift of that moisture so essential to all life. To be sure, two thirds of upland rainfall has been traced to lakes, rivers, growing vegetation, and the soil itself, in an ever recurring program of dew and mist and shower, while it has also been estimated that one quarter of the land surface drains into interior lakes or seas. But they would presently dry up were they not perpetually restored by the inexhaustible reservoir of the oceans. These are the great humidors which moisten the atmosphere to preserve our globe from becoming a universal waste. The carrier winds, however, which distribute that moisture, are anything but impartial, for they deluge some regions while ignoring others. A dry wind may be more parching than burning sunlight. It is such an evil partnership of arid winds and chill ocean currents that gives Peru its famous rainless coast. The Humboldt Current, creeping up from the Antarctic, edges away from the shore, causing a continuous up-welling of cold waters. The fogs and clouds born of contact with tropic surfaces are borne by prevailing westerlies over the heated land. But there, expanding, they not only yield no moisture of their own but suck up what little remains in the parching earth. A similar combination of winds and ocean currents has made so much of western Africa a desert. The cool Benguella Current, flowing northward from the Cape of Good Hope, and the Canaries Current, circling southward past Gibraltar, cause similar upwellings of chill water. This water, with a prevailing temperature of 56 degrees, meets the warm Guinea or Equatorial Current with a temperature of 80, breeding fog and cloud in heated and expanding air, which remains ever thirsty for more moisture.

The influence of clouds upon climate is twofold. Not only are they Nature's sprinkling cans, but vast parasols, as well, against the sun's rays. Where those rays are too abundant, such shade is grateful, but because of them lowering skies are still more dismal in Labrador or Iceland. The Faeroe Islands have but five cloudless days a year!

Showers cool the earth not only directly but by evaporation. Summer in the tropics is sometimes the rainy season. The July heats of India would be unbearable were it not for the deluge of the monsoons. Showers and accompanying evaporation also cool the surface of the sea, although arctic fogs, when rising, may make the sheltered waters perceptibly warmer.

Strabo, noting that temperature declined not only with latitude but with altitude, understood something of the influence of mountain barriers and climatic controls upon plants, animals, and even humans.

Rats and men have been called the only creatures that scorn all zonal restrictions, for they will "go anywhere, live anywhere, eat anything." Both inhabit regions of polar night, the steaming jungles of the Congo, and the arid Australian hinterland. But although mankind can endure the rigors of inhospitable regions, a struggle with Nature for bare subsistence, as Buckle explained, may leave neither time nor energy for nobler achievements, while only favorable environments permit him to develop his full capabilities.

Heat is the life of atoms and of individuals, for the absolute zero of outer space is also absolute death. For man, however, the range between too much and too little is narrow indeed.

The Sahara is credited with the hottest summers on the globe. In Salah, for forty-five consecutive days, the mean daily maximum was 118 degrees in the shade! Once it reached 127. At Aziziya, twenty-five miles south of Tripoli, the thermometer, on September 13, 1922, registered 136, while a reading of 143 has also been reported. In such heats, excessive even for a boiler room or a Turkish bath, man can survive only by imbibing at least five quarts of fluid daily. Surface temperatures that exceed 170 degrees prove that the burning sands of the desert are no mere metaphor. In such dry, hot atmospheres wood splits and leather becomes as hard as board.

Other arid regions are scarcely more endurable. At Barble Bar, Australia, the thermometer registered 90 or above for 151 consecutive days. Death Valley in California is appropriately named, with its Furnace Creek and Funeral Mountains. Perhaps it deserves that title conferred upon it by more than one wilted prospector—"the anteroom to hell." In any case, it seems to offer the hottest monthly temperature with a June mean of 100° F., while once, at least, the thermometer soared to 134. As for the global hot spot the year round, observations covering sixteen years show a mean annual temperature of 86.4° F. for the island of Massawa in the Red Sea—exceptional facilities, one might assume, for acquiring a summer tan.

Excessive cold may be quite as effective a barrier to human progress, although Stefansson has written a book upon the "Friendly Arctic." The site of earth's maximum low is not in frozen Antarctica, but has been located in the Siberian town of Verkhoyansk on the Yana River. Here the thermometer once fell to 94 below zero, a temperature that should satisfy the hardiest Yakut native or even a polar bear. No wonder streams solidify to the bottom, and the surface of the ocean ices over for two hundred and seventy-five miles north of the Yana, farther from shore than anywhere else on earth. Yet people live in Verkhoyansk, where the mean January temperature is minus 58.2 degrees, and the year's average is only 3.3 degrees above zero.

Yet even these temperatures are challenged as a global minimum. Professor Obruchev claims that dubious distinction for Oimekon on the Indigirka River. While his lowest observation during a period of twelve years in this frosty town was only 89.9 degrees below zero, the professor found a January mean of minus 68.3. Sverdrup also, wintering at Goose Fiord on Southwest Ellesmere Land, concluded that the year's average in that lonely place would be 2 degrees below zero in contrast with Verkhoyansk's more genial warmth, some 5 degrees higher. Strict accuracy, moreover, might suggest a yet unknown locality on the great Greenland icecap or even the peak of Everest as possibly still colder.

Violent changes in temperature are also disturbing. Here Verkhoyansk perhaps offers the widest extremes, for in the almost continuous sunshine of summer the thermometer may soar as high above zero as it sinks below in midwinter. In fact the July temperature at Verkhoyansk betters that of San Francisco!

On the other hand, too little change implies monotony, if not stagnation. Quito, Ecuador, shows an annual monthly range of only .3 of one degree. In Bolobo, in the Congo, where the annual range is only 2 degrees, the daily range from noon to midnight is 16. Yet an English engineer once assured me that there were places in the Malayan jungle where the temperature had probably not varied, night or day, as much as three degrees in a century!

Humidity is sometimes as great a problem as temperature. It is not the thermometer which measures discomfort in the dog days. Humidity makes both extreme heat and extreme cold more difficult. The dry cold of the Dakotas and the dry heat of Arizona would be unendurable if linked with too much moisture. But the chief function of water vapor in the atmosphere is, of course, to supply life-giving rainfall.

Here again we encounter wide extremes. The Amazon is the world's great river, not only because of favorable geography but because it drains the most extensive rainy belt on earth. Through great areas the annual precipitation exceeds 80 inches. In vivid contrast, at Iquique, Chile, on the other side of the Andes, not a drop of rain fell for more than four years. Africa also shows strong contrasts. The western slopes of the Cameroons have recorded an annual precipitation of over 412 inches, while for ten consecutive years no measurable rain fall at Wadi Halfa, Egypt, and visible spatters appeared on only 22 days! Death Valley once went 401 days without a drop of moisture; Jaline Island, in the Marshall Archipelago, has 336 rainy days a year. Mountainous regions usually appropriate more than their fair share of moisture. Such is Baguio, in Luzon, which prevalent winds and lofty surrounding terrain have made one of the wettest spots on earth; or the summit of volcanic

Waialeale on Kauai, where the year 1916 registered a rainfall of over 560 inches.

But the one region which best suggests the deluge of Genesis centers around Cherrapunji, in northeastern India. Here the saturated monsoons recoil from the Himalayas to dump their excess moisture. To add to the effect, almost all the annual rainfall, which may reach 905 inches, is concentrated in five months. On a particularly moist day this rainfall measured 41 inches, or nearly three feet and a half. Yet beyond the mountain lie the semiarid plains of Asia interspersed with deserts.

The East Indies seem to be the favored locale of thunder showers, for Buitenzorg, Java, has heard it thunder during 322 of the 365 days of the year.

A combination of ocean currents, prevalent winds, and curious geographical formation has made Australia the most arid of continents. A wet shell partially encloses a vast, dry interior which presents so far unsolved problems in development.

In polar regions, where the cold air neither absorbs nor yields up moisture readily, precipitation is relatively light. Hence the continental icecaps of Greenland and Antarctica, with less snowfall than Scotland, may be actually decreasing. The North Pole is a region of perpetual calm, which extends far south of Latitude 90. Whalers, frozen all winter in arctic ice, have told me that the silence was almost more depressing than the darkness and the cold, though Stefansson and others speak of the growl and crunch of ice and even the audible whirring sizzle of the aurora borealis.

While speculation about the most favorable climate is endless, there seems little doubt about the worst. Aside from lofty mountain peaks, this has been located in Adelie Land, on the edge of Antarctica. Although the cold is less severe than in northern Siberia, the almost continual winds, sweeping downward from the icecap around the South Pole, render living conditions all but impossible. Sir Douglas Mawson, who wintered there, found that the average wind velocity the year around exceeded fifty miles per hour. At times it taxed the capacity of the recording instruments, with an estimated speed of two hundred miles. Such winds, coupled with subzero temperatures, are like a breath from outer space. No wonder Sir Douglas affirmed that a long and happy life elsewhere could hardly compensate for a single year spent in Adelie Land. It is the winds rather than the cold that make the Cape Horn region and the lofty tableland of Tibet so forbidding.

The Caribbean Sea is the playground of the dreaded West Indies hurricanes, that mow swaths of destruction across the tropics. Even more calamitous, because of their wider range and more densely peopled areas, are the typhoons of the Far East. These periodic paroxysms seem to follow a seasonal curve, for though almost unknown in February, and rare in spring, they are relatively frequent from July to November.

Climate has a profound influence upon human health. Pulmonary affections flourish in the enervating heat of the tropics, heart ailments and nerve disorders in the more bracing temperate zones, with their challenge to undue exertion; dampness predisposes to rheumatism, dryness to eye troubles: ailments quite independent of localized germ origins such as malaria or African sleeping sickness.

Recent studies have thrown some light upon the happy medium. S. F. Markham's investigations led him to believe that the best outdoor temperature for men at rest is 75–80 degrees Fahrenheit, with a slight motion of the air. Indoors that temperature would vary with the clothing worn, from 60 to 76, with humidity ranging from 40 to 70.

Dr. Huntington found conditions for the best physical

or mental work quite divergent. Mental processes, he thought, were stimulated in a relatively lower temperature. By plotting the annual growth rings on the stumps of giant sequoia trees, he even linked periods of excessive dryness with mass migrations from Central Asia and corresponding disturbances in Europe.

Ancient civilizations originated in regions now inhabited by backward races. Spreading out from the Nile, the Euphrates, and the Indus River valleys, they clung to the 70th Isotherm, where temperatures neither enervated by their warmth nor depressed by their chill. Modern civilization has flourished best in that global belt which includes New York, London, Paris, and Peking. Here fairly wide fluctuations of both temperature and moisture prevail. Although few would consider such a climate ideal, it seems to have brought out the best in human endeavor.

Buckle, claiming that civilization, like a tree, has its roots in soil and climate, even assigned world religions to the same origin. To him the stern theology of Scotland was a natural product of rocky soil, chill mist, and a diet of oatmeal. On the one hand Norse mythology had its frost giants; on the other, India its Shiva, the destroyer, a deity appropriate to that burning climate. Perhaps the fierce fanaticism of Mohammed's warriors gained impetus from the hot sands of Arabia.

Man has developed both clothing and shelter suited to the climate. Ski enthusiasts dress for the occasion, as do beach loungers at Miami. The Eskimo's furs are a counterpart of the Hindu's loincloth. Within doors temperature may be controlled by steam heat and air conditioning. Even the wattled huts of the East Indies yield coolness and shade, while the igloo, buried in snowdrifts, may harbor tropic heat.

Such adaptability, now that the western march of civilization has girdled the globe, is leading man to branch out toward both the Equator and the poles. Sometimes he has even succeeded in modifying climatic extremes. The felling of forests and draining of muskeg swamps in western Canada has retarded the frost line two weeks or more. Smudge fires in orange groves may raise the temperature above the danger mark, by heating "all outdoors." Irrigation tempers extremes of heat and cold and increases humidity. Conversely, when Mongol raiders destroyed the canals of Babylonia, they transformed a garden into a desert.

Even animals enjoy some escapes from unfavorable climatic conditions. In bitter weather musk oxen and reindeer gather for mutual warmth, while their steaming breath generates a protective cloud above them. Cows, in summer, seek the shade of some great tree, just as marine life plunges beneath the heated surface. Some animals construct homes that fairly rival human edifices for comfort—the beaver, for example. Others hibernate, while many animals and more birds migrate to avoid undesirable seasonal changes.

More fascinating but obscure are speculations over global fluctuations in temperature. That the world was once warmer is proved by coal beds in Greenland and Antarctica; that it was once colder is equally certain from glacial scratches and moraines. Since wide variations over vast intervals of time have prevailed upon this planet, there is little reason to assume that our present climate is static.

Such discussions, however, belong rather to another chapter. Meanwhile, whether this world of ours is growing warmer or colder, the seas, which are the source of so much of our global climate, remain a permanent check against abrupt or extreme variations.

CHAPTER XXXII

Oceans of Ice

In thrilling region of thick-ribbed ice.
SHAKESPEARE

Changing temperatures have profoundly changed the seas. The history of our planet, as geologists decipher it from rock strata, reveals a warm climate interrupted by prolonged yet relatively brief intervals of cold. Then the oceans overflowed as the snows of many winters formed ice fields of continental size. In the most recent of these dismal eras primitive man shivered in drafty caverns, while outside the hairy mammoth and the woolly rhinoceros waded through ever deepening drifts. Millions of square miles where flowers had bloomed were buried beneath ice which scoured the mountains, while it widened and deepened the valleys.

That frozen ocean vastly altered the surface of the earth. The most prominent relic is perhaps the lakes which pit the maps of Minnesota and Finland like the smallpox. These, scooped out, then filled by melting ice, are slowly drying up. Thousands have disappeared, but other thousands remain. Much larger lakes developed, while even our Great Lakes were remodeled. River systems were also reorganized upon a gigantic scale.

Scarcely less noticeable are some of the terminal moraines, scraped from the face of the earth to be piled up at the edges. Cape Cod and Long Island are such moraines. Shallows like Georges and the Grand Banks are remnants of islands thus formed, only to be swallowed up by the sea.

Less pretentious are the winding ridges known as eskers, once river beds in the ice; sand plains, that were former deltas; and those cigar-shaped hills called drumlins, smoothed and molded by the ice. In certain parts of the Northern Hemisphere such remains dominate the landscape.

Innumerable boulders were wrenched loose and scattered broadcast. Moving ice, unlike rivers or currents, can float rocks or run uphill with the thrust of millions of tons behind it. One of the largest recorded boulders in the Western Hemisphere is in the town of Madison in New Hampshire: ninety feet long, forty wide, and thirty-eight high, its weight is estimated at ten thousand tons. Yet a still larger fragment is reported from the banks of the Little Miami, a tributary of the Ohio River. This is a mass of Silurian limestone, just over an acre in extent, from five to seventeen feet in thickness, with an estimated weight of thirteen and a half thousand tons. Yet it was the veriest plaything for the frost giants of the ice age.

Some boulders were left upon quite different rock, so nicely balanced that they can be tilted by the human hand. Traced to the parent ledge, they show the direction of glacial flow, which is also indicated by innumerable scratches.

The effects of so vast an ice invasion were no less marked upon the sea. Such wholesale subtraction of waters wrought a twofold change. The salinity of the oceans was temporarily increased, for the snows which congealed as ice were fresh. But much more significant was a lowering of sea level all over the world. How far this extended is uncertain, for we can only guess at the volume of the ice. Daly thinks the level subsided at least three hundred feet; Professor Shepard hazards an extreme twenty-three hundred. In any case shallow bays were then dry land, while the edges of the continents approached, if they did not surpass, the boundaries of the continental shelves. Hudson Bay, the Baltic, and much if not all the North Sea were dry or filled with solid ice, while innumerable islands appeared which are now submerged. Bridges connecting nearby continental masses were probably established. The Black Sea and the Mediterranean became salt lakes.

Not only did the ice age lower the level of the seas, but there is some evidence that it depressed the surface of the land. Daly believes that Greenland is bowl-shaped under the weight of ice. He also finds that Finland, once buried to a depth of thousands of feet, is rising as the earth crust, long depressed, slowly displays its natural elasticity. Hence he forecasts a future when the Gulf of Bothnia will become— what it was in the late ice age—a fresh-water lake.

We may gain an inkling of this absorbing chapter in earth's history by a glance at the ice fields that remain. For we seem to be emerging from the last glacial period with enormous territories still buried. Ignoring mountain glaciers, mere ice rivers from surplus snows, or even the considerable areas in Iceland and the arctic islands, there are still two great ice fields of imposing size. The Greenland cap, thousands of feet thick, emerges through rocky fiords to break off in those bergs which drift southward to menace navigation. A much more extensive field covers Antarctica, even extending far to sea. The famous Ross Barrier is a sheet of floating ice as large as France, five hundred to fifteen hundred feet in thickness, that drifts away in islands, sometimes fifty miles long, into the circumpolar whirl. In one section of this frozen continent, aptly called the Devil's Graveyard, Admiral Byrd, in a single day, counted over eight thousand bergs.

Ingenious methods have been devised to probe the ice. In Swiss glaciers drilling operations have penetrated the rocky surfaces. These are laborious and difficult, due to the slow but continuous movement of the ice. That magic instrument, the seismograph, designed to trace the origin of earth tremors, is useful here. Daly exploded dynamite upon glacial surfaces to read the seismograph. The tremors through the ice, quite different from those through solid rock, gave a rough cross section. The maximum thickness of Greenland ice, so far examined, is approximately eighty-seven hundred feet, or over a mile and a half.

Conditions in Antarctica are less clearly understood. While the icecap is vastly larger, some five million square miles, there is reason to believe that the depth is less. The Antarctic continent seems to be an inverted bowl some ten thousand feet high. But as lofty mountains are known and a tableland suspected, the average thickness of the ice may not exceed twenty-five hundred feet.

The last great ice age is supposed to have reached its peak some twenty thousand years ago, and to have finished its major melting in about eleven thousand years. Three great ice fields originating in North America had gradually spread outward until they coalesced to cover practically all Canada and much of the United States. At its maximum this super field embraced approximately four million square miles. Its thickness is conjectural, yet there is some evidence for an estimate. The tip of Mount Washington seems to have emerged, but this is far from the ice center. There a thickness of ten thousand feet seems reasonable, in view of the known depth of the smaller Greenland icecap. Professor Shepard even estimates a possible 20,000 feet. Under the force of gravity this enormous mass spread slowly outward from the central foci. Local climates were altered, for an ice field is a region of unbroken winter. Wind currents and storm paths were diverted. The precipitation of moisture from the chill air over the central mass declined to increase around the edges with greater accumulations of snow and ice. And so the slow-moving deluge of death spread southward, beyond the Ohio River and far down the plains of Nebraska and Kansas. Meanwhile in northern Europe a similar panorama was unfolding upon a lesser scale. Somewhere in the Scandinavian territory or over what is now the northern arm of the Baltic, a similar ice field, perhaps 5000 feet thick, spread over northern Europe and a section of Asia, engulfing much of the British Isles and Germany, until at its maximum it covered two million square miles. Meanwhile other ice fields increased, while mountain glaciers crept lower until perhaps twelve million of the fifty-seven million square miles of earth's surface, or rather more than a fifth, was buried. To speak of this tremendous accumulation as an ocean is no exaggeration, for its depth was impressive even from marine standards, and it would have covered nearly half the Indian Ocean.

Geologists, like astronomers, deal in big numbers. Their eras are millions of years. But as estimates are necessarily predicated upon meager data, we find wide disagreement on dates and durations. Over the past million years, however, there is evidence that our Midwestern states experienced five or perhaps six glacial periods, that may have been minor ebbs and flows of one vast icecap whose life span extended over several hundred thousand, perhaps even a million years.

This seeming eternity is only a minor interval in the story of our planet. Moreover, it appears to have been but one of several interruptions in the prevalent global warmth, nor even the most important of these. Still wider areas seem to have been overspread with ice in Permian, and perhaps also in Pre-Cambrian times—dates that range from two hundred million years ago to half a billion!

How do geologists know these things? As ice fields advance, they grind the surface of the rocks into a characteristic boulder clay. This is mixed with pebbles and scratched boulders to form glacial till, which solidifies into tillite. Often such deposits are overlaid with sedimentary rocks whose fossils reveal their later origin. Laboriously, one by one, the geologist turns the pages of the rocks until he gets furtive glimpses into a fabulous antiquity. There are pockets of tillite more than two thousand feet thick that are believed to date back to the most ancient Huronian rocks, perhaps a billion years ago. Such relics are evidences of an Ice Age of terrible severity, even in that remote era.

Mingled with these super ice ages are others of lesser prominence. Some six or seven have been strongly indicated, if not definitely proven. Glacial periods have left some trace upon the rocks far back into Archean times, before the earliest flicker of life upon this planet.

Just why these singular phenomena occurred still baffles the experts. But first let us examine two or three primary facts. It has been pretty definitely established that a lowering of the global climate by ten degrees, if maintained long enough, would bring about an ice age. Continental ice fields are a delicate balance between freeze and thaw, between summer heat and winter cold. Where that balance tends a bit toward winter, ice accumulates to grow by what it feeds upon. Our own climate is affected by the Greenland icecap. We can but dimly appreciate how much the North American weather was disturbed when that icecap extended into Kentucky! In the second place, cold is not the only consideration. Precipitation is quite as essential. At Verkhoyansk, Siberia, although the soil has been reported frozen to a depth of over seven hundred feet, no ice field has ever formed. When North America groaned beneath its white burden, there was no ice field in the colder interior of Alaska. Again, continental icecaps never originate around the North Pole to spread southward. In fact the three foci of the great North American icecap were in the Rocky Mountain region, a point west of Hudson Bay and somewhere in the province of Ontario. From them ice spread in every direction, north as well as south. Elsewhere mountain ranges, prevailing winds, and other conditions prevented any icy accumulation. The winter snowfall was melted by the brief but almost continuous sunlight of summer.

Attempts to explain the origins of glacial periods are threefold: terrestrial, meteorological, and astronomical.

Professor Schuchert has drawn up an elaborate table to prove that ice ages coincide with periods of land elevation. As temperature falls roughly one degree for every climb of three hundred feet, an elevation of three thousand feet would lower local temperature the necessary ten degrees. But there is a vast difference between a global lowering of ten degrees and a merely local one; besides, at least two of the foci of the most recent ice age were in areas of low elevation.

Croll suspected the eccentricity of the earth's orbit, and particularly of the ecliptic. True, the earth wobbles a bit drunkenly. Its axis weaves an irregular orbit among the stars in a period of some fourteen months. This variation of thirty feet may, it has been argued, have been greater once, enough to disturb the balance between summer and winter. However, since glacial periods occurred presumably at the same time, both north and south of the Equator, this explanation seems inconclusive.

Wegener advances his theory of drifting continents. But even he would hardly have claimed that New England was so near the Pole twenty thousand years ago as to support five thousand feet of ice!

More intriguing are meteorological speculations. Chamberlain stressed varying amounts of carbon dioxide in the atmosphere. Though comprising only about 3 volumes in

10,000 volumes of air, this gas imprisons the sun's rays like the glass of a conservatory. At least two hundred times as much carbon occurs in coal beds as is now suspended in the atmosphere. Fluctuations in atmospheric content would, he thought, produce a resultant warmth or chill.

Humphreys emphasized volcanic dust as a modifier of climate. Though true, there is no evidence of any vast outpouring, particularly in the regions where ice accumulated.

Spitaler thought that oceans chilled during the ice age remained cold for great periods, thus lowering the global temperature. Storm centers and wind routes also shifted because of the ice fields, but these are rather results than causes. It has, however, been urged that the Gulf Stream may once have flowed through the Isthmus of Panama to chill northwestern Europe. But how explain the extensive ice fields in South Africa, Patagonia, New Zealand, Tasmania, and Australia, as well as in Central Asia?

Most fascinating of all are forays into space that seek a cause in solar or stellar disturbances. Since the sun is the source of radiant energy, any fundamental alteration would affect the earth's supply. Periods of sunspot activity occur in cycles of approximately eleven years. In other words, our sun is a variable star. May not that variability pursue much wider cycles that swing to greater extremes? The thought is arresting, although there is no present evidence to sustain it.

Interstellar space, in some directions, seems strewn with cosmic dust. As our sun journeys on at a speed of eleven miles per second, it may wander through one of these dust-filled corridors, thus cutting down solar radiation. Here again we find an alluring hypothesis that lacks proof. Civilization is still too young to plot any such celestial calendar.

And now where do these speculations leave us? Most of them must be discarded because they do not explain. Perhaps no one theory suffices; several may be required. Frankly, we do not know enough at present to be sure.

Of more definite interest are changing trends in climate. These have been unmistakable in the past. Coleman found that the loftiest tree in Spitsbergen was a willow scarcely three inches high with leaves half an inch long. Yet there were coal seams not far off. Antarctica also has coal seams and remains of tree trunks 18 inches in diameter! Conversely, in Central India, one of the hottest regions on the globe, there are extensive glacial deposits, while those in South Central Africa extended hundreds of miles to overlap Madagascar. Our global climate certainly has changed.

Is it changing now? Professor Gregory, by a study of date palms and grape vineyards, concludes that the Mediterranean climate is about what it was in Old Testament times. Yet the cedars of Lebanon are growing upon glacial deposits! There is some evidence that grains flourished in medieval Iceland which cannot be grown there now, while ocean ice fluctuates over cycles of a little less than five years. The lost Norse colonies in Greenland may have enjoyed more abundant resources than that region now affords. And yet Dr. Brooks believes that the polar ice fields are receding and that sea levels the world over are rising a fraction of an inch a century. Both Alaskan and Swiss glaciers are melting, while there is reason to believe that the icecap in sullen Antarctica is building up more slowly than it wears away at the edges.

Goldschmidt has estimated that one sixtieth of all ocean water is still locked in existing icecaps. This seems unimportant. Yet the melted waters would fill the entire arctic basin, with the Mediterranean and the Sea of Japan thrown in for good measure!

If another era of unusual warmth should occur, such as brought verdure to arctic islands, this melting ice would inundate every seaport in the world and flood vast continental areas. For it would raise the surface of all the seas at least a hundred feet. Conversely, another glacial period would block every seaport with impassable shoals or dry land, and crush many beneath mile depths of ice.

It has been urged that the intervals between ice ages are noticeably shortening, that the earth is passing through a vast descending cycle where warmth declines and cold grows more intense until our planet will expire beneath an icy shroud. Then, as the sun's rays fail, we may draw over the frozen seas a still colder mantle of solidified air sixty feet thick!

True, such a chill conclusion is only fantastic speculation of what might happen in some far-off aeon. But few episodes in planetary history offer more food for sobering thought than those mysterious periods when oceans of ice overflowed the earth.

CHAPTER XXXIII

Islands

Some unsuspected isle in far-off seas.
ROBERT BROWNING

We are all islanders. Our continents are surrounded by the seas; our globe itself is but an island in space. Convenience, however, classifies as islands land masses bigger than rocks but smaller than continents, a division sometimes vague and elastic.

Largest of islands is Greenland, with an area of 836,000 square miles. It is the refrigerator of the Northern Hemisphere. The Norsemen discovered it and, anticipating modern real estate promoters, called it Greenland. Only scattered relics remain of their lost colonies, although a few white men cling to the rocky western shores with Eskimos farther north.

Most extensive of habitable islands, however, is New Guinea, that sinister semicontinent that projects from the East Indies far out into the Pacific. More than fourteen hundred miles long, if one end were placed on New York City the other would reach nearly to Denver. Much of its three hundred and twelve thousand square miles of area is as dark as Africa and even less explored. First sighted by the Portuguese adventurer, Don Jorges de Menese, in 1526, its mountainous spine shows peaks loftier than the Alps. Home of the most savage and depraved head-hunters, its jungles glitter with gorgeous birds of paradise.

Unequaled among oriental isles, is Java, that tropic Eden, marred by thirty active volcanoes and one hundred and twenty-five volcanic cones. Here the ruins of a once extensive empire crumble in the humid atmosphere. Though much of its surface is uninhabitable, it is the most densely populated region in the world, for within boundaries roughly equal to the state of Pennsylvania are crowded over forty-three million people.

Most notable of island investments is Manhattan, purchased by thrifty Dutchmen for twenty-four dollars and now assessed for something over eight billion. Its population did not all overflow to Brooklyn and the mainland. Instead they evolved a unique architecture to become cliff dwellers in a jungle of skyscrapers.

The Pacific is the Ocean of Islands. They sprinkle its southern area. The main channel of the Atlantic is rather free, but islands cluster in the West Indies and clot the icy arctic basin. Such extensive areas as Baffin Land, Victoria and Ellesmere Islands, now bleak and all but uninhabited, might, if more favorably located, have become the site of whole civilizations.

The Indian Ocean has relatively few islands, except Ceylon and gigantic Madagascar. But in that median territory, where it meets the Pacific, the East Indies, most extensive and far the richest island group on earth, sweep across an arc of forty-five hundred miles.

Island dwellers, lured by the sea, have done more than their share in spreading civilization. Islands breed mariners by necessity. Moreover, protected by the sea, they have enjoyed immunities in a war-ravaged world. Ancient Tyre, though adjacent to the mainland, once withstood a siege of thirteen years by Nebuchadnezzar, King of Babylon. Even Alexander the Great spent nearly a year of his brief life in subduing the formidable fortress before proceeding on his Asiatic conquests. Relative freedom from outside interference permitted England to develop a government founded upon personal liberty. Napoleon scowled at the "wet ditch" of Dover Strait, as did Hitler, more recently, but neither found a way across. Japan was also protected by her narrow seas from the ferocious Mongol invasions of the Middle Ages.

Islands, from remotest times, have been favored of the gods. The Greeks had their Golden Islands of the Hesperides. Perhaps these were the Canary Islands, with their familiar yellow songsters; possibly Madeira, still the land of flowers to jaded Britishers. In islands we seek an ideal climate: the Azores with perpetual spring, or Hawaii, land of unbroken summer. Most of us have turned a wistful glance toward some palm-fringed islet in Balboa's Great South Sea as a refuge from irksome modern life. Like Sancho Panza, we may even covet a small island of our own.

In fancy, then, we might borrow the wings of the albatross or frigate bird for a glance at a few islets peculiarly alluring or forbidding. Isolated ones are always lonely, especially in lonely seas. Such an island, or rather archipelago, lies in a remote area of the Indian Ocean, some two thousand miles southeast of Madagascar. It is called Kerguelen, from the Frenchman Kerguélen-Trémarec who discovered it in 1772. More descriptive of the largest number of the group is its other name—Desolation Island. Eighty-five miles long, with an area of 1400 square miles, roughly that of the state of Rhode Island, it culminates in 6120-foot Mount Ross. The precipitous coast is deeply indented, one fiord, Royal Sound, offering magnificent harborage with twenty miles of landlocked waters. But no ships are anchored there. Penguins and other sea birds pre-empt its sea views, while the beaches are given over to the remnants of a once great herd of sea elephants. Though damp (it rains nearly all the year) the mean temperature hovers about 40 degrees. Strange vegetation flourishes: tussock grass in clumps many feet high, and the queer Kerguelen cabbage that furnished food for such scientific expeditions as that of the *Challenger* and Captain Cook. In 1825, John Neun and three companion sealers were shipwrecked there to pass nearly three years of Robinson Crusoe existence. When their clothing gave out, they sewed new garments from sea leopard skins, with threads of blackfish tendon and buttons of whalebone. Sea elephants furnished the leather for stout moccasins; smoking pipes were fashioned from their teeth—the hollow stems were wing bones of albatross. Purses they made from seal flippers and albatross feet. One of them lived for some time in a hut he fashioned by tilting a whale's skull against an overhanging cliff, reinforced with rafters of whalebone and roofed with sea elephant skins. Their larder of seal meat, fish, and penguin eggs was eked out with Kerguelen cabbage; their nocturnal wanderings were lighted by the "burning mountain," an active volcano. Once one of them nearly lost his life when he sank to the shoulders in a bog hole. They wrote their experiences with splinters of bone, using albatross gall for ink. But numberless such adventurers have lived and died and been forgotten.

From the icebound continent of Antarctica, frozen together and known as Graham Land, a group of islands points like a bony finger toward Cape Horn. They are fringed by a lesser archipelago, the South Shetlands. No one lives on them, save sea birds and occasional seals. Nowhere on earth is there lonelier, bleaker scenery. Most interesting of the latter group is that speck upon the map known as Deception Island. Nearly circular, it rises grandly from the sea. Early voyagers steered through a precipitous passage six hundred feet wide into a landlocked basin one hundred fathoms deep and five miles across. The walls smoked omi-

nously, for Deception Island is the shell of a burned-out volcano that reared above the frozen seas to be engulfed again.
Perhaps it once glared as redly as Mount Erebus, which still
illuminates the southern polar night.

North of Iceland and rather nearer Greenland than the
bluff Norwegian coast is another lonely island, seventeen
miles long by five broad, called Jan Mayen, for the Dutch explorer who landed there in 1614. The Norsemen seemed
to have preceded him, however, for this is perhaps the original Svalbard, or Cold Coast, of their sagas, while Henry
Hudson sighted it in 1607. An Austrian expedition once
spent a year on Jan Mayen, which is dominated by the
colossal volcano Beerenberg, more than eight thousand feet
high and thirty miles in circumference. At various times it
has erupted, like the more famous Hecla in Iceland, to send
lava hissing into the sea, suggesting the "scoriac rivers" in
Edgar Allan Poe's poem *Ulalume*, "That groan as they roll
down Mt. Yaanek In the realms of the Boreal pole."

Stranger still, the waters from the lake which fills the
crater escape as a glacier, a river of ice from the heart of a
dying volcano.

Norway maintains a meteorological station on Jan Mayen
which flashes weather forecasts to the fishermen of Lofoten.

Far into the Arctic, from the mouth of the Yana River,
one of the coldest spots on earth, stretch a group of islands
known as New Siberia. The Russian Sanitov, in 1810,
found that on the nearest of these islands "the whole soil
seems to consist of bones," mainly of the hairy mammoth
and woolly rhinoceros. On another island he discovered a
flint knife and "an axe made of Mammoth tusk." Who left
them there? More modern relics appeared on Kotelny
Island, the remains of a wreck and a hut constructed from
the wreckage. Within was furniture of reindeer antlers, a
spear, and a copper kettle! What seekers of the Northeast

Passage found shipwreck there? On the southern shore of one of these strange islands are the so-called wooden hills. Wrangel thus describes them: "The shore rises twenty fathoms abruptly from the sea. . . . Here are embedded . . . planks in heaps of fifty, sometimes more, sometimes less . . . with the ends cropping out . . . the thickest two and three-fourths inches . . . the wood brittle . . . semi hard . . . of a black color faintly shining . . . imperfectly combustible . . . and with a pitchy smell." He also mentions horns of the woolly rhinoceros, which superstitious natives mistook for the claws of gigantic birds!

Nearly midway in that narrow waistline of the Atlantic, between Africa and South America, rises a singular islet surrounded by ledges called St. Paul's Rocks. The central mass, about sixty feet high, is the perch of sea birds and the eyrie of climbing crabs. Just what it is doing out there in mid-ocean puzzled Darwin, for it does not seem to be volcanic. Is it the remnant of a once larger island or the beginning of a new one? Who knows?

Fifty-six miles southwest of Cape Horn lie those sinister rocks named Diego Ramirez, for the Spanish pilot who first sighted them. The largest, a mile and a half long, towers in sheer cliffs 587 feet high above the stormiest ocean on earth. Great icebergs, torn from the Antarctic Barrier, drift by, with mountainous "graybeards" in an endless procession before howling westerly gales. No one lives on these islands, or could live there. No one ever visits them save wretched seal hunters from Tierra del Fuego. No lighthouse marks their site, but passing ships give them a wide berth. Shipwreck against those pitiless cliffs is certain death!

Tropic heat may be quite as inclement as polar cold. Far off the coast of Ecuador, bisected by the Equator, is a group of volcanic cones called the Galápagos Islands. The largest, Albemarle, is rather more than seventy-five miles in extent.

Often volcanoes pour forth a lush fertility, as in Hawaii and Java; these are only gigantic cinder heaps. Eccentric hermits have tried to live there, but the only permanent residents, aside from sea birds, are huge lizards and still huger turtles, probably the longest-lived of any animal. Some of them weigh several hundred pounds, while at least one individual survived for 165 years! Whalers captured these turtles for fresh meat. Melville, who visited the Galápagos in his wanderings about the South Pacific, said that there the voice of Nature was a hiss!

In the heart of the fabulously rich East Indies rise the sinister peaks of Komodo Island. Though of considerable extent, it has remained largely uninhabited. It is the home of the Komodo lizards, largest of land species, which are sometimes ten feet long and weigh two hundred and fifty pounds. Ferocious as they are repulsive, they attack wild pigs. Sole relic of the bygone age when dinosaurs ruled the world, they may have suggested to the Chinese their national emblem—the dragon. But bizarre life has developed, like rank vegetation, in isolated islands, shut off from the great biological tides that elsewhere swept away the archaic and unfit.

Bird life is particularly characteristic. Mauritius had its great flightless parrot and its ponderous dodo, now both extinct. Largest of recent birds was the moa of New Zealand, which seems to have survived until the Maoris came. Bones of this bird and even fragments of the skin have been found in caves, surrounded by the embers of long extinguished campfires. An ungainly creature, the larger moas were taller and very much heavier than the ostrich. In Madagascar once lived the Aepyornis, which, though not so large as the moa, laid the hugest of all eggs. These, which are eight times the size of an ostrich egg, are occasionally unearthed in bogs. No doubt from one of these eggs sprung the fabled roc of Sindbad the Sailor.

Many islands are entirely pre-empted by birds. Pelicans and cormorants congregate by the millions on the guano islands of Peru. These have been a mine of fertilizer since the days of the Incas. Sometimes a giant condor, sweeping down from the Andes, plows a swath of death through swarming chicks and eggs. Other islands are the home of albatross, penguins, and arctic sea birds.

Islands are also sanctuaries for fur-bearing animals. Most famous are the Pribilofs, shrouded in impenetrable mist in the heart of Bering Sea. Though first sighted by Joan Synd in 1767, they were really discovered by Gerasim Pribilof in 1786. This enterprising Cossack, hearing from natives of great seal rookeries farther north, went to seek them. Though hidden in the fog, he heard the roar of millions of seal voices when miles away. There are four islets in this group, some three hundred miles from the mainland. St. Paul, the largest and site of the most famous of all seal rookeries, Novastoshnok, has an area of thirty-five square miles; the smallest, Walrus Island, has only sixty-four acres. The merciless slaughter of the seals has already been noted. Under governmental restrictions the herds have been largely restored, until at least two million seals now journey annually to the Pribilofs. The males, fierce and aggressive, shift for themselves; but the females, which winter along the California coast, are escorted northward on their three-thousand-mile migrations, by Coast Guard ships. Some four hundred natives share the Pribilofs with arctic foxes and herds of reindeer. From the seal's viewpoint, the fogs are ideal, as they form a canopy against the glare of the arctic sun. A percentage of three-year-old males is annually slaughtered. So far the Pribilofs have yielded a revenue of more than sixty million dollars, or many times the purchase price of all Alaska.

Islands are sometimes the site of unique mineral deposits. Such is Trinidad, in the West Indies, close to South

America. Columbus named it from three sister hills. He sailed through the narrow straits he named the Serpent's Mouth and the Dragon's Mouth, which separate it from the continent, without even suspecting the presence of the mainland. On Trinidad is that bottomless lake of asphalt whose tarry product Sir Walter Raleigh used to calk his ships. Although millions of dollars' worth have been removed, the supply seems inexhaustible.

Certain vegetable products are also associated with islands. The tiny Banda group in the East Indies is the original home of the nutmeg; while Ceylon still has its "cinnamon fields." From prehistoric times Socotra, in the Arabian Sea, has been called the Isle of Frankincense. The Greeks knew it vaguely as Dioscorides. Nearly seventy-five miles long, with a maximum width of twenty, its Granite Mountains, rising above 4600 feet, are clothed nearly to the summits with "incense-bearing" trees. The Arabian geographer Edrisi claimed that Socotra had been visited by an expedition sent by Alexander the Great. Nestorian Christians seem to have flocked there in the Middle Ages, before Mohammedan invasions engulfed them. Somaliland, not far away, was probably the "cinnamon coast" of Ptolemy. Along Socotran cliffs are strange inscriptions cut in the rock, thought to be of Ethiopian origin. Ambergris used to wash ashore and was an article of export. But the "sweet savor" of burning incense has mingled with religious observances from King Solomon's temple to the modern cathedral.

In the Solomons, where populations overflow, the natives have actually constructed small islets in shallow seas. Islands have also been pumped up along the coast of Florida. But man is an indifferent builder compared with the lowly polyps. Many coral islands are clothed in verdure; others, mere sand and rock, have been called "the bleached bones" of islands. Some, rising but a few feet above sea level, are swept clean by typhoons; a few are even swallowed up by high-course tides.

The mutineers on Pitcairn burned all bridges to the civilized world. But even lonelier is Tristan da Cunha, a truncated volcanic cone far down the South Atlantic. Here, shut off for years at a time from the outside world, dwell a few score rugged individualists who, whatever they may miss of excitement, avoid the stresses of our too complex civilization.

Some islands have been put to base uses as gigantic prisons. Of evil memory is Devil's Island (well named), the French penal colony off the malarial jungles of Guiana. And St. Helena will always be invested with the melancholy grandeur of Napoleon I.

Islands offer biologists convenient steppingstones in tracing life to neighboring continents. The marsupials of Australia suggest a link with Asia, that was broken far back in geological time. Wild life in the East Indies hints at former land bridges that alternately rose and were submerged. The tiger and the rhinoceros of Java and Sumatra are unknown in Borneo, but the orangutan of Borneo and Sumatra is alien to Java. Such tangled threads of animal and plant geography are well-nigh numberless.

Of greater interest are human relics. Easter Island, in a remote corner of the Pacific, seems to have developed the only written language in Polynesia. Its forest of stone faces, sometimes twenty feet high, staring out across an empty sea, have hinted at more extensive populations and territories. Disciples of the lost continent of Mu have found here a fertile field. Though their theories are not widely credited, Easter Island remains an ocean enigma.

More interesting than coral islands are those of volcanic origin. Such are the Aleutians that stretch from Alaska in a wide arc toward Asia. Largest of the group is Unimak, called by its Russian discoverers "the roof of Hell." Among its several active craters is Mount Pogrammi, in native dialect, "the Black Destroying Death," from its clouds of volcanic dust and smothering gasses. Most easterly of the chain is Attu, pitted with bomb craters and whitened by the bones of Japanese soldiers.

But perhaps most intriguing of all are those shifting islets which are still being remodeled. Some years ago inhabitants fled Verde Island, off Luzon, because it "seemed to be sinking into the sea." Iwo Jima, the scene of recent bloody history, is one of a group long known as the Volcano Islands. Before the war Pacific Ocean pilots warned shipping of peculiar dangers there, since "in an active volcanic area new ones may appear. In 1903 an islet formed about three miles northeast of Minami, attaining an elevation of 480 feet. In 1904 it had become a low reef less than ten feet high. A new island was formed by the eruption of a submarine volcano on January 25, 1914, two miles in circumference and 400 feet high." In 1916 this island had disappeared and a depth of a hundred and forty fathoms was reported.

In 1880 the United States steamer *Alert* observed an upsurge of ashes with a strong smell of sulphur. At night flames burst forth. Yet when the abysmal fireworks ended, only a crescent-shaped patch of discolored water remained. Later soundings revealed a shoal eight fathoms deep.

From such troubled seas rises Sofugan, known to sailors as Lot's Wife. A sheer pinnacle of rock 326 feet high, it overhangs like a gigantic tooth. Twenty-fathom soundings all around reveal no bottom. Whence arose this grotesque monstrosity? The bursting forth of subterranean fires surely adds novelty to the commoner perils of navigation!

The Aleutians also present an example of fusing and disappearing islands in Bogoslof. When discovered in 1790, it was a jagged mountain now called Castle Island. In the late

1880s a new formation, Fire Island, rose smoking from the seas some distance away. Between 1905 and 1907 two other peaks appeared. By 1908, however, both had vanished, leaving a black ridge thirteen hundred feet high connecting Fire with Castle Island.

Such episodes may explain islands that seem to have been swallowed up like ships in the night. Ganges Island, in the Pacific, appears on many maps, yet Japanese investigations, before the war, reported a depth of nearly a thousand fathoms. Entire island groups have been lost. No doubt crude methods of recording latitude and longitude have been largely at fault, but known changes in the ocean floor prove that such disappearances may not be wholly mythical.

Vitus Bering, sailing back through the narrow strait which bears his name, discovered the two islands known as the Diomedes. The lesser, Little Diomede, is of special interest. A sheer rock rising abruptly from the sea, it presents a table-land about two miles long by one wide. Around the single landing place the Russian Kobelev, in 1779, found 160 natives living in curious stone huts. Wales, Alaska, the point on North America nearest to Asia, looms sullenly across a twenty-two-mile stretch of water. Diomede's beetling cliffs, towering thirteen hundred feet, are favorite nesting places for myriads of murres, cormorants, kittiwakes, and puffins. Three miles farther off is Great Diomede; somewhere between runs the boundary line that separates America from the Union of Soviet Republics. How nearly do two world empires of divergent races, languages, and systems of government approach in the Diomedes! Will their Gibraltar-like flanks ever bristle with guns? To indulge in such speculations in a world still prostrate from the last war is merely to avoid their ominous implications. Surely it would be a tragedy to disturb the harmless sea birds.

CHAPTER XXXIV

Capes—The Turning Points of History

Round the cape of a sudden came the sea,
And the sun looked over the mountain's rim.
                                    BROWNING
He saw them, headland after headland stretch
Far on into the rich heart of the west.
                                    TENNYSON
A forked mountain or blue promontory
With trees upon it.
                                    SHAKESPEARE

Capes are turning points in history. Like giant fingers thrust into the sea, they have always beckoned voyagers to what lay beyond. Shakespeare caught the glamor in his matchless line, "To unpath'd waters, undream'd shores." This is the lure of the unknown.

Many capes have appropriate names. What word could better describe the 500-foot cliff that marks Scotland's northernmost limit than Cape Wrath? A sand prong on the Carolina coast is properly identified as Cape Fear; a rocky bluff in Washington as Cape Disappointment; while a world of meaning clusters about the southernmost tip of Greenland—Cape Farewell!

Perhaps no other cape has so changed the "tide in the

affairs of men" as that bold headland called Good Hope. Like an eagle's talon, it projects some fifteen miles into the sea, a mountainous ridge terminating in sheer cliffs eight hundred feet high. From their verge one may look due north along the west coast of Africa, whence came the Portuguese, urged on by the vision of Prince Henry the Navigator, then, turning, gaze due east—toward India and the Orient.

Perhaps the Phoenicians saw it long ago on that voyage that Herodotus relates, while it was sparsely inhabited by the Hottentots and the animallike Bushmen. But its European discoverer of record was Bartholomew Diaz, when in 1487 he was forced by his mutinous crew to turn back from a point some hundreds of miles farther east. He had been blown entirely around the cape, and saw it only on his return. He called it Cabo Tormentoso—the Cape of Storms —which his grateful monarch changed to the familiar name of our geographies. Vasco da Gama was wounded by a native assagai while reconnoitering in the neighborhood, an incident which did not improve his savage temper; a pocket beach under the cliffs is named for him.

Pigafetta, returning with Magellan's sole surviving ship, the *Vittoria*, viewed the cape with disfavor. He wrote, "It is the largest and most dangerous Cape in the world. We were nine weeks near that Cape with our sails hauled down because we had the west and northwest winds in our quarter, and because of a most furious storm. Finally, by God's help, we doubled that Cape." Sir Francis Drake was more favorably impressed, for he called it "the noblest headland in the world."

While they held this strategic point, the Portuguese controlled the commerce of the Orient. But it slipped from their feeble fingers, permitting the Dutch to build a rich colonial empire on the ruins of former monopoly. During the wars of Napoleon the English seized the region, leaving the problem of English-Boer discord to vex posterity.

In the old days the site of what is now Capetown was a port of call for all ships to replenish their water supplies and buy provisions from the natives. Perhaps the most interesting mementos are the post office stones still exhibited in the local museum. These stones informed later comers where letters were cached from natives, a curious news center, the germ of a hundred romances.

Good Hope, however, is not the tip of Africa. Cape Agulhas, about a hundred miles east, stretches a full degree farther south. I once arose early to survey it in the dim morning light, a vast cliff five hundred feet high, the apex of a continent.

Cape Horn is quite as prominent in the log of the windjammer. For it was known to sailormen the world over as Cape Stiff, and a passage westward in winter was the supreme test of seamanship.

This chill rock was known, of course, to native Yahgans of Tierra del Fuego, and their degenerate neighbors, the Hausch, or kelp eaters. But what white man first saw its forbidding cliffs is still debated.

Magellan was not that man, for he found a shorter way through the straits which bear his name. Its western outlook upon the Pacific is marked by Cape Desire. Pigafetta notes its discovery: "We sent a well equipped boat up the strait to explore. The men returned within three days and reported that they had seen the Cape and the Open Sea. The Captain-General wept for joy and called that Cape, Dezeado, for we had been desiring it for a long time." Having battled his way through a dangerous passage three hundred and ten miles long, we can imagine Magellan's relief at viewing his Mare Pacifico.

Cape Horn is a cliff 1391 feet high, the tip of Horn Island some five miles long. The South American Pilot states its latitude—55 degrees 59 minutes south. It marks the extreme continental reach toward the South Pole, thirteen hundred miles beyond the Cape of Good Hope, 600 miles farther south than Stewart Island, off New Zealand.

Sir Francis Drake has long been credited with its discovery. Driven far off the western end of the Strait of Magellan in a storm, he landed upon some island where—in his own words—he "came finally to the uttermost part of the land toward the South Pole—the extreme edge or cliff." He even reached over this cliff so that he might be "further to the southward upon it than any . . . man has yet known." The rough map drawn by one of his companions, however, and his description differ widely from that of Horn Island. There are many other islands along that wild coast. Drake's priority has been challenged. But his name remains in the tempestuous waters that separate South America from Antarctica, known as Drake Strait. Reisenberg is particularly critical, claiming that this water is not a strait anyway, Drake never sailed upon it, and probably never even saw it! However that may be, Schouten, the Dutch navigator, seeking a new route to the Indies, first negotiated the cape. His logbook carries an entry for January 29, 1616. "Cape Hoorn is rounded in 57 degrees 48 minutes south, rounded at 8 P.M." His latitude was in error, his longitude more so. Note that he named this famous promontory for his home port, Hoorn, and a companion ship, burned on the Patagonian coast. But its familiar shape has shortened the choice of its discoverer to the more expressive Cape Horn. Here at last was that rock which Drake at least thought he visited when he called it "the uttermost Cape—where the Atlantic Ocean and the South Sea meet in a most wide and free scope." But enough of controversy over this memorable landmark of the seas.

Another turning point in history is that grim headland which Richard Hakluyt called "the dreadful and misty North Cape." The wild Lapps may have known this mountainous islet on the Norwegian coast, but Octhere, the Northman, was the first explorer of record who ever rounded it by sea. In describing his voyage, which occurred about the year 900, he found, upon sailing northward, that "the coast turned toward the east," then, after four days' sail, "the coast turned toward the south." This is an untutored Viking's outline of that hazardous route around the Scandinavian Peninsula to the White Sea.

Summer tourists in the land of the midnight sun know little of the hardships which beset early voyagers. Sir Hugh Willoughby, sailing from England in 1553 for the Northeast Passage, rounded the cape successfully, only to perish with all his ship's company somewhere on the pitiless coast beyond. Richard Challenger, in the companion ship *Bona Ventura*, survived to tell how he "held on his course toward that unknown part of the world . . . and came at last . . . where he found no night at all but a continuall light and brightness of the sun shining clearly upon the huge and mighty sea."

In 1580, Captain Arthur Pet followed on the same quest in a tiny vessel of 40 tons. His course was set first "to the North Cape," and thence onward to Cathay. He reached Novaya Zemlya only to be forced back by impassable ice. His associate, Captain Jackman, in a ship of 20 tons, was lost on the return, "somewhere in the North Sea."

Willem Barents, sailing from Amsterdam in 1596, also rounded North Cape, but after spending a winter in the Arctic, succumbed to cold and privation while trying to cross from Novaya Zemlya to the mainland in an open boat.

Now that Russia is developing the "ice-free" Murmansk coast, far more shipping will doubtless pass North Cape.

For it is not only the gateway to the Arctic, but from the viewpoint of Moscow it is the gateway to the Atlantic—and beyond.

Less well known to us but tragic in its history is that bleak projection that marks the northernmost tip of Asia. Here the Taimir Peninsula, with its skeletal ridge—the wild Byrranga hills, from 2000 to 3000 feet high—thrusts boldly out into the Arctic in one of the most desolate regions on earth. Yet it was the goal of early navigators, for it barred the northeast pathway to China. It terminates in "a low promontory which a bay divides into two, the eastern arm projecting a little farther to the north than the western." Thus wrote Baron Nordenskjöld, on his voyage around northern Asia in the good ship Vega in 1878–79.

On August 19, 1878, he said, "A dark, ice free cape peered out of the mist in the northeast. . . . We had now reached a great goal, which, for centuries, had been the object of unsuccessful struggle. . . . For the first time a vessel lay at anchor off the Northern most cape of the Old World. . . . There was no glacier . . . no inland lakes . . . no perpendicular cliffs, no high mountain summits . . . a landscape the most monotonous and the most desolate I have seen in the far north." A polar bear, waddling along the beach, turned disgustedly inland. His private preserves were being invaded. The explorer remained about a day, erected the customary cairn, observed "distant hills perhaps 300 meters high." The cape, he remarked, was named for "Chelyuskin, who may have been there." Nordenskjöld knew but imperfectly what has since come to light, an episode in one of the most thrilling chapters of exploration.

Peter the Great, a year before his death, had sent Vitus Bering to explore the shores of the Pacific. This work was carried on with even greater zeal by the Czarina Anna. For seventeen years the Russian court was thronged with savants eager to map the most inaccessible regions. Bering was retained as chief, but with many subordinates. The formidable Taimir Peninsula was attacked from both the west and the east. From the west little was accomplished, but from the Lena River, on the east, Lieutenant Prontchishev sailed along the coast and almost but not quite attained his goal. His crew, however, became exhausted from handling frozen ropes and battling ice, and the discouraged leader finally succumbed to his many hardships. His mate, the Cossack Chelyuskin, after incredible exertions, regained the mouth of the frozen Olenek River, where the lieutenant's young wife also died and was buried in the same grave with her husband. Here what was left of the party spent a terrible winter in half-submerged huts. From his wrecked vessel, Chelyuskin returned to the Lena, then overland to Moscow for instructions. Ordered to return, he served this time under Lieutenant Laptjev. The new expedition set out from Yakutsk, provisioned for two years. Exploring the coast, they built signal towers. At the base of one of them they unearthed a mammoth's tusk. Forced back to the Khatanga River, they spent the winter with wild Tunguses who kept reindeer. The following year they again braved those fearsome seas, only to have their little ship caught in the ice and swept far off by gales. Freezing over, the ocean offered them a bridge to the beach. The men, carrying heavy loads, staggered for twenty-five days across the desolate country to the Khatanga River, where they wintered once more. Baffled in his attempts, Laptjev, the following year, decided to return to the Yenisei River and attack the peninsula from the west. Temporarily blinded by an eye infection, he was unable to reach the coast. But Chelyuskin, setting out in sledges, surveyed the coast, not hitherto observed, and sometime between May 1 and July 20, 1742, stood upon that barren bastion described by Nordenskjöld. Six years of hardship, seldom equaled and perhaps never surpassed, are commemorated in the name—Cape Chelyuskin.

A baggy peninsula called Boothia juts northward two hundred and fifty miles from the Canadian coast into the swarming islands of the arctic region. John Ross, leading one of many English expeditions to open up the famous Northwest Passage, first explored it in 1831. It is of special interest, for inland from its frozen shores lay the magnet of all compass needles, the North Magnetic Pole. The Murchison Promontory, a bleak frontage of nearly twenty miles along narrow Bellot Strait, marks the northernmost tip of the continent. This, Ross also established on his tour of investigation.

Asia was once supposed to join America. Peter the Great authorized Bering to learn the facts. These, though unknown to him, had already been established by another Cossack, Simon Dezhnev, quite as daring and intrepid as Chelyuskin. On the banks of the Kolyma River, Dezhnev learned from a wandering Chukchi of another great stream that flowed west into a different ocean. This was the Anadyr, which empties into Bering Sea. Fired by the zeal of the explorer, with the added lure of rich furs and walrus ivory, Dezhnev sailed down the Kolyma with seven boats, announcing that he would bring back two hundred and eighty sable skins, the Golden Fleece of the Far North. Four boats, discouraged at horizons of unending ice, turned back. Another was wrecked and the crew distributed between the remaining two. These became separated in a storm, but both kept on. No complete account survives, for these Cossacks were little more communicative than the Vikings. They were men of deeds, not words. But Dezhnev mentions "the great Tchukotsky Noss where the natives wore ornaments of Walrus Ivory through their pierced lips." This was

East Cape, which the Chukches still inhabit. These curious disks, or labrets, usually of ivory, sometimes of jade, are worn through two holes pierced in the upper lip. Stefansson observed one several inches in diameter. As for noss, Hakluyt learned long before from Russian travelers that "noss signyfyeth a nose, and therefore they call all capes or points that reach into the sea the same name."

Sailing through the strait, later named for Bering, Dezhnev overran his mark and suffered shipwreck. Returning overland, however, to the mouth of the Anadyr, he built a new boat and discovered a "walrus bank," probably a shoal crowded by these huge creatures. This involved a bloody dispute with other Cossacks. Meanwhile the companion boat seems to have reached Kamchatka, where the natives at first received the survivors kindly, supposing them to be gods. Discovering their error, they killed the strangers, a death perhaps more merciful than the usual shipwreck, cruel exposure, and starvation.

After 1654 all records of Dezhnev disappear. In what nameless grave he lies, whether on land or sea, will probably never be known. But his name survives, at least upon Russian maps, in that formidable "noss" which he rounded on the first recorded voyage in the Pacific from the north.

More than sixty years later, in 1711, the Cossack Popov traveled overland to this cape, where he observed, "opposite the promontory may be seen extending on both sides in the direction both of the Kolyma and the Anadyr an Island called by the Chukches, the 'Great Land.'" Some had visited this land in their canoes and found there unfamiliar trees, evidence of one of those countless migrations which have flowed across that narrow strait for thousands of years. Vitus Bering, groping through the fog, observed "a high mountain where Chukches lived," East Cape. This, according to the coast survey, rises twenty-eight hundred feet.

The smoky sea and narrow strait are named for him, but the bold "noss" is an enduring monument to Dezhnev. It marks the nearest approach of the Old World to the New: the meeting of two vast empires—our own and Russia's.

Captain Cook, in his last great voyage, also penetrated Bering Strait, but enjoyed that rarity for the latitude, a clear day. He wrote, "We had the opportunity of seeing at the same moment the remarkable peaked hill, near Cape Prince of Wales on the Coast of America, and the East Cape of Asia, with the two connecting islands of St. Diomede between them."

In the changing panorama of world affairs, to speculate about the future may be futile. But these promontories, only thirty-six miles apart, hidden in fog and washed by icy currents, may yet become memorable turning points in history.

CHAPTER XXXV

Romantic Trade Routes

Where'er in mart or on the main
With peaceful flag unfurled
She helps to wind the silken chain
Of commerce round the world.

WHITTIER

Trade is the lifeblood of civilization. Commodities gathered from the whole world have made possible ever advancing standards of material well-being. Even more important are those intangibles which stimulate cultural growth: customs, political institutions, scientific discoveries, literature, art, and religious convictions.

A casual glance at a globe might suggest the erroneous inference that trade expands freely in every direction. On the contrary, international commerce has always flowed through definite channels.

On land these have often been determined by such physical features as the Khyber Pass, the one available approach to India from the north, as was the narrow gateway of Thermopylae to ancient Greece. Less clearly defined but equally compelling factors determined the trade routes across Turkestan through which the commerce of China trickled intermittently to the Western world. Another natural passage across a continent was the Oregon Trail. Political upheavals have proved greater barriers than mountains or deserts. When the huge Mongol Empire broke to pieces, overland trade routes to the Far East were effectually barricaded, to be still further restricted when the Turks conquered the Near East.

A straight line is seldom the shortest distance between trade centers. Because trade, like water, seeks its lowest level, an economic one, the cheapest route has usually been preferred no matter what the distance. Hence the superiority of waterways has always been recognized. It is less expensive to load cargoes on ships than on pack mules or camels; a fundamental advantage that neither railroads nor auto trucks have overcome.

Navigable rivers are the most inviting of highways. Lakes and streams which afforded easy portages enabled Canadian fur traders to exploit a virgin wilderness. Where rivers have not followed the desired direction, canals have proved serviceable substitutes. The Grand Canal of China was one of the main arteries of that great country, rivaling in importance the Yangtze and the Hwang Ho. The Erie Canal, connecting the seaboard with the undeveloped West, established New York City as our greatest port, while the Suez and Panama canals have probably had a greater influence upon water routes than the discovery of a new ocean.

Although land barriers are obvious enough, commerce would seem to enjoy untrammeled freedom on the sea. But here again trade routes are almost as rigidly marked as rivers, for the oceans of the globe offer many features of advantage or disadvantage to voyagers.

In olden times winds were the important consideration. The galleys that Strabo encountered at Myos Hormos awaited the favoring monsoon to bear them to India. Magellan and Sir Francis Drake veered far out of their way to pick up the trade winds across the Pacific. Not many decades ago a sailing vessel, buffeted by westerly gales off Cape Horn for more than three months, gave up the struggle to sail eastward to Australia around the world. Absence of wind was also a hazard, for the ship becalmed in the doldrums invited the miseries of thirst and even starvation. Navigators also learned to follow or to avoid ocean currents.

Although steam has partially overcome such restrictions, it has not conquered them. Transatlantic liners still bear to the southward to escape the perils of arctic ice. Besides, vital necessities—coal, fuel oil, and docking facilities—are so concentrated at strategic points that England, at war, could coerce neutral shipping into fixed routes across oceans supposedly free. Half the ocean shipping of the world is engaged regularly in the North Atlantic.

Sea lanes converge like spider webs at such great ports as London, New York, and Tokyo. Usually, though not always, they follow a great circle. But the disabled vessel, unequipped with radio, which drifts far from ocean highways faces ominous possibilities. Vast areas of global waters are visited only at rare intervals; vast areas have never been visited at all!

And yet international commerce has always been more important than it seemed. On the wall of a rock-hewn tomb in Thebes, which dates back to 1500 B.C., are painted five ships which, the inscription informs us, sailed to "the Land of Incense" (the East African coast). They brought back "heaps of myrrh, resin, ebony, pure ivory, gold, cinnamon wood, eye cosmetics, apes, monkeys, skins of the southern panther" (leopards) and other exotic products. At a later date the maritime empire of the Arabs extended southward to Mozambique and thence to India. The Romans maintained some intercourse with India and even China. By laborious stages, across toilsome years, the merchandise of the Orient invaded the West. Silk was introduced into Byzantium, while from some remote source, shrouded in fable, came perfumes and pearls and spices.

An interesting memento of commerce in the Middle Ages is a baptismal font in the Church of St. Sulpice in Paris. It is the shell of a ponderous mollusk that weighed between three and four hundred pounds, the Tridacna, or giant clam, of the Moluccas. Sent as a present to Francis I of France by a Mohammedan potentate, what romance might be woven into its wanderings halfway around the world! Hoisted into some nameless canoe by pearl divers among coral reefs, a Malay craft may have borne it on the first lap of the long voyage westward, or was it a Chinese junk? Perhaps a Tamil trader took it to Ceylon, whence a leaky Arab dhow conveyed it on the hazardous voyage through the Erythraean Sea. Some grunting camel ferried it across the Syrian Desert to be transshipped to a Turkish or Genoese galley. How long the journey was, or the time involved, what possible shipwreck, what bloody clashes between scimitar and kris can never be known. But this trophy of the sea remains a witness to the commercial enterprise of the period.

Few achievements have been greater stimulants to progress than the discovery of new trade routes. Irked by Turkish restrictions and the Mediterranean monopoly of Italian cities, Columbus steered boldly west to seek the Indies. But all unwittingly he fetched up against the broadside of the Americas, a land mass thousands of miles long that barred further progress in that direction. To circumvent this barrier taxed the exploring skill and resourcefulness of western Europe for centuries.

Meanwhile the Portuguese, climaxing a hundred years of effort, rounded Africa to establish the most famous trade route of all history. With fortress-guarded harbors like Algoa and Delagoa bays, they controlled that route long enough to create a brilliant but transient empire. The Spaniards, claiming most of the Western Hemisphere, found their unwieldy dominions a positive hindrance to Far

Eastern commerce. Hence Magellan sought and found to the southward a break in that formidable land mass which gave precarious access to the Orient by a route enormously lengthy and hazardous. He did, however, establish a "bridge-head" on the farther shores of the Pacific in the Philippine Islands. To reach these new dominions the Spaniards found the Panama route more feasible, a preference strengthened by the conquest of Peru. And so Spanish galleons voyaging through the Caribbean transshipped their wares across the isthmus for another long journey to Cebu or Callao.

The Dutch, become a great maritime power by their successful struggle for independence, chafed at such barriers. Fearing the vengeance of the Spaniards in the Strait of Magellan, Schouten, reaching farther south, rounded Cape Horn. If this were not so favorable as the more traveled route around Good Hope, it offered a greater challenge to seamanship. In fact the discoveries of Magellan and Schouten may have suggested to Keats those "Magic casements, opening on the foam Of perilous seas in faery lands forlorn."

For a time the restless Dutch sought still other outlets to wider world horizons, but wisely abandoned them when, having wrested southern Africa from the Portuguese, they appropriated the latter's richest possessions in the East Indies.

Meanwhile England, then a poor country which pastured sheep to export their wool, awakened to the possibility of world commerce. In 1497, John Cabot, another Genoese, bore the British flag to the mainland of North America. Unfortunately he also bequeathed to posterity the vision of a new seaway to the Orient, that ill-starred Northwest Passage, which was destined for generations to enlist a maximum of heroic enterprise for a pitiful minimum of result.

It was Martin Frobisher, in the reign of Queen Elizabeth, who pioneered in those icy seas that separate Labrador from

Greenland, where the smallest of his three tiny ships, of only 10 tons burden, foundered in 1576. In 1585, John Davis led the first of three similar expeditions, to be remembered in Davis Strait, the gateway to that sector of the Arctic. Henry Hudson also turned aside from notable discoveries to explore that vast bay which bears his name and was destined to become his grave.

For a time its evil waters beckoned other voyagers into a great natural cul-de-sac—quests not entirely fruitless since they opened up that empire of lake and forest so long controlled by the Hudson Bay Company.

The charter granted in 1670 by Charles II to "the governor and company of adventurers trading into Hudson's Bay" required their co-operation in the discovery of the Northwest Passage. In the pursuit of this alluring prospect many lives and much treasure were expended. Samuel Hearne, following the Coppermine River to its mouth in 1771, was the first white man to reach the Northern Ocean by land. In 1789, Alexander Mackenzie voyaged in a canoe down a great river which he hoped would lead to the Pacific, only to observe whales spouting off its ice-encumbered delta. He called it the River of Disappointment, but his own name has long since been substituted instead. Incidentally, he did reach the Pacific in 1793 by following the Fraser River westward, the first man to cross the continent north of Mexico.

Meanwhile England sent many a gallant ship through the maze of islands which guards the northern passages. In 1819, William Parry nearly succeeded when his ship was frozen in the ice off Melville Island. He had unwittingly forced his way into what was later called McClure Strait, almost within sight of the open Beaufort Sea. Returning, he claimed the reward of £5000 offered by Parliament to anyone who sailed the polar seas westward beyond the 110th Meridian. Another adventurer, John Ross, in 1831 rounded desolate Boothia Peninsula, the northernmost tip of the continent, to locate the North Magnetic Pole.

Most memorable in a long list of tragedies was the fate that overtook Sir John Franklin and his party. Operating from Canadian territories, Sir John had already mapped much of the bleak coast line, but he hoped, by approaching from the eastward, to win the reward of twenty thousand pounds promised by the King of England to "any ship which discovered the Northwest Passage." Setting out in 1845 with 129 officers and men, he almost but not quite succeeded. Through winding channels choked by floes and shoals he fought his way until crushed in the ice and forced to abandon his two ships, the *Erebus* and *Terror*. No complete record has ever been recovered, for the party perished to the last man. From fragmentary evidence it appears that Sir John himself perished in that strait which cuts off huge Victoria Land from the continent. Some of his men were observed by Eskimos dragging a boat over the ice. A few reached the mainland not far from the eastern limit of Franklin's previous explorations. They seem to have fallen, one by one, and frozen where they fell.

Lady Franklin exhausted her personal fortune and was ably assisted by the governments of both Great Britain and the United States in equipping relief expeditions. Although too late to bring aid to the doomed party, these mapped some ten thousand miles of seacoast and succeeded in piecing together the loose ends of the Northwest Passage. In 1850, Lieutenant McClure, in the stout ship *Investigator*, separated from his superior, Captain Collinson, coasted eastward from Bering Strait along Alaska and Canada. Crossing Beaufort Sea, he entered the strait now named for him, where he wintered in a rocky cove on Banksland. Climbing a lofty hill, he looked out into Melville Sound, which Parry, approaching from the opposite direction, had entered thirty years before. Though also forced to abandon ship, and kept a prisoner in the Arctic for three winters, McClure eventually returned to England to share in the ten thousand pounds of prize money distributed among his officers and crew, and to be duly knighted and acclaimed as the discoverer of the Northwest Passage.

Various straits and bays and islands of this frozen region commemorate the names of a few of those who dared to brave the Arctic. Some emulated William Baffin, who, leaving England in 1616, penetrated far northward, adding vastly to scientific knowledge. Others, like Simpson and Dease, followed Canadian rivers to the sea to map long stretches of ice-encrusted coast lines. In recent years the labors of Stefansson, Sverdrup, MacMillan, and others have made the world more familiar with those lonely regions. But it was not until the present century that any single expedition succeeded in navigating the full length of the Northwest Passage.

That honor fell to Roald Amundsen, a Norwegian who inherited all the daring and resolution of Eric the Red. At college he had thrilled when a lecturing professor called the forcing of the Northwest Passage the "supreme adventure." Some years elapsed until June 1903, when Amundsen with six kindred spirits stole away from Tromso in the dead of night to avoid troublesome creditors. His vessel was the tiny *Gjoa* of 47 tons, variously described as "a sloop, a sealer and a herring boat." Besides her sails she was equipped with a thirteen-horsepower auxiliary engine for emergencies. Escaping shipwreck by an eyelash, she was frozen in the ice for three successive winters. En route the party took time to revisit the site of the North Magnetic Pole. One man succumbed to hardship and exposure, but the others eventually reached Bering Strait and the Pacific. The goal of more than three centuries of bitter struggle was at last attained.

Although the Northwest Passage has lost its former significance, sections are still patrolled by stout supply boats of the Canadian Government and the Northwest Mounted Police. Whalers also frequent those dreary channels, home of floes and blizzards, the scene of so much superhuman exertion and suffering.

Less advertised but really more accessible was the Northeast Passage, along the arctic shore line of Eurasia. Fortunately the perils of this route were sufficiently revealed by the experiences of Barents and Willoughby and Pet, coupled with the incredible hardships of Russian explorers, to deter other intruders into that treacherous ocean. In 1915 the Russian Vilkitski, sailing from Bering Sea, covered in reverse direction the course followed by Nordenskjöld, the Finnish Swede, more than forty years before. This was a challenge to Amundsen, who started westward from Norway in July 1918. After passing Asia's northernmost tip, Cape Chelyuskin, his ship was frozen in the ice, and he himself suffered serious accident. His right shoulder, broken by a fall, was not properly set for months; he was nearly suffocated by the fumes from a stove; he was knocked down in an encounter with a white bear and was saved only by his faithful dogs. When, frozen in the ice for a second winter, the *Fram* broke her propeller, five natives helped navigate the disabled vessel to Seattle.

Powerful icebreakers now crunch sea lanes through the floes of the Northeast Passage, while meteorological stations send out informative flashes. Stefansson thinks the entire route is navigable, except during winters of unusual severity. The rush of settlers to frozen tundras and barren hills now rivals the influx of homesteaders into the American Northwest. The Murmansk coast, haunt of a few nomadic

Lapps, boasted in 1938 a population of 130,000. The trapping village of Igarka on the Yenisei had become a boom town of 20,000; swarms of prospectors were pouring into the gold fields of the Lena; wheat was maturing two hundred miles beyond the Arctic Circle; northern Siberia had become a vaster edition of the Dakotas and Alberta.

Boldest of all sea routes to the Far East pointed straight across the North Pole. Yet it was advocated by Sebastian Cabot, Henry Hudson, and many others, who listened to tales from hardy whalers of ice-free seas warmed by the Gulf Stream. Though long since abandoned as a commercial prospect, the lure of the pole continued on purely scientific grounds. Here America entered the list with numerous competitors: Grinnell, Greely, Kane, Hayes, De Long, and others, culminating in Robert E. Peary, who, after many heartbreaking failures, finally reached the pole on April 6, 1909.

And was that route so impracticable? To ships, yes; to airplanes—but that is another story.

Here again the irrepressible Amundsen entered the picture. Not content to be the only man who ever sailed through both the Northwest and the Northeast passages, this doughty Norseman sought fresh conquests. And so, on December 14, 1911, accompanied by four companions on skis and fifty-two Eskimo dogs, he planted his country's flag upon the South Pole. To be sure, Shackleton had blazed that trail, but Amundsen's superior management and organization succeeded where the unfortunate Scott, who also reached the pole little more than a month later, perished among his lifeless companions on the return journey.

Having stood upon one end of the global axis, Amundsen must needs observe the other also. On May 11, 1926, he flew from Spitsbergen in a dirigible, circled the North Pole, then continued on the first successful voyage across that frigid sea to Alaska. On this polar excursion he was pre-ceded, by two days only, by Commander, now Admiral, Byrd, who three years later also flew by airplane to the South Pole.

In June 1928 a Russian hamlet caught a faint SOS from the Nobile dirigible wrecked upon arctic ice. In the disas-trous landing Nobile himself suffered a broken arm and leg with other injuries. Although not on friendly terms with the Italian explorer, Amundsen volunteered to go in search of him. Before setting out he remarked that he had always hoped to die on some high mission in the Arctic. His wish was granted, for the seaplane which bore him on this final adventure was never heard from again.

CHAPTER XXXVI

The Oceans in a Changing World

> Roll on, thou deep and dark blue ocean, roll!
> Ten thousand fleets sweep over thee in vain;
> Man marks the earth with ruin,—his control
> Stops with the shore.
>
> BYRON
>
> This precious stone set in the silver sea,
> Which serves it in the office of a wall
> Or as a moat defensive to a house,
> Against the envy of less happier lands,
> This blessed plot, this earth, this realm, this England.
>
> SHAKESPEARE

The seas have had a profound influence upon world affairs. Not infrequently they have determined the rise and fall of nations. The basis of Great Britain's might is mainly oceanic. One cause of Russia's restlessness and seeming aggressiveness is an "ocean hunger," which has never been satisfied. America, with the passing of her clipper ships, seemed to fall into a prolonged apathy. But with distant bases now established in the two major oceans, she has become definitely "sea-minded."

From the chaos of international relationships, a pseudo science called Geopolitik has emerged. Adolf Hitler and his advisers gave it a sinister reputation. Yet, baldly stated, it merely recognizes the essential unity of our globe and its possible dominance by certain areas, strategically located.

Our industrial age requires two things: raw materials and world markets. Both confer upon a nation greatness and enduring prosperity; both demand access to the sea.

Global conflicts always resolve into a struggle for sea power. Napoleon, long invincible on land, was foredoomed to failure, for Waterloo was an inevitable result of Trafalgar. In the far greater conflict of 1914 and its bloodier aftermath, sea power proved even more decisive.

While armies can be cut off from essential supplies, navies continue to levy economic tribute upon the world. Moreover, they can enlist the support of nations remotedly situated, just as Great Britain twice gained the decisive co-operation of America. Sea power, in the long run, can stifle land power, no matter how formidable or brilliantly directed.

This has not always been the case. Egypt might have mastered the eastern Mediterranean and disputed with Babylonia the western shores of the Indian Ocean. But though familiar with ships, both remained essentially land powers. The great moguls never appreciated the extensive Indian seacoast, but fell easy victims to nations which did. English dominance spread inland from the key seaports of Bombay, Madras, and Calcutta.

The greatness of Knossus, in Crete, was maritime, but it was rather the Phoenicians who proved the importance of a merchant marine. The power of Athens was based upon the "wooden walls" of her war galleys, and had she learned the wisdom of benevolent leadership, she might have imposed upon the ancient world a more enlightened dominion than that of Rome. Sea power enabled Carthage to challenge the Romans, and only when the latter took to the sea was their supremacy assured.

When the Roman Empire began to disintegrate, the Emperor Constantine, with farsighted judgment, chose Constantinople for his capital, a city that could easily be invested from land but never conquered while it retained control of the narrow straits and neighboring waters. How impregnable was this position is written in the almost fabulous history of that Byzantine stronghold, the metropolis of the Middle Ages, which remained, until its final overthrow in 1453, the last unravished remnant of the Roman Empire and the eastern bastion of Christendom against Mohammed.

Like the Romans, the Turks, though natural soldiers, took to the sea in their swift, piratic craft, to harass western Europe for centuries. Sea power also brought opulence to Venice and Genoa, and gave the Normans, though few in numbers, a position of prominence in world affairs.

Elsewhere sea power has been equally successful. It enabled those island empires originating in Sumatra and Java to dominate vast areas; and it spread Arab culture down the coast of Africa, beyond the Strait of Mozambique.

Sea power gave Portugal its brief but glamorous mastery of the Orient, and made Spain the foremost nation in the world. Only when her merchant marine had been riddled by Dutch and English adventurers did the glorious age of the Spanish galleon fall into eclipse.

This sea power was, as we have already observed, entrenched in the possession of strategic trade routes. The struggle for the mastery of these trade routes and the search for possible new ones was long one of the central motifs in the confused pattern of international affairs.

An ancient chronicle relates how "Offa, King of Mercia, after a glorious reign of thirty-nine years, bequeathed to England the useful lesson that he, who will be secure on land, must be supreme at sea." Britain, without a navy of her own, had fallen an easy prey to the Romans, the Anglo-Saxons, the Danes, and the Normans. That lesson was well learned by pioneers like Sir Francis Drake and other marauding sea kings, whose fighting ships, manned by skilled seamen, laid the foundation of the British Empire. Their lusty challenge still echoes in those proud boasts that "the sun never sets upon British possessions" and "Britannia rules the waves."

Control of neighboring seas has long been an accepted and jealously guarded right of nationalism. In Venice the most gorgeous annual pageant depicted the marriage of the city to the Adriatic Sea. The Danes formerly levied tribute on all who passed the narrow Baltic Straits. English policy has assigned a vital importance to the waters which separate the white cliffs of Dover from the Continent, and never hesitated to resort to arms, if need be, to prevent an aggressive power from obtaining a foothold there.

All nations control purely coastal waters. International law has recognized the "three-mile limit," which has sometimes been extended to twelve miles or even the more elastic "from headland to headland." Recently President Truman has laid claim, on behalf of the federal government, to mineral products from submerged areas out to the very edge of the continental shelves. International disputes have led nations still farther asea, where valuable fisheries were involved, like those of the Grand Banks of Newfoundland or the halibut grounds in the Pacific. In short, there has always been an urge to extend jurisdiction beyond recognized bounds. For international law, poorly defined at best, is a frail barrier against national acquisitiveness.

However nations might wrangle over coastal waters, they have usually upheld the "freedom of the seas." England alone has remained the great dissenter. Her far-flung colonial empire and her control of trade routes, particularly the Suez Canal and the Cape of Good Hope, guarded by such fortresses as Gibraltar, Malta, and Singapore, have given her an overlordship of the oceans unparalleled in history. To be sure, this dominion of funnel and sail and coaling station has been discreetly veiled in the guise of amicable commerce, but the power has been there and war has brought it into sharp relief.

We fought Great Britain in 1812 over that very issue. Freedom of the seas was one of President Wilson's fourteen points. It was repeated in the Four Freedoms—meaningless phrase—which President Roosevelt and Winston Churchill broadcasted during the recent war. But whatever her commendable restraint in normal times, Great Britain, driven to extremity, has never hesitated to use her naval might as though the oceans of the world were her exclusive property. All this is a far cry from the policy enunciated by Queen Elizabeth, when she protested to the Spanish ambassador, "Neither can a title to the ocean belong to any people." But Spain then held the upper hand and England had not yet become the dominant maritime power.

Access to the sea has been the motivating policy of more than one modern nation, and a bottling up of such natural aspirations has proven quite as explosive as superheated steam. Austria's refusal to allow Serbia such an outlet fanned that smoldering resentment which flared up in the assassination of the Austrian archduke and lighted the conflagration of global war. Poland's failure to grasp the importance of the Baltic coast line led to her fall from a position once greater than Russia's to complete helplessness and dismemberment. It was Hitler's closing of the Polish Corridor which was the occasion, if not the cause, of the last Great War.

Japan's attack upon Pearl Harbor gave her temporary control of the Pacific and the opportunity to acquire, for a brief time, a huge colonial empire. Her insular position, moreover, made her almost immune from direct attack, nor would her sudden collapse have occurred without a new note in warfare, the bomber and the atomic bomb!

Now that our globe is controlled by three superpowers, the British Empire, the Russian Empire, and the United States, it is of the first importance to note how sea power ranks in that new world which has not yet crystallized from the wreckage of the old.

First of all, Great Britain's command of the oceans no longer rests upon superior naval might. America's navy is now the most formidable in the world and American resources quite sufficient to maintain that superiority. Great Britain, however, still holds her ancient trade routes and many strategic positions like Aden, which guards the eastern approach to the Suez, and Hong Kong, called the key to the China Seas. Her vast empire, however, has been subjected to tremendous stress and strain: Ireland has become almost a separate government; South Africa is bedeviled with a Boer discord and native discontent; India is a seething volcano of unrest; while that remote continent, Australia, with a sturdy independence, has problems of its own.

Meanwhile America, richest of nations, with extensive frontage on two oceans, finds her sea power enormously expanded. Strategic bases, obtained from England, with certain rights in Greenland and Iceland, have greatly extended her sphere in the Atlantic. In the Pacific, while granting the Philippines independence, she retains a benevolent oversight of their affairs. Moreover, the island bases wrested from Japan, added to her already considerable holdings in Hawaii, Samoa, and elsewhere, assure a commanding position. That she will ever selfishly exploit that maritime empire is unthinkable, but it should give her a decisive influence in advancing international justice.

Russia is the question mark whose shadow falls like a red smear across two continents. From the viewpoint of Geopolitik, her position is impregnable. She is the dominant "heartland" of continental size. Her resources in forest, farm, and mine are incalculable. Her population, increasing rapidly, is healthy, strong, and vigorous. Out of Asia have swept those white invasions of the past which created modern civilization: the Greek, the Roman, the Celt, the German, and now, last of all, the Slav. If Russia were content, within her limitless horizons, to remain a great land power, to work out amid her steppes and tundras the revolutionary ideas which have obsessed her people, the world might well await the outcome in sympathetic interest. But Russia has always reached out toward the sea. Peter the Great built that city now called Leningrad, as a "window opening upon Europe." Catherine the Great extended her coast line along the Black Sea. Smaller nations—Estonia, Latvia, Lithuania, with a generous slice of Poland—were absorbed to expand her Baltic area. For centuries the czars dreamed of seizing Constantinople. Napoleon once blocked that ambition, remarking, "He who controls India and Constantinople controls the world." His was a truly global viewpoint.

When Russia moved too aggressively in that direction, England and France effected a temporary check in the Crimean campaign. But the grand project merely slumbers, as is revealed by insistent pressure upon Turkey. For in all her extensive seacoast Russia has no first-class harbor free from winter ice or other obvious disadvantage.

Meanwhile, in the Far East, Cossack adventurers pushed her frontiers to the shores of the Pacific—and beyond. By the middle of the last century Russia, having acquired Alaska, was claiming coastal territory down to the middle of California. Fortunately such remote possessions were little valued at Moscow, and the Alaskan purchase preserved this continent for its original settlers.

The recent war, which involved the whole world in universal madness, has eliminated the only two strong powers that were natural barriers to Russian expansion. The destruction of Germany has allowed Slavic influence to penetrate Central Europe to a degree that is disturbing to Great Britain. The collapse of Japan has removed the last effective bar to Russia's interference in Manchuria and China. Moreover, by her aggressive attitude in Iran, Russia is reaching down toward the Indian Ocean, an expansion that Great Britain has never ceased to oppose. Let her evident thrusts seaward be crowned with success, let her land resources be supplemented with a corresponding power at sea, and she might, should she care to do so, exert an influence in world affairs beyond Hitler's wildest dream.

Meanwhile there is one part of the oceans that she does largely dominate—the polar sea. We have noted, all too briefly, the development of her vast Siberian borders and her ice-free Murmansk coast. These, to be sure, seem remote to us, but are they? A new ocean is rapidly being explored— the ocean of the air. When the Wright brothers stood upon Kill Devil Hill to launch the first airplane flight, they fairly outdid Balboa when he caught his historic glimpse of the Pacific, for they sighted a global ocean.

Roughly two thirds of all land areas lie north of the Equator. Roughly nine tenths of the world's population resides there. Almost all the great financial and manufacturing centers are still farther to the north—beyond the 30th parallel of latitude. That shortest of all routes from east to west—across the pole—so long locked in ice against trading ships, is no such barrier to the pilots of the air.

When Amundsen first crossed that sea in a dirigible in 1926, his flight was quite as momentous as the voyages of

Columbus and Magellan. Within a year Russian airplanes had followed suit, one landing in Washington State, another far down into California. And that was before the building of the long-flight, superbombers of today!

Stefansson, who spent years in the Arctic, where he foraged like a native upon the country, thinks that winter flying there is safer than anywhere else on earth. Snowfall is scanty and storms infrequent, for they breed farther south, where warmer winds and waters mingle. Accurate weather forecasts are now obtainable, for Russia has meteorological stations scattered along her vast frontiers, while there are similar stations in northern Canada, Greenland, Iceland, and elsewhere. Moonlight affords sufficient illumination through at least half the polar night, while the innumerable frozen lakes which dot the Canadian wilderness are ideal landing fields.

When Hitler, standing on Dover Strait, announced, "There are no more islands," he made a prophetic utterance. The congressman who remarked during the war that America had only two friends, the Atlantic and Pacific oceans, was looking east or west. Had he glanced to the north, he would have observed a troubled sea of looming possibilities. One can almost hear the echo of Pindar's stately ode, "Not going by ship nor on foot could you find the wonderful way to . . . the Hyperboreans." For distances that ships could not traverse by years of battling with the ice, or sledging parties reach over the illimitable floes, the airplane can span in a single night.

It was an overwhelming air force that crushed Germany and Japan. Perhaps it would be well to retain that force, for, to paraphrase the wisdom of King Offa, "He who would protect his cities from rocket guns and blockbusters must be supreme in the air."

In the dizzy tempo of our times the oceans have lost

something of their former defensive value. Henceforth they are linked with the growing navies of the air. But at least one corner of the seas, long reckoned of little worth, is assuming a menacing importance. That is the icebound North Atlantic, still called the Arctic. The boundary between the Soviet Empire and Alaska, which narrows to three miles between the Diomedes in Bering Strait, may well be ignored in the knowledge that the polar sea everywhere can now be bridged at a single lap. Perhaps this Arctic, rather than the Pacific, is destined to become the ocean of the future.

Around it meet the three dominant powers: the British Empire, Russia, and the United States, all mutually involved, all readily accessible, all equally vulnerable. The narrowing meridians of longitude unite at the pole. One glance at that strategic point should cause a deal of sobering thought. It should teach a world, bitter, avaricious, and brutal, that only through international peace can civilization survive. For in that temple where worshipers still bow before the idols of racial superiority and imperialistic greed is a blind Samson that could bring the entire edifice crashing down in ruin—the atomic bomb!

Index